For Kay

Blackstone's Guide to the

RACE RELATIONS (AMENDMENT) ACT 2000

Henrietta Hill

OXFORD
UNIVERSITY PRESS

OXFORD
UNIVERSITY PRESS

Great Clarendon Street, Oxford OX2 6DP

Oxford University Press is a department of the University of Oxford.
It furthers the University's objective of excellence in research, scholarship,
and education by publishing worldwide in

Oxford New York

Athens Auckland Bangkok Bogotá Buenos Aires Cape Town
Chennai Dar es Salaam Delhi Florence Hong Kong Istanbul Karachi
Kolkata Kuala Lumpur Madrid Melbourne Mexico City Mumbai Nairobi
Paris São Paulo Shanghai Singapore Taipei Tokyo Toronto Warsaw

with associated companies in Berlin Ibadan

Oxford is a registered trade mark of Oxford University Press
in the UK and certain other countries

Published in the United States
by Oxford University Press Inc., New York

A Blackstone Press Book

British Library Cataloguing in Publication Data
Data available

Library of Congress Cataloging in Publication Data
Data available

ISBN 1-84174-268-6

1 3 5 7 9 10 8 6 4 2

Typeset by Style Photosetting Ltd
Printed in Great Britain
on acid-free paper by
Antony Rowe Ltd, Chippenham and Reading

Contents

Foreword by Lord Lester of Herne Hill QC

The inquiry into the failures of the police service in the wake of Stephen Lawrence's racist murder drew attention to a long-standing anomaly — the exclusion from the Race Relations Act 1976 of liability by the police and other public authorities for discrimination done in their capacity as public authorities. That extraordinary anomaly was the result of a majority decision of the House of Lords in *Amin* interpreting the statutory language with the austerity of tabulated legalism.

The Lawrence report recommended that the full force of the Race Relations Act be extended to apply to the police service, but it was ambiguous as to what it meant by 'the full force'. The Government responded by agreeing to close the *Amin* gap in respect of public authorities generally and not only the police service, but only for acts of direct discrimination. Ministers and their advisers did not want courts and tribunals to be empowered to decide whether policies which hit disproportionately at ethnic minorities (or other vulnerable groups) were objectively justifiable.

Eventually, after a broad-based campaign in the House of Lords and beyond, the Government relented and agreed to extent the Act to cover indirect as well as direct discrimination by public authorities, to place public bodies under positive duties, and to make consequential amendments to the legislation against sex and disability discrimination. An EU directive will require a similar approach to sexual orientation, religious and age discrimination in employment, covering indirect as well as direct discrimination.

The Race Relations (Amendment) Act 2000 closes the *Amin* gap as well as places public authorities under a positive duty to promote equality and good race relations.

This useful book places the new Act in its political and legal context, discussing the Parliamentary debates and examining the Act's interaction with existing legislation, including the Human Rights Act and Article 14 of the European Convention on Human Rights.

The Guide recognises the practical importance of the Government's acceptance that indirect, as well as direct, discrimination should be unlawful in the provision of public services. Without the full application of the Race Relations Act, it would remain lawful for officials, the police, immigration services, the Inland Revenue, the Benefits Agency and many other public authorities to operate practices and procedures having an unfair and disproportionate adverse impact on ethnic minority groups.

Together with the positive duty imposed on certain authorities to 'have due regard to the need to eliminate unlawful racial discrimination and to promote equality of opportunity', the new law should prompt them to audit their practices and procedures and to take a proactive approach to equality. Chapter 6 of the Guide emphasises the need for the Government to define the specific duties to be imposed on those bodies subject to the Act's general duty to promote equality. It also highlights the important role of the Commission for Racial Equality in giving guidance and monitoring and enforcing the new law.

The new Act represents a significant change in our now twenty-five year old equality legislation. The EU Race Directive and EU Framework Directive, which prohibits discrimination in employment and occupation on the grounds of age, religion, belief, disability and sexual orientation, will require wider legislative changes. As the last chapter of the Guide recognises, further reforms are necessary not only to the Race Relations Act but also to the whole panoply of UK anti-discrimination legislation.

Preface

The Race Relations (Amendment) Act 2000 is the most significant development in British race relations legislation for a quarter of a century. It puts into place a key recommendation of the Macpherson Report, namely that the prohibition on race discrimination in the Race Relations Act 1976 should extend to the police, but goes further by extending the 1976 Act to all public authorities. Individuals are given new rights under the Act to challenge race discrimination by public authorities in the courts. Certain public authorities are also placed under a new, broader general duty to eliminate discrimination and promote equality in the services they provide to the public. The Commission for Racial Equality will have the power to enforce new specific duties on certain authorities if they do not comply with their obligations to promote equality. The Act is important for all practitioners frequently involved in claims against state bodies, such as those practising in the fields of criminal justice, actions against the police and prisons, discrimination, immigration and asylum, housing, mental health and clinical negligence. The key provisions of the Act came into force on 2 April 2001, with full implementation by way of secondary legislation scheduled for late 2001/early 2002.

CONTENTS

Chapter 1 of the book sets the scene by explaining the history of ethnic diversity in Britain, the developments in the human rights movement which recognised protection from racial discrimination as a human right, the scope of the previous Race Relations Acts and the motivation for the 2000 Act.

Chapter 2 explains which public authorities are covered by the new prohibition on racial discrimination and gives examples of the sorts of functions which are included. Chapter 3 sets out what types of discrimination by public authorities are prohibited under the new s. 19B, gives some examples of each type of discrimination and explains how the new s. 19B interacts with the other provisions of the 1976 Act and the Human Rights Act 1998. Chapter 4 sets out the scope of each of the exceptions from the new s. 19B prohibition on discrimination and the general exceptions to Part III of the Act which will continue to apply to the new s. 19B.

Chapter 5 explains the concepts of vicarious and secondary liability under the Act, including the new vicarious liability which attaches to chief officers of police. Chapter 6 details the new general duty and specific duties on certain public bodies to promote equality and the introduction of mechanisms for the Commission for Racial Equality to give guidance as to the duties and to enforce them as necessary. Chapter 7 explains how the Act extends the protection from discrimination in the field of public appointments.

Chapter 8 explains the procedures open to an individual under the Act, namely (i) a complaint to a county/sheriff court or immigration tribunal in relation to discrimination by a public body contrary to the new s. 19B; and (ii) an application for judicial review alleging a failure by a public body to comply with its general duty to promote racial equality under the new s. 71 or unlawful discrimination in public appointments contrary to the expanded s. 76.

Chapter 9 concludes the book with a summary of some of the initial responses to the Act, and information about developments in European discrimination law and their implications for domestic law in the near future.

The Appendices contain the full text of the 1976 Act as amended by the 2000 Act, some of the key Hansard debates, the new style questionnaire under s. 65 of the 1976 Act, some precedents for statements of case, and the Appendices from the Consultation Paper which list the public bodies bound by the new positive duties.

ACKNOWLEDGMENTS

I would like to thank all those people who discussed the Act with me, helped me to understand it and inspired me to think about it.

In particular, my thanks go to Barbara Cohen at the Commission for Racial Equality and Heather Williams at Doughty Street for encouraging me to consider the implications of the Act for criminal justice at our Discrimination Law Association lecture; to Ann Dummett for her work with the Immigration Law Practitioners Association on the immigration exemption, and for her invaluable assistance with the drafts of Chapter 4 dealing with these provisions; to Chitra Karvé at the Commission for Racial Equality for her support during her days at Liberty, and for her comments on the draft of Chapter 6 on the new general and specific duties; to Meera Yagnik and Kirsten Lampe for their research assistance on the Hansard debates and the public authorities test; to Gaby Charing at the Discrimination Law Association for involving me in the Association's response to the Consultation Paper on the Act; to Zoë Gillard at Liberty for enabling me to discuss the Act with experienced civil actions against the police practitioners at Liberty's seminar on the Act; to Michael Rubinstein for giving me the opportunity to lecture on the Act to a wide range of solicitors and other professionals; and to Keir Starmer for encouraging me to approach Blackstone in the first place, and at whose evening at King's College (with Francesca Klug) the idea for the book was formed.

My thanks also go to the clerks and staff at Doughty Street Chambers for giving me the space to write the book. In particular, Christine Kings, Michelle Simpson, Mia Hakl and Alison Gerry (then Seaman) were a great help in organising the seminars on the Act, at which the intellect and experience of my colleagues and the solicitors who instruct us invariably raised new and interesting issues for me to grapple with while writing.

I would also like to thank my family — my mother Carol and brother Oliver — for their support during the writing of the book, as always. Sadly my grandmother, Kay, passed away while the book was still at the proof stage, and it is to her memory — especially her request for signed copies for Christmas presents — that the book is dedicated. My friends in London and elsewhere kept me sane while typing away, and TB — as always — provided the endearing voice of reason during the writing process.

My thanks also go to Alistair, David, Jeremy and Ruth at Blackstone.

Finally, I would like to thank Lord Lester of Herne Hill QC for his strident comments on the Act during the Parliamentary debates; for his (successful) encouragement of the Government to ensure that indirect discrimination was covered by the Act; and for agreeing to write the Foreword to the book.

I have aimed to state the law as at 10 September 2001. Any mistakes are — of course — mine.

Henrietta Hill
Doughty Street Chambers
September 2001

Table of Cases

Chapter One
Introduction to the Race Relations (Amendment) Act 2000

1.1 INTRODUCTION

The Race Relations (Amendment) Act 2000 ('the 2000 Act') is the fourth substantial piece of legislation aimed at improving race relations in Great Britain. Its significance lies in its extension of the prohibition of race discrimination to public functions not previously covered and its broadening of the positive duties on public bodies to eliminate discrimination and to promote racial equality. This Chapter explains the history of ethnic diversity in Britain, developments in the human rights movement which recognised protection from racial discrimination as a human right, the previous Race Relations Acts and the motivation for the 2000 Act.

1.2 HISTORY OF MIGRATION TO GREAT BRITAIN

In Chapter 1 of his Consultation Paper on the implementation of the 2000 Act, 'New Laws for a Successful Multi-Racial Britain' (February 2001), the then Home Secretary summarised *Roots of the Future, Ethnic Diversity in the Making of Britain*, a 1996 book by the Commission for Racial Equality. In that book, the Commission had traced the last 40,000 years of migration to Great Britain, and the economic and social benefits to Britain which this brought. These successive waves of migration began with the arrival of the Bronze Age migrants who came from north-west Europe. They were followed between 1000 and 150 BC by the Celts (descended from the dwellers of the Russian steppes) and between 43 and 410 AD by the Romans. The fall of their Empire was followed by large scale invasions by Angles, Saxons, Jutes, Frisians, people from what is now northern Germany, southern Denmark and the northern parts of the Netherlands. Norse culture was added by the Viking invasions between 800 and 1000 AD and French influence increased by the Norman invasion of 1066.

The first Jewish settlements flourished under the protection of William the Conqueror, and between 1550 and 1660 Protestant refugees fleeing religious persecution in mainland Europe found safety in Britain. Between 1555 and 1883 the slave trade resulted in an increase in the number of peoples from Africa in

Britain, while the demand for seafarers in the merchant navy and servants brought people from India and China. The Irish population in Britain grew significantly between the 1830's and 1850 as a result of rural poverty and famine in Ireland. During the First and Second World Wars several million Indians enlisted in the British Army and many settled here afterwards. Large numbers of West Indians, Africans (from those countries which are now Zambia, Zimbabwe, Malawi, Kenya, Uganda, Zanzibar and Tanzania), Poles and Czechs also fought for Britain in the Second World War and remained when the war was over. Many more from the Caribbean, India and Pakistan migrated to Britain after the war under government programmes which encouraged immigration to provide the workforce which would assist with post-war reconstruction.

1.3 THE HUMAN RIGHTS MOVEMENT AND RACE DISCRIMINATION

Alongside the development of post-war multi-ethnic Britain, the human rights movement was growing in the international sphere. Britain played a key role in this movement, which recognised that the prohibition of discrimination on any ground, including racial grounds, was vital to the protection of human rights. A general protection from discrimination was enshrined in the Universal Declaration of Human Rights 1948, Articles 1, 2 and 7, the International Covenant on Civil and Political Rights 1966, Articles 2(1), 3 and 26 and the American Convention on Human Rights 1969, Articles 1 and 2. Similarly, the European Convention on Human Rights and Fundamental Freedoms 1950, Article 14 provided a broad protection from discrimination in the enjoyment of the other Convention rights on any ground, including race, colour, language, religion, political or other opinion, national or social origin, association with a minority, property, birth or other status. A specific Convention providing more detailed protection from discrimination on racial grounds, the International Convention on the Elimination of All Forms of Racial Discrimination, entered into force in 1969 (although the UK did not ratify it until much later). In addition, the European Court of Justice sought from the outset to interpret European Community law in accordance with the European Convention on Human Rights, including Article 14 (see *Case C-260/89 ERT* [1991] ECR I-2925).

1.4 THE RACE RELATIONS ACTS 1965, 1968 AND 1976

By the early 1960's, racism and racial inequality in Britain were rife. Signs outside lodgings reading 'No dogs, no Irish, no blacks' were not uncommon. Neither was it unusual for people to be refused service in shops and restaurants solely because of their race or the colour of their skin. Racism was also openly a feature of electoral campaigns, such as the one in 1962. The causes of this poor state of race relations are complex, but may well have been rooted in the ideology of national, cultural, religious and economic supremacy inherent in the British colonial experience (see, further, the commentaries extracted at R. Townshend-Smith, *Discrimination Law: Text, Cases and Materials* (Cavendish, 1998) at pp. 5–14).

The Race Relations Act 1965 was the first legislative attempt to improve race relations in Britain. The 1965 Act prohibited discrimination in places such as hotels, public houses, restaurants, theatres, public transport and any place maintained by a public authority. The Race Relations Act 1968 outlawed discrimination in other areas.

The Race Relations Act 1976 ('the 1976 Act') prohibited race discrimination in employment, training and education, housing, the provision of goods, facilities and services and certain other specified activities including public appointments made by Ministers and Government Departments. The 1976 Act abolished the Race Relations Board and the Community Relations Commission and established the Commission for Racial Equality. The Commission was given a statutory duty to work towards the elimination of discrimination, to promote equality of opportunity and good relations between persons of different racial groups generally and to keep under review the working of the Act. To assist with that aim the Commission was also given strategic powers of enforcement. The 1976 Act also placed a statutory duty on local authorities and on specified local educational bodies to promote racial equality.

1.5 THE MOTIVATION FOR FURTHER RACE RELATIONS LEGISLATION

1.5.1 Gaps in coverage provided by the Race Relations Act 1976

The Race Relations Acts 1965, 1968 and 1976 undoubtedly helped change behaviour and attitudes and made a significant contribution to racial equality in Great Britain, especially in the employment sphere. However, aside from the fields of education and housing, there was an inherent limit to how far the 1976 Act could apply to public authority functions. Over time, these gaps were widened by case law as the Courts adopted a narrow interpretation of which public functions were in fact covered by the Act as 'goods, facilities and services'.

In general, it was decided that in respect of public authorities, the Act only applied where the act done was at least similar to an act that could be done by a private person (*R* v *Entry Clearance Officer, Bombay, ex parte Amin* [1983] 2 AC 818). For example, it had been held that the Act did cover the granting of tax relief and giving of advice on tax matters by Inland Revenue officers, and the decisions and activities of a local authority concerning children in its care, but did not extend to immigration control functions (*Savjani* v *Inland Revenue Commissioners* [1981] QB 458; *Conwell* v *London Borough of Newham*, EAT, Charles J presiding, 8 July 1999; *R* v *Entry Clearance Officer, Bombay, ex parte Amin* [1983] 2 AC 818). It had also been held that while a constable would be providing a service when giving directions to a member of the public, he or she would not be providing a service when making an arrest, exercising stop and search policies, or otherwise enforcing the law (*Farah* v *Commissioner of Police for the Metropolis* [1998] 2 QB 65). Similarly, although the allocation of work in prisons was held to come under s. 20, it was very unlikely that the operation of prison discipline would do so (*Alexander* v *Home Office* [1998] 1 WLR 968). In addition, private organisations carrying out public functions, such as transporting prisoners or assisting immigration control, were excluded from the scope of the Act.

The decision in the key case of *Amin* was widely criticised by respected commentators such as David Pannick and John Gardner (see the extracts from their commentaries in A. McColgan, *Discrimination Law Cases and Materials* (Hart, 2000) at pp. 234–236). Lord Lester has since described *Amin* as 'arbitrary, irrational and confusing' and such that, if the Law Lords had the opportunity to reconsider the decision, it is likely that they would reverse it (Hansard HL, 11 January 2000, col. 546). In debates about the 2000 Act, it was widely felt that the case law in this area was uncertain and only clarified the position in relation to particular cases and in a piecemeal fashion (see, for example, Lord Bassam, Hansard HL, 14 December 1999, col. 128; David Liddington MP, House of Commons Standing Committee D, 11 April 2000, p. 3).

1.5.2 Growing ethnic diversity in Great Britain

By the late 1990's, the ethnic population of Great Britain was increasingly diverse. The 1991 Census had indicated that the largest ethnic minority population lived in the south-east, while urban areas in the West Midlands, Yorkshire, Humberside, north-west England, Cardiff and Glasgow also had significant ethnic minority populations. The Census also showed that nearly half of the ethnic minority population present in Britain had been born here. The 1999 Labour Force Survey data showed the ethnic diversity of modern day Britain as follows: white (93.5%), black Caribbean (0.9%), black African (0.7%), black other (non-mixed) (0.2%), black mixed (0.3%), Indian (1.6%), Pakistani (1.2%), Bangladeshi (0.5%), Chinese (0.2%) and other (0.9%) (see the Consultation Paper on the 2000 Act, paras. 1.5 and 1.6).

There was also diversity between the backgrounds and experience of Britain's ethnic minority groups. This manifested itself in the complex geographical distribution of different groups which had, for example, led to high levels of segregation in some places between different groups and between those whose origins lie in different parts of the Indian subcontinent or the Caribbean. There was also a significant difference between those groups whose first language was English, that is those from the West Indies and some Asian groups, and those who had little or no knowledge of English on arrival. Further, those of Afro-Caribbean origin were very likely to come from a notionally Christian background whereas Asians were predominantly Muslims, Hindus and Sikhs. There may also have been significant cultural differences between older people from ethnic minorities for whom the ideas and values of the land they left may continue to be very significant in their lives, and younger people, born and brought up entirely in the UK. (See, further, R. Townshend-Smith, *Discrimination Law: Text, Cases and Materials* (Cavendish, 1998) at pp. 1–4).

1.5.3 Evidence of continued inequality in access to public life

There was, however, increasing concern at the lack of access by ethnic minorities to public life. There was little ethnic diversity in the highest public appointments, such as Generals in the Army or High Court Judges, and the Home Secretary indicated that at the time of his Consultation Paper on the 2000 Act, less than 2% of Senior Civil Servants and about 3% of teachers were from ethnic minorities, out of about 7% of the working population (Consultation Paper, para. 1.14).

1.5.4 Evidence of continued inequality in access to public services

There was, more significantly, a growing body of research and evidence suggesting that equality had not been achieved in the way in which public authorities developed and implemented policies and the means by which they provided services to those from ethnic minorities. At the forefront of this evidence was the Macpherson Inquiry into the racist murder of Stephen Lawrence, a young black man who died on 22 April 1993 and whose killers have yet to be held accountable. The Inquiry was set up on 31 July 1998 ‘to inquire into the death of Stephen Lawrence on 22 April 1993 to date, in order particularly to identify the lessons to be learned for the investigation of racially motivated crime’. It held 69 days of public hearings, heard 88 witnesses and received some 100,000 pages of evidence. The first part of the Inquiry covered the police investigation into the murder and the second part dealt with the wider lessons to be learned.

The evidence which the Inquiry heard revealed the extent of shortcomings in the services provided by public bodies to ethnic minorities and in the employment prospects open to them. The Commission for Racial Equality, for example, submitted evidence referring to the levels of dissatisfaction with the criminal justice system which it had found among ethnic minority groups. This evidence included complaints regarding discrimination in the ways the police exercised their powers or failed to act when the victim was from an ethnic minority. The Commission said it felt ‘hampered’ in its work by the fact that the Race Relations Act 1976 did not extend to the police’s law enforcement role. In its Third Review of the 1976 Act published on 9 June 1998, the Commission recommended that this position be changed (*Select Committee on Home Affairs, The Inquiry into Matters Arising from the Death of Stephen Lawrence Part Two: Evidence Submitted by the Commission for Racial Equality*, paras 1.2, 1.4 and 3.1).

1.5.5 The Macpherson Report and its implementation

The Macpherson Inquiry’s findings were published on 24 February 1999 (Cm 4262-I). The central and most important issue for the inquiry was racism and whether and how that affected the handling of the case. It was observed during the Parliamentary debates on the 2000 Act that, although Lord Scarman in his 1981 Report into the Brixton disorders had considered the notion of ‘institutional racism’, it was the Macpherson Inquiry which had brought this concept into the wider domain (Lord Bassam, Hansard HL, 14 December 1999, col. 149). The Inquiry defined institutional racism as ‘. . . the collective failure of an organisation to provide an appropriate and professional service to people because of their colour, culture or ethnic origin. It can be seen or detected in processes, attitudes and behaviour which amount to discrimination through unwitting prejudice, ignorance, thoughtlessness, and racist stereotyping which disadvantage ethnic minority people’. The Inquiry found that, applying that definition, ‘. . . institutional racism exists within . . . both the Metropolitan Police Service and in other Police Services and other institutions countrywide. . .’.

The Report made 70 recommendations to the Government. These included changes to the police discipline regime, the setting of clear objectives by police forces for dealing with racist crimes better, the setting of targets for the recruitment and promotion of ethnic minority police officers and a more equitable use of police stop-and-search powers. Recommendation 11 adopted the recommendations of the Commission for Racial Equality’s 1998 Report, to the effect that: ‘the full force of the Race Relations legislation should apply to all police officers, and that Chief

Officers of Police should be made vicariously liable for the acts and omissions of their officers relevant to that legislation'. However the Report had also made clear that it did not believe that such problems of discrimination in services were confined to the police, but that equality of access was an issue all public institutions needed to face. The Report said: 'if racism is to be eliminated from our society there must be a co-ordinated effort to prevent its growth. This needs to go well beyond the police services . . . it is incumbent upon every institution to examine their policies and practices to guard against disadvantaging any section of our communities'.

In introducing the Report to Parliament, the Home Secretary indicated that he would adopt Recommendation 11 in its entirety, and take it further — namely to extend the 1976 Act to cover not only the police, but also to cover all public services such as the civil service, the immigration service and the national health service. He justified this by saying that:

> In my view, any long-established, white-dominated organisation is liable to have procedures, practices and a culture that tend to exclude or to disadvantage non-white people. The police service, in that respect, is little different from other parts of the criminal justice system — or from Government Departments, including the Home Office — and many other institutions. . . . Companies and other organisations in the public sector have long been subject to this litigation, but so far the Government have failed to keep their own house in order. The Macpherson Inquiry has demonstrated the failings of one very important public institution, the police service. The police service have a special responsibility in our society, because day by day they are the immediate guardians of fairness and justice; but we would be deluding ourselves if we believed that the issues thrown up by the inquiry affect only the police, for the report's implications go much wider. The very process of the inquiry has opened all our eyes to what it is like to be black or Asian in Britain today, and the inquiry process has revealed some fundamental truths about the nature of our society — about our relationships one with another. Some of those truths are uncomfortable, but we must confront them (Hansard HC, 24 February 1999, cols. 391–393).

On 23 March 1999 the Home Office published its 'Stephen Lawrence Action Plan', the means by which it undertook to take the recommendations of the Macpherson Report forward. The Stephen Lawrence Steering Group oversees the implementation of the Action Plan. This Group is chaired by the Home Secretary and is comprised of members from inside and outside Government, including representatives from the Commission for Racial Equality, the Race Relations Forum, the Association of Police Authorities, the Association of Chief Police Officers, the Superintendents' Association, HM Inspectorate of Constabulary, the Metropolitan Police, the Black Police Association and the Crown Prosecution Service. In Scotland, the Deputy First Minister and Minister for Justice chair an equivalent group for the Scottish Executive's Action Plan in devolved matters (Home Office Press Release 100/99, 24 February 1999; Consultation Paper, Introduction, para. 3). The Government has since provided two Annual Reports on its progress in implementing the Action Plan.

1.5.6 The Government's Response to the Commission for Racial Equality's Third Review of the Race Relations Act 1976

On 14 July 1999 the Government announced its response to the Commission for Racial Equality's Third Review of the 1976 Act. When published on 9 June 1998 this report had contained 57 proposals for reform, and the Home Secretary had consulted on the proposals until 18 December 1998. He received many responses from Race Equality Councils and others directly involved in assisting ethnic minorities. In his response to the Report, the Home Secretary reiterated the Government's commitment to extending the 1976 Act.

He also stressed that '. . . the public sector should promote race, gender and disability equality . . . the legislative and non-legislative options will be explored . . .'. He also indicated that clarification of the definition of 'indirect discrimination' was desirable, to reflect developments in European legislation; and that improvement was needed to the compensation arrangements for indirect racial discrimination in line with that in the Sex Discrimination Act. He also made clear that it was desirable, subject to careful assessment of the relative benefits and burdens, to maintain consistency between the equality regimes by extending the EC Burden of Proof Directive's provisions to cover race discrimination legislation (see, further, Chapter 9). Insofar as the Commission for Racial Equality's powers were concerned, he felt that the Commission should have new powers to suggest changes to practices and procedures where an investigation has shown evidence of unlawful racial discrimination and that it should be able to act more strategically than it could do at that time in relation to carrying out formal investigations. The Home Secretary also undertook to keep the position of statutory ethnic monitoring by businesses under review.

The Government's response to the Commission's Third Review of the Race Relations Act 1976 was announced as part of a strategic package of measures on equality that the Government is taking forward. On the same day, the then Minister for the Cabinet Office, Dr Jack Cunningham, announced the Government's response to the Better Regulation Task Force's review of anti-discrimination legislation. This included a commitment to harmonisation of the provisions of the Race Relations Act 1976, the Sex Discrimination Act 1975 and the Disability Discrimination Act 1995. The Education and Employment Secretary, David Blunkett also announced the Government's response to the Equal Opportunities Commission's report 'Equality in the 21st Century' (Home Office Press Release 219/99, 14 July 1999).

1.5.7 The Government's Equality Statement

The Government issued a composite 13-point Equality Statement on 30 November 1999, setting out its work towards eliminating discrimination on grounds of race, sex, disability, age and religion. The aims of the Government in improving race relations were explained in terms of both the moral case for prohibiting racial discrimination (derived from the basic human right to be treated with equality and fairness) and its economic and social justification (the need to ensure that everyone's potential can be utilised) (point 1 of the Equality Statement). These two themes were repeated in the Consultation Paper on the 2000 Act (paras 1.1 and 1.2).

The inclusion within the Race Relations (Amendment) Bill of the prohibition on discrimination by public bodies was an important part of the Equality Statement (point 6); as was the need to encourage public bodies to promote racial equality (point 4). There was already a duty on the public sector in Northern Ireland to promote equality of opportunity and the Equality Statement indicated that the Government would be 'looking at and learning from' the operation of that legislation. A commitment to increasing ethnic minority representation in public bodies and the Civil Service was reiterated (point 5); and it was announced that research had been commissioned into the scale and nature of religious discrimination and the extent to which it overlaps with race discrimination (point 11) (Cabinet Office Press Release 274/99, 30 November 1999; Consultation Paper, Appendix 1).

1.6 PASSAGE OF THE RACE RELATIONS (AMENDMENT) ACT 2000 THROUGH PARLIAMENT

The Race Relations (Amendment) Bill was introduced into the House of Lords on 2 December 1999.

At that stage the Bill only included the extension of the prohibition on direct race discrimination to public functions not already covered, and the concomitant right of individuals to complain of unlawful discrimination in the Courts. The Government had made a commitment to place a statutory duty on public authorities to promote equality 'as soon as legislative time permits' but such a duty was not included in the Bill at this stage (Home Office Press Release 403/99, 3 December 1999). The Commission for Racial Equality had been critical of this 'serious defect in the Bill' and Lord Lester, Baroness Whittaker, Lord Ahmed, Lord Dholakia and others had urged the Government to bring the positive duty into the Bill as soon as possible (Hansard HL, 14 December 1999, cols. 143, 164 and 170). Almost every speaker in the second reading in the Lords also expressed concern about the fact that the Bill did not extend to indirect discrimination (see, for example, Lord Cope, Hansard HL, 14 December 1999, col. 137; Lord Lester, Hansard HL, 14 December 1999, col. 141; Baroness Howells, Hansard HL, 14 December 1999, col. 150; Lord Avebury, Hansard HL, 14 December 1999, col. 159; Lord Ahmed, Hansard HL, 14 December 1999, col. 165; Lord Dholakia, Hansard HL, 14 December 1999, col. 169). At the House of Lords Committee stage, Lord Lester and others argued strongly for amendments to include indirect discrimination and the positive general duty (Hansard HL, 11 January 2000, col. 544–567; Hansard HL, 13 January 2000, col. 773–778; for a summary of the arguments advanced as to why the exclusion of indirect discrimination was incompatible with the UK's international commitments and the Human Rights Act, see Colm O'Cinneide, 'The Race Relations (Amendment) Act 2000', [2001] P.L. Summer 220 at 224, note 21).

On 27 January 2000, when the Bill was still at the House of Lords Committee stage, Lord Bassam announced that the Act would be extended to cover indirect race discrimination. He also announced that the Government would bring forward the amendment to the Bill to include a positive duty to promote equality on the face of the Bill (rather than leaving it to secondary legislation), leaving room for consultation on how the duty would operate in practice and how it would be enforced. Both these amendments were to be brought forward at Commons

Committee stage. Lord Bassam indicated that although the Government had always been in favour of such an extension of the Act in principle, there had been a concern to ensure that such a provision would be effective without leaving public bodies open to routine legal challenge in circumstances where their policies were entirely proper. The debates since the Bill was published, had, he said convinced the Government that '. . . on balance, the risk of spurious challenge is outweighed by the principle of including indirect discrimination in respect of public sector functions in the Bill. . .'. The Act, he said, would therefore extend to areas such as the implementation of central and local government's regulatory, economic and social policies and law enforcement in respect of indirect as well as direct discrimination (Hansard HL, 27 January 2000, col. 1673). The Bill passed to the Commons on 3 February 2000.

The amendments necessary for the inclusion of indirect discrimination were agreed as the Bill completed its Committee stage in the House of Commons on 2 May 2000 (Hansard HC, 13 April 2000, Standing Committee D, (am) part 3 and (pm) parts 1–2). The amendments necessary for the inclusion of the positive duty to promote equality were also agreed (Hansard HC, 2 May 2000, Standing Committee D, parts 1–5 and 8–10). The amendment meant that there would be a broader general duty on public authorities to eliminate discrimination and promote race equality and further specific duties would be imposed by order after consultation had taken place on the details. It was made clear that this positive duty extended to '. . . both the internal organisation of public authorities and delivery of their services'. Home Office Minister Mike O'Brien, in announcing the amendment, anticipated that incorporating a duty to promote race equality would '. . . send a strong message about the importance the Government attaches to race issues . . .' and that the duty itself would mean that '. . . race equality must be central to policy development and implementation' (Home Office Press Release 111/2000, 3 May 2000).

During the passage of the Bill, on 2 October 2000, the Human Rights Act 1998 came into force, bringing the protection from racial discrimination in the enjoyment of Convention rights in the European Convention on Human Rights 1950, Article 14 into domestic law.

The Bill completed its passage through the Commons on 30 October 2000. After this, it went back to the Lords for consideration of the amendments made in the Commons. The Bill received Royal Assent, and became an Act of Parliament, on 30 November 2000. The Act came into force on 2 April 2001, save that for the purpose of the imposition of a requirement or the giving of an immigration authorisation under s. 19D(3), s. 1 came into force on 26 March 2001 (see the Race Relations (Amendment) Act 2000 (Commencement) Order 2001 (SI 2001/566)).

1.7 CORE PROVISIONS OF THE ACT

The 2000 Act does not replace the 1976 Act but strengthens and extends its scope.

The stated main aim of the Act is to stress the 'special responsibility' on public bodies as employers, policy makers and service providers to deliver race equality, 'set the pace' on race equality and 'lead by example'. Further, by outlawing discrimination in all public functions, '. . . the Government is setting a minimum standard for public authorities. It is signalling that race discrimination in the performance of public functions is unacceptable. It must be avoided' (Consultation Paper, paras 1.18 and 2.12).

Section 1 of the 2000 Act inserts a new s. 19B into the 1976 Act, outlawing race discrimination by all public authorities (as defined) in the exercise of their functions. All forms of race discrimination (direct discrimination, indirect discrimination and victimisation) are included, and the existing protections against discrimination and the exceptions thereto in Parts II and III of the 1976 Act are unaffected. As the 2000 Act merely inserts these additional sections into the 1976 Act to create new forms of prohibited discrimination, except where explicit alternative provision is made, all the current enforcement provisions of the 1976 Act apply to the new s. 19B. The individual's remedy for unlawful discrimination is by way of a complaint to the county court (or sheriff court in Scotland), and the existing provisions in relation to remedies, the commission for Racial Equality's powers, time limits and exceptions apply.

Section 1 also inserts new ss. 19C–19F into the 1976 Act. The new ss. 19C and 19F provide that judicial and legislative acts and decisions not to prosecute or to discontinue criminal proceedings are exceptions to the new s. 19B. The existing defence of prior statutory authority for discrimination under s. 41 of the 1976 Act is preserved by the new s. 19C. The new s. 19D provides that in certain immigration and nationality functions, discrimination is permitted on the grounds of nationality or ethnic or national origin (but not race or colour) provided it is authorised by a government minister acting personally, or an immigration official in accordance with a statutory or ministerial authorisation. The new s. 19E requires the Home Secretary to appoint a person who is not a member of his or her staff to act as a monitor of the exception in relation to immigration and nationality cases.

Section 2 sets out the new positive statutory duties on public authorities by inserting new ss. 71 and 71A–71E into the 1976 Act. The new s. 71(1) sets out the broader 'general duty' on public bodies listed in Schedule 1A of the Act to have due regard to the need to eliminate unlawful racial discrimination and to promote equality of opportunity and good relations between persons of different racial groups. Section 71(5) gives the Home Secretary power to add to the list of bodies in sch. 1A. The new s. 71(2) provides for 'specific' duties for the better performance of the general duty, which can be imposed on all or some of the listed public authorities by the Home Secretary or the Scottish Ministers. The new s. 71A sets out some limitations to the general duty and the new s. 71B makes special provision for the general duty in Scotland and Wales. The new s. 71C authorises the Commission for Racial Equality to issue Codes of Practice for the better performance by bodies of their positive duties, and such Codes will be admissible in evidence. The new ss. 71D and 71E set up the procedural mechanisms by which the Commission can enforce compliance with the specific duties (by serving a compliance notice and, in default of compliance with that, applying to the county or sheriff court).

Section 3 widens the protection against discrimination in public appointments in s. 76 of the 1976 Act.

Section 4 inserts a new s. 76A into the 1976 Act to make Chief Officers of Police liable for acts of discrimination by officers under their direction or control. A new s. 76B sets out a list of other police bodies to whom the new s. 76A applies.

Section 5 inserts new s. 57(4A)–(4C) into the 1976 Act setting out certain procedural provisions where a complaint of unlawful discrimination under s. 19B is made in relation to a criminal investigation. It provides that no remedy other than damages or a declaration (in Scotland, a declarator) is available unless a court is satisfied that the remedy concerned would not prejudice a criminal investigation or decision to institute criminal proceedings. It also provides a presumption that a county or sheriff court, on application, will grant an adjournment (in Scotland, a sist) of a race discrimination case, if it would prejudice a criminal investigation. It also permits the respondent to such a claim to defer answering a question on the claimant's questionnaire served under s. 65 of the 1976 Act if to answer it would cause such prejudice.

Section 6 inserts a new s. 57A into the 1976 Act to the effect that complaints of racial discrimination in certain immigration and nationality decisions will be heard (with human rights complaints) as part of 'one-stop' immigration appeals by the Immigration Appellate Authorities.

Section 7 removes the provision in s. 69(2)(b) of the 1976 Act by which a Ministerial certificate could be conclusive of the fact that an act of discrimination was done for the purposes of national security. Section 8 inserts a new s. 67A into the 1976 Act providing a procedure by which courts can determine such issues of national security.

1.8 TIMETABLE FOR IMPLEMENTATION

The provisions of the Act outlawing race discrimination in all public functions, outlawing race discrimination in public appointments not previously covered, applying the general duty to promote equality to certain listed bodies, making Chief Officers of Police vicariously liable and limiting the circumstances in which safeguarding national security can be used to justify discrimination came into force on 2 April 2001. The outstanding matters are the addition of bodies to which the 'general duty' to promote equality applies and the extension of 'specific duties' to promote equality. The Home Secretary began public consultation on these areas on 22 February 2001 in *New Laws for a Successful Multi-Racial Britain* (February 2001). The closing date for responses was 15 May 2001.

The Home Secretary had initially hoped that secondary legislation extending the list of bodies to which the general duty applies and imposing specific duties on listed public bodies would be made in July 2001, that the Commission for Racial Equality's Codes of Practice would be laid before Parliament in the summer of 2001, and that the specific duties to promote race equality would come into force in November 2001. There has been some slippage to the timetable, perhaps caused by the intervening General Election. As at 25 July 2001, Ministers were considering the 290 responses which had been received during the consultation period, and were working on the detail of the Orders to bring the specific duties into effect.

At the time of writing, the Home Office website on the Act (www.homeoffice.gov.uk/raceact) indicated that it was hoped to lay the orders before Parliament as soon as possible after the Summer recess, in October 2001.

Chapter Two
Public authorities and public functions covered by the new prohibition on racial discrimination

2.1 INTRODUCTION

Section 1 of the Race Relations (Amendment) Act 2000 inserts a new s. 19B into the 1976 Act to the effect that 'It is unlawful for a public authority in carrying out any functions of the authority to do any act which constitutes discrimination'. Chapter 3 explains what sorts of acts will constitute 'discrimination' for the purposes of the new s. 19B. This Chapter explains which public authorities are covered by the new section and gives examples of the sorts of functions which are included.

2.2 WHAT IS A PUBLIC AUTHORITY FOR THE PURPOSES OF THE NEW SECTION 19B?

The original version of the Race Relations (Amendment) Bill proposed that only those bodies which were specified in the Act or by the Home Secretary would be subject to the prohibition on discrimination in the new s. 19B. Even at that stage, however, it was clear that the new s. 19B was going to extend to a large number of bodies. In introducing the Bill in the Lords, Lord Bassam said: '[t]his provision applies to all functions that are not already covered by the Act; in other words where functions are already covered by another provision of the Act, that coverage will not change. The new section will have a very wide application . . .' (Hansard HL, 14 December 1999, col. 129). In debates during the passage of the Bill, however, it was suggested by many that the 'list' approach would provoke uncertainty. The Government was urged to adopt the definition of 'public authority' in the Human Rights Act 1998 for the sake of consistency (see, for example, Baroness Whittaker, Hansard HL, 14 December 1999, col. 16; Lord Lester, Hansard HL, 11 January 2000, col. 534; Lord Avebury, Hansard HL, 11 January 2000, col. 536; Baroness Howells, Hansard HL, 11 January 2000, col. 537; Lord Avebury, Hansard HL, 26 January 2000, col. 1685; Fiona Mactaggart, Hansard HC, 9 March 2000, col. 1272; Hansard HC, 13 April 2000, Standing Committee D, parts 1–3). This approach was eventually adopted (although the positive duties under the Act remain subject to the 'list' method) (Hansard HC, 30 October 2000, col. 526).

The new s. 19B therefore adopts the approach taken in the Human Rights Act and offers no finite list of public authorities bound by the Act, but simply gives a generic definition of what the public authority classification does and does not include. Under s. 19B(2)(a), 'any person certain of whose functions are functions of a public nature' is a 'public authority' except those listed in s. 19B(3), namely: either House of Parliament; a person exercising functions in connection with proceedings in Parliament; the Security Service; the Secret Intelligence Service; the Government Communications Headquarters; and any unit or part of a unit of any of the naval, military or air forces of the Crown which is for the time being required by the Secretary of State to assist the Government Communications Headquarters in carrying out its functions. Section 19B(4) further provides that in relation to a particular act, 'a person is not a public authority by virtue only of s. (2)(a) if the nature of the Act is private.'

The definition of 'public authority' under both the Human Rights Act and the 2000 Act is deliberately wide in that it includes anyone whose work involves functions of a public nature, including private sector organisations. It also has only limited exceptions, and is certainly much wider than those bodies which have traditionally been susceptible to judicial review. The ministerial statements about this provision in the 2000 Act confirm that the definition of 'public authority' is deliberately wide (see the overviews of the Act on the Home Office's website for it: www.homeoffice.gov.uk/raceact/overview.htm and www.homeoffice.gov.uk/raceact/bilingen.htm).

A threefold classification is generally used to determine whether a body is a public authority for the purposes of the Human Rights Act 1998, and it is likely that the same approach will be taken to public authorities under the Race Relations (Amendment) Act 2000. This approach groups bodies into 'pure' public bodies, 'hybrid' bodies and private bodies.

2.2.1 'Pure' public bodies

During the passage of the equivalent provisions in the Human Rights Act through the House of Lords the Lord Chancellor commented that: 'In many cases it will be obvious to the courts that they are dealing with a public authority. In respect of government departments, for example, or police officers, or prison officers, or immigration officers, or local authorities, there can be no doubt that the body in question is a public authority. Any clear case of that kind comes in under [s. 6(1)] . . .' (Hansard HL, 24 November 1997, col. 811). A similar approach will be taken under the 2000 Act. Its provisions therefore clearly extend to all those public bodies who have traditionally been regarded as such, including central and local government, the NHS, licensing authorities, the police, the Prison Service and the Probation Service. In education, the Act will continue to apply to all schools and colleges maintained by local education authorities or education authorities (in Scotland), independent (fee paying) schools and colleges, further education colleges, special schools, early years provision, universities, local education authorities and governors of schools and colleges and school boards (in Scotland).

2.2.2 'Hybrid' bodies

'Hybrid' bodies are those under s. 19B(2)(a), namely those 'certain of whose functions are functions of a public nature', a concept again taken directly from s. 6(3)(b) of the Human Rights Act. The aim of the latter section was described by the Lord Chancellor as including '. . . bodies which are not manifestly public authorities but some of whose functions only are functions of a public nature. It is relevant to cases where the courts are not sure whether they are looking at a public authority in the full-blooded sense with regard to those bodies which fall into the grey area between public and private. The Bill reflects the decision to include as "public authorities" bodies which have some public functions and some private functions . . .'. The Lord Chancellor gave Railtrack as an example of a body with a mixture of public and private functions. When carrying out its functions relating to safety, it would qualify as a public authority; but when carrying out its functions as, for instance, a property developer by engaging in a private transaction such as the disposal or acquisition of land it would so qualify. Similarly a private security company would be exercising public functions in relation to the management of a contracted out prison but would be acting privately when, for example, guarding commercial premises. Doctors in general practice would be public authorities in relation to their NHS functions, but not in relation to their private clients.

The 'public functions' test is one which has been used in the judicial review field to identify which bodies can be susceptible to review. Therefore, while s. 6 of the Human Rights Act must be given 'a generous interpretation', it is clearly inspired by the approach developed by the courts in identifying which bodies and activities are subject to judicial review. That approach requires consideration to be given not only to whether the body performs public or governmental functions, but also to the source of the power of the body and whether it is legislative or not. Consideration must also be given to whether the body is publicly funded in respect of the functions it is exercising, whether it is institutionally or structurally controlled by government, whether the government would have had to intervene if the body in question did not exercise those functions, and whether there is a consensual element (such as a contract) in the relationship between the individual and the body. Applying those tests, media regulators, city regulators, health service bodies, educational bodies and professional bodies have been held to be subject to judicial review. (See, further, R. Gordon and T. Ward, *Judicial Review and the Human Rights Act* (Cavendish, 2001) at pp. 38–47; R. Clayton and H. Tomlinson, *The Law of Human Rights* (OUP, 2000) at pp. 186–204; A. Lester and D. Pannick, *Human Rights Law and Practice* (Butterworths, 1999) paras 2.6.3–2.6.4; S. Grosz, J. Beatson and P. Duffy, *Human Rights: The 1998 Act and the European Convention* (Sweet & Maxwell, 2000) at pp. 60–71; and R. Pillay, 'Public Authorities under the Human Rights Act', JUSTICE conference paper, 28 June 2001.)

However, the class of hybrid bodies under the Human Rights Act or the Race Relations (Amendment) Act is wider than the class of bodies which have been held to be susceptible to judicial review, largely because of the origins of both Acts in human rights jurisprudence. In relation to the Human Rights Act, the Lord Chancellor said: 'When we were drawing up the Bill, we noted that the Convention had its origins in a desire to protect the individual against the abuse of power by the state, rather than to protect one individual against the actions of another . . . we wanted a realistic and modern definition of the state so as to provide a correspondingly wide protection against the abuse of human rights. Accordingly, liability under the Bill would go beyond the narrow category of central and local government and the police — the organisations that represent the minimalist view of what constitutes the state'. The Government also intended the meaning of 'public authority' under the Human Rights Act to correspond with the notion of state responsibility under the European Convention on Human Rights (Lord Hardie, the Lord Advocate, Hansard HL, 5 February 1998, col. 794 and Jack Straw, Hansard HC, 17 June 1998, cols. 406, 432, 433). This jurisprudence has held, for example, that states cannot escape liability under the Convention simply by asserting that an individual or body entrusted with public functions has acted ultra vires. States are strictly liable for the conduct of their subordinates and cannot shelter behind their inability to ensure that their will is respected (*Ireland* v *UK* (1979–80) 2 EHRR 25 at para. 159). Similarly, states cannot absolve themselves from responsibility by delegating their obligations to private bodies or individuals (*Van der Mussele* v *Belgium* (1984) 6 EHRR 163).

The 2000 Act will therefore extend to private or voluntary agencies carrying out such public functions as running schools, prisons or immigration detention centres, escorting remand prisoners to and from courts, enforcing parking controls, assisting with immigration control or providing residential care. It seems accepted that the general provision of education by schools and universities (those that are not provided by pure public authorities in any event) will amount to a public function, but it is unclear where the line will be drawn with regard to more specialist education, such as in small private colleges or specialist classes. Insofar as other bodies are concerned, the extent to which the classification of a 'hybrid' body 'cuts across' what has been traditionally regarded as the public/private law divide is a developing area. Test cases under the Human Rights Act are currently seeking to re-visit pre-October 2000 decisions finding that a body is not performing a public function. In *Donoghue* v *Poplar Housing and Regeneration Community Association Limited* [2001] EWCA Civ 595, the Court of Appeal held that the role of the respondent housing association in providing accommodation for the applicant and then in seeking possession of it was so closely assimilated to that of the local housing authority that the housing association was a public body for the purposes of the Human Rights Act. Similarly, in *Wallbank* v *Parochial Church Council of Aston Cantlow* [2001] EWCA Civ 713, it was held that a Parochial Church Council, which enforced a common law liability on the applicants as lay owners of rectory land to defray the cost of repairs to the parish church, was a public body for the purposes of the Human Rights Act. By contrast, in *(1) Elizabeth Heather (2) Martin Ward (3) Hilary Callin* v *(1) Leonard Cheshire Foundation (2) HM Attorney-General* [2001] EWHC Admin 429, it was held that an association which provided care homes for disabled people was not such a body. Although the *Leonard Cheshire* case is under appeal, practitioners seeking to determine whether a body is public, hybrid or private for the purposes of a claim under the 2000 Act would be assisted in that task by considering the approach taken in these cases under the Human Rights Act.

2.2.3 'Pure' private bodies

These are bodies with no public functions which are not caught by the Human Rights Act or the Race Relations (Amendment) Act 2000. They are not therefore bound by statutory obligations in the Acts and cannot be held accountable in a court for a breach of Convention rights or unlawful race discrimination.

There has been much debate, however, as to how far there will be a 'horizontal' effect of the Human Rights Act. This relates partly to the extent to which the increasing awareness of human rights standards will be accepted by private individuals as a benchmark for their behaviour. It is likely that there will be a similar debate as to how far the positive duties to eliminate discrimination and to promote equality under the 2000 Act will also influence the actions of 'pure' private bodies. In its general guidance on the Act, *Strengthening the Race Relations Act* (December 2000), the Commission for Racial Equality hinted at this, saying: 'This [Act] is targeted at the public sector — hospitals, schools, police, local councils, government ministers — but the standards expected of public bodies should influence practice in the private sector'. The Government also urges public authorities to identify with their private sector partners which of their functions contracted out to them are 'functions of a public nature'. Those partners are also urged to take action to reduce the risk of claims of unlawful race discrimination (Consultation Paper, para. 2.24).

2.3 WHAT SORT OF FUNCTIONS ARE COVERED BY THE NEW SECTION 19B?

Again, the approach taken by the 2000 Act is wide. The new s. 19B simply applies to 'any functions' of the authority. Perhaps unsurprisingly given its breadth, s. 19B does not provide any further examples of which functions are covered. The CRE's general guidance document *Strengthening the Race Relations Act* (December 2000), the Home Secretary's Consultation Paper (para. 2.13), and the website for the Act (www.homeoffice.gov.uk/raceact/outracdi.htm) however, give the following examples of the sorts of public functions which must be exercised without discrimination:

(a) The police — functions relating to criminal investigations, stop and search, arrest, bail and detention of suspects, assisting victims and controlling demonstrations.

(b) The regulatory and law enforcement powers of bodies such as Customs and Excise, local authority officers, tax inspectors, Trading Standards officers and the Health and Safety Executive, including the collection of taxes, the investigation of benefit fraud and inspections of residential care homes.

(c) The Prison Service — core functions such as the allocation of prisoners, the imposition of discipline and punishments and the searching of visitors.

(d) The Probation Service — core functions such as the preparation of pre-sentence reports and the commencement of proceedings seeking revocation of community sentences.

(e) Immigration — the core functions of the Immigration and Nationality Directorate of the Home Office, such as the decisions of immigration and entry clearance officials, and the functions of private bodies performing immigration functions, such as running immigration detention centres (although the extent of the prohibition of discrimination on grounds of nationality, ethnic or national origin (as opposed to race or colour) is narrower in the immigration context, as is explained in Chapter 4).

(f) Licensing authorities — the granting of licenses such as those for street trading, gaming and liquor licenses.

(g) Mental health authorities — determinations such as those for compulsory detention under the Mental Health Act 1983.

The Consultation Paper notes (at paragraph 2.23) that the absence of any central or comprehensive list of the public functions has a deliberate aim, namely to ensure that public authorities recognise that good governance requires them to review their functions and identify them for themselves. That, the Consultation Paper hopes, will enable steps to be taken if necessary to reduce the risk of claims of unlawful race discrimination in the newly covered areas. The Government urges public bodies to take this step although rightly comments that it will ultimately be for the courts to decide whether a body is performing a public function within the meaning of the new provisions.

Chapter Three
Types of discrimination by public authorities prohibited by the Act

3.1 INTRODUCTION

As explained in Chapter 2, s. 1 of the Race Relations (Amendment) Act 2000 prohibits race discrimination by public authorities by inserting a new s. 19B into the Race Relations Act 1976 ('the 1976 Act'). This Chapter sets out what types of discrimination by public bodies are prohibited under the new s. 19B, gives some possible examples of each type of discrimination and explains how the new s. 19B interacts with the other provisions of the 1976 Act and the Human Rights Act 1998.

The new s. 19B fits into the scheme of Part III of the 1976 Act which prohibits discrimination in employment (ss. 4–15), education (ss. 17–19), the provision of goods, facilities and services (s. 20), housing matters (ss. 21–24) and by associations other than trade unions (ss. 25–26) (for further commentary on these provisions, see section 3.5 below). The same statutory mechanisms for establishing whether or not there has been unlawful discrimination therefore apply to claims under the new s. 19B. The Act first declares what constitutes 'discrimination' (ss. 1–3) and then specifies in what circumstances discrimination is unlawful (one of which is the new s. 19B). It is necessary first to consider whether the body whose acts are to be challenged has committed an act of discrimination as defined, and then, but only then, consider whether that act is rendered unlawful by one of the later provisions of the statute (*Chiu* v *British Aerospace plc* [1982] IRLR 56). By analogy with the construction of the Sex Discrimination Act 1975 (see *Cornelius* v *University College of Swansea* [1987] IRLR 141), for the purposes of the Act, 'discrimination' may be either racial discrimination or discrimination by way of victimisation (s. 3(3)). 'Racial discrimination' can be either 'direct' or 'indirect' although these terms are not used in the Act itself. In simple terms, discrimination is said to be 'direct' when it is overt, explicitly on grounds of race; discrimination is 'indirect' when it is hidden behind a more or less plausible facade; where the discrimination is ostensibly on other grounds, but has the effect of discriminating on grounds of race. A claim which simply refers to 'discrimination' has been held sufficient to cover a complaint of both forms of discrimination in s. 3(3) (*Quarcoopome* v *Sock Shop Holdings Ltd* [1995] IRLR 353, EAT).

'Victimisation' is defined in s. 2 of the 1976 Act and essentially involves discrimination against an individual by reason of the efforts they have previously made to enforce their, or someone else's, rights under the Act.

3.2 DIRECT DISCRIMINATION

As the Commission for Racial Equality's website points out, discrimination is not the same as racial prejudice or racism. 'Prejudice literally means "pre-judging" someone — knowing next to nothing about them but jumping to conclusions because of some characteristic, like their appearance. Racism is the belief that some "races" are superior to others — based on the false idea that different physical characteristics (like skin colour) or ethnic background make some people better than others'. Discrimination, by contrast, occurs when someone is 'treated less favourably on grounds of their colour, race, nationality or national or ethnic origin' (see www.cre.gov.uk).

Section 1(1)(a) of the 1976 Act, which defines what is generally known as 'direct discrimination', adopts this distinction, providing that a person discriminates against another for the purposes of the Act if 'on racial grounds he treats that other less favourably than he treats or would treat other persons'. This is because, as the Commission points out, 'The Race Relations Act is concerned with people's actions and the effects of their actions, not their opinions or beliefs . . .'. Discrimination may, nevertheless consist in treating people differently simply by virtue of a difference in their racial group or on the basis of attributes stereotypically associated with their racial group. Discrimination under s. 1(1)(a) comprises two elements: (a) treatment which was less favourable than the treatment which was (or would have been) accorded to another person, and if so (b) that the less favourable treatment was on racial grounds (*Glasgow City Council* v *Zafar* [1998] ICR 120 at 123, Lord Browne-Wilkinson).

3.2.1 Less favourable treatment

To decide the issue of less favourable treatment, it is necessary to consider whether the complainant was treated less favourably by the respondent than the respondent treated or would have treated someone of a different racial group in the same or relevantly similar circumstances — i.e. one must compare 'like with like' (*Marks & Spencer plc* v *Martins* [1998] ICR 1005). This means that in order to prove that an individual has suffered direct racial discrimination, he or she will have to compare the treatment he or she received, and about which he or she is complaining, with that which is (or would be) accorded to someone not of his or her racial group. It is therefore helpful, although not essential, to give an example of someone from a different ethnic group who, in similar circumstances has been treated more favourably than the person complaining of discrimination.

However, whether the comparison is actual or notional, s. 3(4) makes clear that 'A comparison of the case of a person of a particular racial group with that of a person not of that group under section 1(1) must be such that the relevant circumstances in the one case are the same, or not materially different, in the other'. Therefore, for the purposes of the comparison, the relevant circumstances of the complainant and of the person (actual or notional) with whose treatment (actual or notional) he is comparing his own must be the same or not materially different. To take an example, a person who claims he has been discriminated against by being refused a loan will have to compare his treatment with that of someone of comparable financial standing. By analogy with the 'like with like' provision in the Sex Discrimination Act 1975, it is generally true that the relevant circumstances of one individual cannot be said to be different from that of someone belonging to another racial group, where the differentiating factor is itself connected with race or nationality (*Showboat Entertainment Centre Ltd* v *Owens* [1984] IRLR 7, per Browne-Wilkinson J at 10). However, where action taken is 'race-specific' it is unnecessary to make any comparison with how others were treated (*Sidhu* v *Aerospace Composite Technology Ltd* [2000] IRLR 602, CA). In *Chief Constable of the Kent Constabulary* v *Jimi Kufiji* (EAT, Judge Peter Clark presiding, 4 May 2001), for example, it was held that the sending of a postcard which made a derogatory comment about black women was racially-specific behaviour.

It is not necessary to show that a person openly expressed an intention to treat someone else less favourably on racial grounds, or intended to discriminate at all (*R* v *Commission for Racial Equality, ex parte Westminster City Council* [1984] IRLR 230). It is possible in many circumstances to infer a discriminatory motive from all the circumstances in which the treatment was given. It does not have to be shown that the discriminator acted solely out of racial prejudice. As long as racial grounds were a substantial cause of his action, it is open to the court to find that there has been unlawful discrimination. Where other factors play a part, the court must decide whether the racial element was an operative cause (*Owen & Briggs* v *James* [1982] IRLR 502 [1982] ICR 618, CA). However, a lack of knowledge on the part of the alleged discriminator of the racial origin of the person in respect of whom it is said there has been discrimination will be material to a finding of whether the alleged discriminatory act was done on racial grounds (*Simon* v *Brimham Associates* [1987] IRLR 307, [1987] ICR 596, CA).

Section 1(2) of the Act makes clear that segregation is less favourable treatment, although this only applies if there is deliberate segregation — the mere fact of segregation is not necessarily sufficient (*Furniture, Timber and Allied Trades Union* v *Modgill*; *Pel Ltd* v *Modgill* [1980] IRLR 142, EAT).

3.2.2 'On racial grounds'

Section 3(1) defines 'racial grounds' as meaning '. . . any of the following grounds, namely colour, race, nationality or ethnic or national origins . . . .'. 'Nationality' was added to the 1976 definition to meet a restrictive interpretation of the earlier definition (see *Ealing London Borough Council* v *Race Relations Board* [1972] AC 342, HL and *Tejani* v *Superintendent Registrar for the District of Peterborough* [1986] IRLR 502, CA). It is now established that 'ethnic origins' is wider than 'racial origins'. Discrimination against a member of an 'ethnic minority' can be taken as encompassing religious and cultural differences as well as strictly racial differences.

In *Mandla* v *Dowell Lee* [1983] IRLR 209, for example, a headmaster refused a Sikh boy a place at his school because the boy insisted on wearing a turban. The Court of Appeal held that Sikhs were a group defined by religion, not birth and that discrimination against wearers of the turban might be religious discrimination but it was not racial discrimination; 'ethnic origins' was synonymous with 'racial origins'. The House of Lords reversed this, unanimously holding that in modern usage 'ethnic' was wider than 'racial', though 'ethnic' had the flavour of race; Sikhs were a group defined by common ethnic origins, and were thus a 'racial group' within the 1976 Act.

In *Mandla*, Lord Fraser set down these guidelines for establishing whether a group can constitute an ethnic group within the meaning of the 1976 Act:

> . . . it must, in my opinion, regard itself, and be regarded by others, as a distinct community by virtue of certain characteristics. Some of these characteristics are essential; others are not essential but one or more of them will commonly be found and will help to distinguish the group from the surrounding community. The conditions which appear to me to be essential are these:—(1) a long shared history, of which the group is conscious as distinguishing it from other groups, and the memory of which it keeps alive; (2) a cultural tradition of its own, including family and social customs and manners, often but not necessarily associated with religious observance. In addition to those two essential characteristics, the following characteristics are, in my opinion, relevant; (3) either a common geographical origin, or descent from a small number of common ancestors; (4) a common language, not necessarily peculiar to the group; (5) a common literature peculiar to the group; (6) a common religion different from that of neighbouring groups or from the general community surrounding it; (7) being a minority or being an oppressed or a dominant group within a larger community, for example a conquered people (say, the inhabitants of England shortly after the Norman conquest) and their conquerors might both be ethnic groups. . . . A group defined by reference to enough of these characteristics would be capable of including converts, for example, persons who marry into the group, and of course excluding apostates. Provided a person who joins the group feels himself or herself to be a member of it, and is accepted by other members; then he is, for the purposes, of the Act, a member. . . . In my opinion, it is possible for a person to fall into a particular racial group either by birth or by adherence, and it makes no difference, so far as the 1976 Act is concerned, by which route he finds his way into the group.

Prior to *Mandla, in Seide* v *Gillette Industries Ltd* [1980] IRLR 427, EAT it was held that discrimination against Jews could be racial discrimination, although as the editors of *Harvey on Industrial Relations and Employment Law* ('*Harvey*') point out (at paragraph 847), that was a different matter; for Jewishness usually implies ties of blood, and so Jews can be regarded as a racial group even in the narrower sense.

In *Commission for Racial Equality* v *Dutton* [1989] 1 All ER 306, CA, the Court of Appeal, applying *Mandla* v *Dowell Lee*, found that gypsies could constitute a 'racial group' under the 1976 Act by virtue of their shared history, geographical origin, distinct customs, language derived from Romany and, as with Sikhs, a common culture. By contrast, in *Crown Suppliers (PSA) Ltd* v *Dawkins* [1993] ICR 517, CA, Rastafarians were held not to fall within the definition of a separate ethnic group. Neill LJ observed that the *shared* history of Rastafarians (as opposed to the rest of the Afro-Caribbean community) went back only some 60 years, and thought that though they were a separate group they were not a separate group as defined by reference to their ethnic origins.

Muslims, denoting a group of persons united only in their religious beliefs, do not constitute a race. Thus acts of discrimination against Muslims cannot be held to amount to discrimination on 'racial grounds' (or 'ethnic origins'). But action taken which causes detriment to Muslims as a class (such as, in the employment sector, a refusal to allow time off work to celebrate a religious festival — *J H Walker Ltd* v *Hussain* [1996] IRLR 11, EAT) may be productive of indirect discrimination against persons from a particular racial group.

It has recently been held that discrimination between the constituent national groups found within the UK (the Scots, the English, the Welsh) constitutes racial discrimination on the grounds of 'national origins' (*Northern Joint Police Board* v *Power* [1997] IRLR 610, EAT). The EAT held that whether a group could be defined by reference to its national origins depended on whether there were identifiable elements, both historically and geographically, which at least at some point in time reveal the existence of a nation. Purely regional identities would not fall within the definition although it is perhaps debatable whether the Cornish and Northern Irish would be protected by the Act (see, further, *Harvey*, at para. 848.01).

It has been held that racial discrimination can include treating a person less favourably because of the colour of someone else with whom the victim of discrimination has associated. In *Showboat Entertainment Centre Ltd* v *Owens* [1984] IRLR 7, for example, a white employee who was dismissed for refusing to carry out an instruction from his employers to exclude young blacks from an entertainment centre successfully complained of discrimination on the basis that she had been discriminated against by virtue of her association with the black people. *Zarczynska* v *Levy* [1978] IRLR 532 and *Weathersfield Ltd* v *Sargent* [1999] IRLR 94 are similar examples.

3.2.3 Examples

The following are examples of the sorts of direct discrimination which would be unlawful by virtue of the new s. 19B:

(a) racist harassment or assault of black inmates while in prison or police custody;

(b) treating racist assaults, racist harassment of local authority tenants or racist bullying in schools less seriously if the victim is black rather than white;

(c) requiring only black patients to produce their passports before they can receive hospital treatment;

(d) assuming that all black prisoners are aggressive and therefore subjecting them to harsher discipline than white prisoners;

(e) refusing to admit a black pupil to school when a white pupil would be admitted, or excluding a black pupil from school in circumstances where a white pupil would not be so excluded;

(f) making poorer quality social services or special education needs provision for those from certain ethnic groups;

(g) a deliberate policy of assigning two inmates of the same racial group to double cells in prison, thereby segregating them from other inmates.

For a commentary on how the Act could be used to challenge racially discriminatory sentencing, see Sarah Ricca, 'Dealing with Discrimination', *The Times*, 5 June 2001. Further examples of direct discrimination which would be unlawful by virtue of the new s. 19B but which would also constitute unlawful discrimination under the Human Rights Act are given at section 3.6.3 below. See also Section 1 of the Commission for Racial Equality's publication, *The General Duty to Promote Racial Equality: Guidance for public authorities on their obligations under the Race Relations (Amendment) Act 2000* (April 2001). Helpful extracts of cases and commentary on direct discrimination and 'racial grounds' can also be found in A. McColgan, *Discrimination Law Cases and Materials* (Hart, 2000) at pp. 35–64 and pp. 413–433 and in R. Townshend-Smith, *Discrimination Law: Text, Cases and Materials* (Cavendish, 1998) at pp. 111–117 and 139–151).

3.3 INDIRECT DISCRIMINATION

Indirect discrimination aims to challenge discrimination which is not immediately apparent, but which results from the operation of apparently neutral actions or events, requirements or conditions, policies or procedures. It is caused by treatment which may be described as equal in a formal sense as between different racial groups, but which is discriminatory in its effect on one particular racial group. It is currently prohibited by s. 1(1)(b) of the 1976 Act, which provides that a person discriminates if:

> (b) he applies to that other a requirement or condition which he applies or would apply equally to persons not of the same racial group as that other but—
>
> (i) which is such that the proportion of persons of the same racial group as that other who can comply with it is considerably smaller than the proportion of persons not of that racial group who can comply with it; and
>
> (ii) which he cannot show to be justifiable irrespective of the colour, race, nationality or ethnic or national origins of the person to whom it is applied; and
>
> (iii) which is to the detriment of that other because he cannot comply with it.

This definition will need to be amended by 19 July 2003 in order to comply with the broader definition of indirect discrimination in the new European Community Race Directive (as to which, see Chapter 9). It may be amended before then, given that the definition of indirect discrimination in sex discrimination law is due to be amended on 12 October 2001, as a result of similar European Community developments in sex discrimination law. (See the Sex Discrimination (Indirect Discrimination and Burden of Proof) Regulations 2001 (SI 2001/2660) laid before Parliament on 20 July 2001 and due to come into force on 12 October 2001, although implementation of the relevant EU Directive (Directive 97/80 on the burden of proof in cases of discrimination based on sex) was actually required by 22 July 2001.) The Discrimination Law Association had submitted in the consultation process on the proposed changes in sex discrimination that the Government should adopt a uniform approach and amend the definition of indirect discrimination for all cases (employment, goods and services) under the sex and race Acts, but the Government declined. The only definition so far changed is that for employment cases under the Sex Discrimination Act. A change in the definition for non-employment sex cases and for race cases may nevertheless be forthcoming before 2003. What follows is therefore a statement of the law as at the date of writing, but practitioners should be aware that change is imminent in this area.

A four-step analysis for establishing whether indirect racial discrimination as defined by the 1976 Act has taken place was suggested by the EAT in *Tower Hamlets London Borough Council* v *Qayyum* [1987] ICR 729. First, it was necessary to identify the colour, race, nationality or ethnic origin of the applicant; secondly, whether there was, for relevant purposes, a racial group of similar colour or nationality or ethnic origin as the applicant; thirdly, whether or not there had been a requirement or condition which was imposed generally irrespective of race or nationality or ethnic origin; and finally, determine whether the proportion of the racial group to which the applicant belonged and to which the requirement or condition applied was considerably smaller than the relevant comparable proportion of the indigenous group. In the EAT's view, once the process had been exhausted, it became a comparatively simple matter to ascertain whether the relevant proportion of the ethnic minority group could comply with the requirement or condition.

3.3.1 'Racial group'

'Racial group' is defined in a similar way to 'racial grounds' (above). By s. 3(1), 'racial group' means '. . . a group of persons defined by reference to colour, race, nationality or ethnic or national origins, and references to a person's racial group refer to any racial group into which he falls . . .'. The EAT in *Tower Hamlets London Borough Council* v *Qayyum* stressed how important it is to identify clearly the racial group for the purpose of comparison to determine proportional inability to comply with a condition or requirement. The meaning of 'racial group' and especially 'ethnic origins' has been authoritatively expounded by the House of Lords and the Court of Appeal in *Mandla* and *Dutton* (see 3.2.2 above). Further, by s. 3(2), 'The fact that a racial group comprises two or more distinct racial groups does not prevent it from constituting a particular racial group for the purposes of this Act'. Therefore, for example, 'East European' could include Poles, Hungarians, Czechoslovaks and so on, and 'Czechoslovak' could be considered to comprise several separate racial groups, Bohemians, Moravians, Slovaks, etc (see, further, *Harvey* at para. 868).

3.3.2 Requirement or condition

In the employment context, it is necessary to decide whether the employer has imposed a 'requirement or condition' which is likely to impose an absolute bar on members of some particular racial group as against others rather than a preference (*Perera* v *Civil Service Commission and the Department of Customs and Excise* [1983] IRLR 166; *Meer* v *London Borough of Tower Hamlets* [1988] IRLR 399,

CA). The same concept will apply in relation to claims under the new s. 19B — in other words, are the functions of the public body operated in such a way that there is a bar on people of certain racial groups from benefiting from those functions in the same way as others? A requirement or condition does not have to be express or conscious. It can arise from a public body's standard practice, by analogy with the employment sphere, where indirect discrimination can be made out if a promotions procedure is inherently likely to work in a discriminatory way (c.f. *Watches of Switzerland Ltd* v *Savell* [1983] IRLR 141, EAT). The phrase 'requirement or condition' should be construed as widely as possible to ensure that discriminatory practices are eliminated, in accordance with the purposes of the Act (*Clarke* v *Eley (IMI) Knoch Ltd* [1982] IRLR 482, EAT). However, the implementation of the EU Race Directive, and its definition which includes practices as well as provisions or criteria, will mean that the requirement of a 'must' expounded in cases such as *Meer* will no longer apply, and that the approach in cases such as *Falkirk* v *White* [1997] IRLR 560 will be more appropriate (see further, Gay Moon, 'Indirect Discrimination', JUSTICE conference paper, p. 9).

3.3.3 Proportion who can comply with the condition or requirement

To show indirect discrimination, it is necessary to show that the requirement or condition has a disproportionate effect on the members of one racial group as against others. The requirement or condition must be such that the proportion of one racial group is considerably smaller than the proportion of other racial groups who can comply. What is being looked for is the *proportion* of the respective groups who can comply, not the *numbers* or *ratios* of them (see *Perera* v *Civil Service Commission and the Department of Customs and Excise* [1982] IRLR 147).

It will be a matter for the court to choose an appropriate section of the population for comparison, to see if an allegation of indirect discrimination is made out, and the court's selection of the pool will generally only be overturned on appeal if the choice of pool is perverse (see, for example, *Pearse* v *City of Bradford Metropolitan Council* [1988] IRLR 379, EAT; *Greater Manchester Police Authority* v *Lea* [1990] IRLR 372, EAT).

In *Perera*, the EAT expressed concern about the use of statistics to prove cases of discrimination:

> However, there remains the root problem that, by any normal statistical standard, the only statistical evidence laid before the tribunal is in fact inadequate. It is based on a very small sample from a very small number of non-typical offices. Is it therefore right to hold that the complainant has proved his case? We found this a very difficult point. On the one hand the burden is on the complainant to prove his case and, viewed in isolation, the statistics produced do not prove it. On the other hand it is most undesirable that, in all cases of indirect discrimination, elaborate statistical evidence should be required before the case can be found proved. The time and expense involved in preparing and proving statistical evidence can be enormous, as experience in the United States has demonstrated. It is good policy to require such evidence to be put forward unless it is clear that there is an issue as to whether the requirements of s. 1(1)(v)(i) are satisfied. With some hesitation we have come to the conclusion that in this

> case the complainant has proved his case . . . '[because the employers chose neither to adduce statistical evidence in rebuttal, nor to demonstrate that the complainant's incomplete statistics gave a distorted picture'.

In *Rutherford* v *Harvest Town Circle* (EAT, Lindsay P, 10 July 2001), the EAT affirmed that, following *R* v *Secretary of State for Employment, ex parte Nicole Seymour-Smith and Laura Perez* [1999] ICR 859, [2000] 1 WLR 435, in less obvious cases of indirect discrimination, it is appropriate to use more than one form of comparison, in terms of numbers and proportions from disadvantaged and non-disadvantaged groups. The implementation of the Race Directive will also mean that statistics will not always be necessary where disadvantage from indirect discrimination is obvious.

Following *Mandla*, the issue of whether a person 'can comply' is to be judged not by asking whether a person can *in theory* comply but whether he can in *practice* comply, consistently with the customs and traditions of the racial group to which he belongs.

3.3.4 Detriment

A person cannot complain of a discriminatory practice unless it affects him personally. In the context of the new s. 19B, this would mean that an individual would need to have been directly affected by an allegedly discriminatory policy or practice, rather than merely offended and concerned by it. The implementation of the Race Directive will, however, mean that a policy or practice which 'would put' an individual at a disadvantage could constitute indirect race discrimination.

3.3.5 Justification

By s. 1(1)(b)(ii) of the Act, a requirement or condition does not constitute indirect discrimination if it is justifiable in the circumstances. The issue of 'justification' is notoriously difficult. It is essentially for the respondent to show that he could not reasonably be expected to discontinue his discriminatory practice. Justification is an issue of fact — '. . . one that has been left by Parliament to the industrial tribunals [and by analogy, the county courts] whose function it therefore is to reflect the attitude of society as a whole regarding the degree of justification required to make distinctions of race or sex tolerable in an employment context . . .' (*Raval* v *Department of Health and Social Security and the Civil Service Commission* [1985] IRLR 370). This makes it difficult to overturn a finding on justification on appeal, and means that it can be hard to give advice on what is or is not likely to satisfy the justification test.

The editors of *Harvey* suggest that the 'flavour' of justification as considered in *Mandla* was that 'convenience' or 'preference' for a discriminatory policy would not be sufficient to meet the test for justification; but that it would not be necessary to go as far as showing that there was a 'necessity' for it. They continue by explaining how initially the EAT proposed a stringent test for justification, but that later cases indicated that the onus was no more than the ordinary balance of probabilities, and also that the necessity involved was no more than reasonable necessity. For a helpful summary of these cases, see *Harvey*, paras. 904–926. More recently, in *R* v *Secretary of State for Employment, ex parte Nicole Seymour-Smith and Laura Perez* [2000] 1 WLR 435 at 450, Lord Nicholls said, obiter, that:

> The burden placed on the government in this type of case [admittedly one of sex discrimination] is not as heavy as previously thought. Governments must be able to govern. They adopt general policies, and implement measures to carry out their policies. Governments must be able to take into account a wide range of social, economic and political factors. . . . If their aim is legitimate, governments have discretion when choosing their method to achieve their aim. National courts, acting with the benefit of hindsight, are not to impose an impractical burden on governments which are proceeding in good faith. Generalised assumptions, lacking any factual foundation, are not good enough. Governments are to be afforded a broad measure of discretion.

In *Mandla*, it was suggested that if a school was faced with an allegation of racial discrimination on the grounds that suitable meals were not provided for those of a certain religion, the school might well be able to justify the policy on the grounds that it was prohibitively expensive to provide the necessary meals. It is hard to predict how justification will be interpreted under the new s. 19B. However, what perhaps can be said in relation to discrimination claims under the new s. 19B is that attempts to justify indirect discrimination on the grounds of resources will have to be met with a greater level of scrutiny if the new s. 19B is to have any real impact.

3.3.6 Examples

The following are examples of the sorts of indirect discrimination which might be unlawful by virtue of the new s. 19B:

(a) A requirement that all pupils must not wear headgear could exclude Sikh boys who wear a turban, Jewish boys who wear a yarmulka or Pakistani girls who wear a hijaab (headscarf), in accordance with cultural and religious practice.

(b) The way in which the catchment area for a popular school is drawn if the effect of it is to exclude an estate with a high proportion of ethnic minority families, as well as a road in which there is a hostel for asylum seekers, if there is no non-racial justification for the way the map is drawn.

(c) A condition for securing bail that the defendant had a fixed employment or fixed address, which would disproportionately affect gypsies.

The issue of whether or not police stop and search patterns which appear to be discriminatory can be challenged as indirect discrimination is one of debate. For the Government view (in the negative), see the comments by the Parliamentary Under-Secretary of State for the Home Department, Mike O'Brien, at the House of Commons Standing Committee stage of the Bill (Hansard HC, Standing Committee D, 13 April 2000 (morning)).

Further examples of indirect discrimination which would be unlawful by virtue of the new s. 19B which might also constitute unlawful discrimination under the Human Rights Act are given at section 3.6.3 below. See also Section 1 of the

Commission for Racial Equality's publication, *The General Duty to Promote Racial Equality: Guidance for public authorities on their obligations under the Race Relations (Amendment) Act 2000* (April 2001). For further cases and commentary relating to indirect discrimination, see A. McColgan, *Discrimination Law Cases and Materials* (Hart, 2000) at pp. 65–125 and R. Townshend-Smith, *Discrimination Law: Text, Cases and Materials* (Cavendish, 1998) at pp. 266–319).

3.4 DISCRIMINATION BY WAY OF VICTIMISATION

Section 2(1) states that a person discriminates by way of victimisation if he:

> treats the person victimised less favourably than in those circumstances he treats or would treat other persons, and does so by reason that the person victimised has—
>
> (a) brought proceedings against the discriminator or any other person under this Act; or
>
> (b) given evidence or information in connection with proceedings brought by any person against the discriminator or any other person under this Act; or
>
> (c) otherwise done anything under or by reference to this Act in relation to the discriminator or any other person; or
>
> (d) alleged that the discriminator or any other person has committed an act which (whether or not the allegation so states) would amount to a contravention of this Act, or by reason that the discriminator knows that the person victimised intends to do any of those things, or suspects that the person victimised has done, or intends to do, any of them.

Victimisation does not occur unless the reason why the person was treated less favourably was one of the grounds set out in s. 2(1).

Victimisation essentially means treating someone less favourably because of the efforts they have made to enforce their rights under the 1976 Act, by doing a 'protected act'. The 'protected acts' are bringing proceedings under the Act (whether against the alleged perpetrator of victimisation or someone else), giving evidence or information in connection with any proceedings brought under the Act, otherwise doing 'anything under or by reference to' the Act (such as serving a s. 65 questionnaire in a case of suspected discrimination) in relation to the alleged perpetrator of victimisation or someone else and alleging facts which would constitute a breach of the Act (whether by the alleged perpetrator of victimisation or someone else). Insofar as the latter is concerned, it is not necessary to assert in so many words that there has been a breach of the Act; it is enough that the allegation is made that the relevant act was done. However, by s. 2(2), s. 2(1) does not apply to treatment of a person by reason of any allegation made by him if the allegation was false and not made in good faith. The phrase 'do . . . by reference to' the Act is capable of a wide meaning (see *Kirby* v *Manpower Services Commission* [1980] 3 All ER 334). The House of Lords recently held that victimisation can be proved without establishing the bad faith of the alleged discriminator (*Nagarajan* v *London Regional Transport* [1999] IRLR 572, HL). For further cases and comments on victimisation, see A. McColgan, *Discrimination Law Cases and Materials* (Hart, 2000) at pp. 126–136.

3.5 INTERACTION OF THE NEW SECTION 19B WITH DISCRIMINATION ALREADY PROHIBITED BY THE 1976 ACT

The 1976 Act already outlaws discrimination by public authorities in certain types of education (ss. 17–19), in housing matters (ss. 21–24) and by associations (other than trade union-type organisations) (ss. 25–26). The provisions outlawing discrimination in the provision of goods, facilities and services (s. 20) also extend to public authorities to the extent that the act done was at least similar to an act that could be done by a private person (*Savjani* v *Inland Revenue Commissioners* [1981] QB 458; *R* v *Entry Clearance Officer, Bombay, ex parte Amin* [1983] 2 AC 818; *Farah* v *Commissioner of Police for the Metropolis* [1998] 2 QB 65). Discrimination by public authorities which is rendered unlawful by these sections will almost certainly constitute discrimination under the very broad new s. 19B, although there may be some cases where only the 'old' provisions apply. This might apply, for example, where there is a dispute in a 'services' case as to whether the body providing the service was a public authority for the purposes of the new s. 19B, or not, in which case reliance could only be placed on the old s. 20. Practitioners therefore need to be aware of the scope of the old provisions.

3.5.1 Education

By s. 17 of the 1976 Act, it is already unlawful for the 'responsible body' of an educational establishment

> to discriminate against any person:
> (a) in the terms on which it offers to admit him to the establishment as a pupil; or
> (b) by refusing or deliberately omitting to accept an application for his admission to the establishment as a pupil; or
> (c) where he is a pupil of the establishment—
> (i) in the way it affords him access to any benefits, facilities or services, or by refusing or deliberately omitting to afford him access to them; or
> (ii) by excluding him from the establishment or subjecting him to any other detriment.

The educational establishments in England and Wales covered by s. 17 are any such establishments maintained by a local education authority, independent schools (which are not special schools), special schools not maintained by local education authorities, universities, and any other establishments providing full-time or part-time education which are designated under s. 24(1) of the Sex Discrimination Act 1975 for the purposes of the corresponding provisions of that Act. The Secretary of State for Education and Science has made an order designating the following establishments: certain independent polytechnics in London, certain establishments which receive grants from the Department of Education and Science, certain establishments which receive grants from the University Grants Committee, certain establishments which are assisted by local authorities; and certain independent establishments of further education. The responsible bodies who must not discriminate are the local educational authority, managers or governors of the establishment, the proprietor of the school or the governing body of the university, as appropriate. The Secretary of State for Wales has also made an order designating certain educational establishments which receive grants from the Welsh Office. Similar provisions apply in Scotland to prohibit discrimination by educational establishments managed by education authorities, those in respect of which the managers are for the time being receiving grants under s. 75(c) or (d) of the Education (Scotland) Act 1962, universities, independent schools and any other educational establishment providing full or part-time school education or further education. The responsible bodies are, again, the education authority, the managers of the educational establishment, the governing body of the university or the proprietor of the school.

Section 18(1) of the 1976 Act makes it unlawful for a local education authority, in carrying out such of its functions under the Education Acts 1944 to 1975 as do not fall under s. 17, to do any act which constitutes racial discrimination. Section 18(2) makes similar provision for Scotland. For example, discrimination in the award of discretionary grants under s. 2 of the Education Act 1962, or in the provision of facilities for social and physical recreation under s. 53 of the Education Act 1944, would be covered by s. 18.

Under the 1976 Act, there were special arrangements for the enforcement of ss. 17 and 19 against establishments and bodies in the public sector of education. These have now been changed by the 2000 Act (see Chapter 8).

3.5.2 Goods, facilities, services and premises

Section 20(1) of the 1976 Act makes it unlawful for any person concerned with the provision (for payment or not) of goods, facilities or services to the public or a section of the public to discriminate against a person who seeks to obtain or use those goods, facilities or services, (a) by refusing or deliberately omitting to provide him with any of them; or (b) by refusing or deliberately omitting to provide him with goods, facilities or services of the like quality, in the like manner and on the like terms as are normal in the first-mentioned person's case in relation to other members of the public or (where the person so seeking belongs to a section of the public) to other members of that section.

Section 20(2) gives the following as examples of the facilities and services mentioned in subs. (1):

(a) access to and use of any place which members of the public are permitted to enter;
(b) accommodation in a hotel, boarding house or other similar establishment;
(c) facilities by way of banking or insurance or for grants, loans, credit or finance;
(d) facilities for education;
(e) facilities for entertainment, recreation or refreshment;
(f) facilities for transport or travel;
(g) the services of any profession or trade, or any local or other public authority.

Section 20 applies only to discrimination by persons who are concerned with the provision of goods, facilities and services to the public or a section of the public. Thus the section does not apply where the transaction is one of a purely private and personal nature. By s. 75(1) of the Act, s. 20 applies to acts done by or for the purpose of a Minister of the Crown or government department, or on behalf of the Crown by statutory bodies or office-holders, in the same way as it applies to acts done by a private person.

Section 20 therefore applies to anyone providing goods, facilities or services to the public, for example, in hotels, shops, banks, insurance companies, financial services, cinemas, theatres, bars, restaurants, pubs, places of entertainment or refreshment, transport and travel services, and services provided by any local or public authority and by any profession or trade; and makes it unlawful for any such organisation to discriminate by, for example, refusing an individual their services on racial grounds, or giving the individual their services on less favourable terms or conditions than offered to people of other racial groups.

3.5.3 Housing

By s. 21(1) of the 1976 Act it is unlawful for a person, in relation to premises in Great Britain of which he has power to dispose, to '. . . discriminate against another— (a) in the terms on which he offers him those premises; or (b) by refusing his application for those premises; or (c) in his treatment of him in relation to any list of persons in need of premises of that description'. This provision does not apply to a person who owns an estate or interest in the premises and wholly occupies them unless he uses the services of an estate agent for the purposes of the disposal of the premises, or publishes or causes to be published an advertisement in connection with the disposal (s. 21(3)). By s. 21(2), it is unlawful for a person, in relation to premises managed by him, to '. . . discriminate against a person occupying the premises— (a) in the way he affords him access to any benefits or facilities, or by refusing or deliberately omitting to afford him access to them; or (b) by evicting him, or subjecting him to any other detriment'.

By s. 22, there is an exception from ss. 20(1) and 21 for 'small dwellings' as defined.

Section 23 provides further exceptions in that ss. 20(1) and 21 do not apply to discrimination which is rendered unlawful by any provision of Part II or s. 17 or 18, or to discrimination which would be rendered unlawful by any provision of Part II but for any of the following provisions, namely ss. 4(3), 5(1)(b), 6, 7(4), 9 and 14(4) (s. 23(1)). Further, s. 20(1) does not apply to anything done by a person as a participant in arrangements under which he (for reward or not) takes into his home, and treats as if they were members of his family, children, elderly persons, or persons requiring a special degree of care and attention (s. 23(2)).

By s. 24(1), it is unlawful for a landlord or other person whose licence or consent is required for the disposal of premises in a tenancy to discriminate against a person by withholding the licence or consent. This provision does not, however, apply if the person withholding the licence or consent or a near relative of his resides and intends to continue residing on the premises, and there is in the premises accommodation which he or she shares with others who are not members of his or her household and the premises are small premises as defined (s. 24(2)). 'Tenancy', for the purposes of s. 24, is defined at s. 24(4).

The net result of these provisions is that, subject to the owner-occupiers exception in s. 21(3) and the 'small premises' exception in s. 22(1), it is unlawful for anyone (including a public body) selling, letting or managing property (including business premises) to discriminate in any of the following ways:

(a) in the terms on which individuals are offered the premises;
(b) by refusing to let someone buy the premises;
(c) by treating a prospective tenant or purchaser differently from others who want to rent or buy;
(d) by refusing to transfer a lease to someone;
(e) by denying someone access to any benefits or facilities at the premises;
(f) by evicting someone or subjecting them to other disadvantages.

3.5.4 Discrimination by associations (other than trade union-type organisations)

Section 25(1) of the 1976 Act prohibits discrimination by:

> . . . any association of persons (however described, whether corporate or unincorporate, and whether or not its activities are carried on for profit) if—
> (a) it has twenty-five or more members; and
> (b) admission to membership is regulated by its constitution and is so conducted that the members do not constitute a section of the public within the meaning of section 20(1);
> and it is not an organisation to which section 11 applies [namely a trade union-type organisation].

By s. 25(2) it is unlawful for such an association, in the case of a person who is not a member of the association, to discriminate against him, (a) in the terms on which it is prepared to admit him to membership; or (b) by refusing or deliberately omitting to accept his application for membership. By s. 25(3), it is unlawful for such an association, in the case of a person who is a member or associate of the association, to discriminate against him, (a) in the way it affords him access to any benefits, facilities or services, or by refusing or deliberately omitting to afford him access to them; or (b) in the case of a member, by depriving him of membership, or varying the terms on which he is a member; or (c) in the case of an associate, by depriving him of his rights as an associate, or varying those rights; or (d) in either case, by subjecting him to any other detriment. Whether or not a person is a 'member' or an 'associate' of such an association can be determined by reference to the definition of these terms in s. 25(4).

By s. 26, those associations whose 'main object' (to be determined by reference to the 'essential character' and 'all relevant circumstances') is to enable the benefits of membership to be enjoyed by persons of a particular racial group defined otherwise than by colour are exempted from s. 25 for acts which would otherwise constitute discrimination other than on grounds of colour. In other words, there is a limited exception from s. 25 for those groups whose main purpose is to benefit a particular racial group.

For a good overview of the scope of these provisions, see the Home Office Guide to the Race Relations Act 1976, which can be found at www.homeoffice.gov.uk/

raceact/guide.htm and 'The Law' section of the Commission for Racial Equality's website at www.cre.gov.uk. See also A. McColgan, *Discrimination Law Cases and Materials* (Hart, 2000) at pp. 216–239, which includes cases decided under the education provisions, statistical information showing the disparate treatment of ethnic groups in relation to housing and extracts and commentary on 'services' cases. See also R. Townshend-Smith, *Discrimination Law: Text, Cases and Materials* (Cavendish, 1998) at pp. 371–383.

3.6 INTERACTION OF THE NEW SECTION 19B WITH THE HUMAN RIGHTS ACT 1998

Article 14 of the European Convention on Human Rights provides that: 'The enjoyment of the rights and freedoms set forth in this Convention shall be enjoyed without discrimination on any ground such as sex, race, colour, language, religion, political or other opinion, national or social origin, association with a minority, property, birth or other status'. Article 14 is incorporated into UK domestic law as one of the 'Convention rights' in sch. 1 to the Human Rights Act 1998, which came into force on 2 October 2000.

3.6.1 Discrimination prohibited by Article 14

The open text of Article 14 is its most significant aspect, in that it applies to '. . . discrimination on any ground . . .'. The Article catalogues a range of possible grounds '. . . sex, race, colour, language, religion, political or other opinion, national or social origin, association with a minority, property, birth . . .' but the use of the phrases 'such as' and 'other status' makes clear that the categories are not closed. This is a substantial improvement on domestic law prior to the coming into force of the Human Rights Act, which was generally limited to protection from discrimination on grounds of sex, marital status, race and disability.

'Other status' in Article 14 has been interpreted to include sexual orientation (*Dudgeon* v *UK* (1981) 4 EHRR 149; *Sutherland* v *UK* [1998] EHRLR 117), age (*N* v *UK*, App. No. 11077/84, 49 DR 170), illegitimacy (*Inze* v *Austria*, Series A, No. 126 (1988) 10 EHRR 394; *Marckx* v *Belgium* (1979–1980) 2 EHRR 330), marital status (*Rasmussen* v *Denmark* (1985) 7 EHRR 371), trade union status (*National Union of Belgium Police* v *Belgium*, Series A, No. 19 (1975) 1 EHRR 578), poverty (*Airey* v *Ireland* (1979–1980) 2 EHRR 305) and disability (*Malone* v *UK* [1996] EHRLR 440). Military status, conscientious objection to military service, professional status and imprisonment are also covered (See Harris, O'Boyle and Warbrick, Law of the European Convention on Human Rights (Butterworths, 1995, p. 470). Arguments can also be made that acts of discrimination by reason of physical attributes, geographical location, or education are also within its scope.

Article 14 therefore clearly includes the Race Relations Act concept of 'racial grounds' as a prohibited ground of discrimination, but is also of much broader application, and would include, for example, groups only defined by their religion.

However, as is the case under the Race Relations Act, it must be shown that any difference in treatment is based on the characteristic identified. In *Van der Mussele* v *Belgium* (1984) 6 EHRR 163 a trainee barrister alleged a breach of Article 4 (forced labour) in conjunction with Article 14 on the grounds that, unlike apprentices in other professions, he was obliged to complete a certain amount of voluntary legal work in order to qualify. The Court rejected his claim on the basis that as there were significant differences between the different professions he was not comparing 'like with like' and therefore discrimination was not made out. Similarly the Court has held that comparing married and unmarried couples (*Lindsay* v *UK* (1986) 49 DR 181), juveniles and adult prisoners (*Nelson* v *UK* (1986) 49 DR 170) or category A and low-security prisoners (*X* v *UK*, Commission, 9/12/92, unreported, cited in Starmer, *European Human Rights Law* (LAG, 1999) at p. 688) is not comparing 'like with like'.

Further, Article 14 does not prohibit all kinds of discrimination. Similarly to the notion of justification under the Race Relations Act, the jurisprudence of the Convention recognises that differential action may be appropriate but distinctions have to be soundly and objectively based (*Belgian Linguistics* case (1968) 1 EHRR 252, para. 10). Whether there is such justification depends on the aim and effect of the measure and whether there is a reasonable relationship of proportionality between the means employed and the aim sought to be realised. The burden of proof is on the applicant to show a difference in treatment — it then shifts to the state authority in question to justify the difference. As it is put in EC law, 'comparable situations are not to be treated differently and . . . different situations are not to be treated alike unless such treatment is objectively justified' (*Case 203/86, Kingdom of Spain* v *Council of the European Communities* [1988] ECR 4563, para. 25).

3.6.2 Dependent nature of Article 14

The wording of Article 14 makes it clear that, unlike provisions such as Article 26 of the International Covenant on Civil and Political Rights, it does not provide a 'free-standing right' to protection from discrimination. What it does mean is that when exercising *the other Convention rights*, an individual has the right not to be discriminated against on any ground, including those listed in the Article. The scope of the protection from discrimination in Article 14 is therefore limited to those rights embodied in the Convention and its Protocols. It can only be invoked in conjunction with one of the other Convention rights and in that sense is 'dependent' on them.

However, a breach of Article 14 can be found even where there is no violation of a substantive right (*Belgian Linguistics* case (1968) 1 EHRR 252, para. 9). What is required is that the action in question falls 'within the ambit' or the 'subject-matter' of another Convention right (*Rasmussen* v *Denmark* (1985) 7 EHRR 371; *Family K and W* v *Netherlands*, App. No. 11278/84, 43 DR 216 (1985)). In other words, although there can never be a breach of Article 14 alone, there can be a breach of it when considered alongside another Convention article even if there would be no violation of that Article taken alone. Examples of this principle in operation are:

(a) *X* v *Netherlands* (1971) 38 Coll Dec 9 and *X* v *Netherlands* (1973) 16 Yearbook 274 — the Court was willing to consider claims raising issues of discrimination in welfare benefits while rejecting the notion that the benefit in question was a 'possession' within the meaning of Protocol 1, Article 1.

(b) *Schmidt and Dahlstrom* v *Sweden* (1979–80) 1 EHRR 632 — the applicants complained of a number of detrimental measures aimed at members of a trade union which had sanctioned strike action. The Court found that although the measures involved — retroactive salary increases — did not in themselves engage Convention rights, they were 'linked' to the rights of trade unions to protect their members' best interests under Article 11 and therefore it was appropriate to consider the issue of discrimination.

(c) *Abdulaziz, Cabales and Balkandali* v *UK* (1985) 7 EHRR 471 — the applicants, women who were lawfully settled in the UK, complained that unlike men who were so settled, their spouses were refused permission to join them in the UK. The Court found that although that there was no violation of Article 8 taken alone, there was a breach of Article 14 in conjunction with Article 8. The Court took no issue with the restriction on the admission of non-national spouses to the UK in principle but agreed that it was unlawfully discriminatory to permit entry to the spouses of males but not of females.

Further, issues of discrimination may arise even in areas where states are not obliged to provide specific protection. Where a state chooses to provide a greater protection than is necessary to 'secure' the right in question, Article 14 applies to all aspects of the right in question. A classic example of this was given in the *Belgian Linguistics* case (1968) 1 EHRR 252, para. 9) when the Court indicated that although Article 6 did not compel States to institute a system of appeal courts, once the state had done so (and therefore gone beyond what Article 6 obliged it to do), it would violate that Article, in conjunction with Article 14, if it excluded certain persons from these remedies without a legitimate reason for doing so while making them available to others in respect of the same type of action.

3.6.3 Examples

The *Schmidt* case, in particular, shows that there may only need to be a 'very loose' relationship between Article 14 and another Convention right to trigger the Article 14 non-discrimination provisions (See Starmer, *European Human Rights Law* (LAG, 1999) at p. 686). This means that it is necessary to look beyond the most obvious applications of the substantive Articles before deciding whether an argument based on discrimination under Article 14 can be made; and that there is perhaps more potential for discrimination claims under the Human Rights Act than has perhaps so far been realised. The following are some examples of possible complaints which could be argued to be unlawful by both the new s. 19B and the Human Rights Act:

(a) *Article 14 together with Article 5 (right to liberty):* (i) a mental health detention in circumstances where evidence showed that someone of a different racial group would not have been so detained; (ii) the imposition of conditions of bail which would not have been imposed but for a person's nationality and which could not be justified on the facts of the case.

(b) *Article 14 together with Article 6 (right to a fair hearing):* a decision to apply to the court for a defendant to be kept in handcuffs during his or her trial, when someone from a different ethnic group would not have been so treated.

(c) *Article 14 together with Article 8 (right to respect for family and private life):* a housing allocation which meant a family of a certain ethnic group was forced to share rooms or was separated, when a family from a different ethnic group would not have been so treated.

(d) *Article 14 together with Article 9 (religious freedom):* a refusal to provide prisoners of a certain ethnic origin with the food required by their religious beliefs in the absence of justification.

Chapter 8 explains the procedure by which race discrimination under the Human Rights Act 1998 can be challenged, and how this interacts with claims under the Race Relations Act 1976 (as amended) and other causes of action.

3.7 TERRITORIAL EXTENT OF THE NEW SECTION 19B

By the new s. 27(1A) of the 1976 Act (inserted by sch. 2, para. 3 of the 2000 Act), in its application to the granting of entry clearance (within the meaning of the Immigration Act 1971), s. 19B applies in relation to acts done outside the United Kingdom, as well as those done within Great Britain.

3.8 OTHER PROVISIONS RELEVANT TO THE NEW SECTION 19B

3.8.1 Discriminatory practices

The prohibition on indirect discrimination is complemented by s. 28 of the 1976 Act, which deals with 'discriminatory practices'. A 'discriminatory practice' is the application of a requirement or condition which results in an act of discrimination which is unlawful by virtue of any provision of Part II or III taken with s. 1(1)(b), or which would be likely to result in such an act of discrimination if the persons to whom it is applied included persons of any particular racial group as regards which there has been no occasion for applying it (s. 28(1)). By s. 28(2), a person acts in contravention of this section if and so long as (a) he applies a discriminatory practice; or (b) he operates practices or other arrangements which in any circumstances would call for the application by him of a discriminatory practice. The kind of practice against which this provision is directed is one which embodies a condition or requirement which has to be complied with before some benefit can be obtained, and which would amount to indirect discrimination if it were applied to a person of a particular racial group seeking the benefit. However, the condition or requirement may be so effective a deterrent to persons of the racial group in question applying for the benefit that no such person ever applies. Consequently, no such person is ever refused the benefit, so no unlawful indirect discrimination occurs. The Act makes practices embodying such conditions or requirements unlawful even though as explained, there may have been no act of unlawful indirect discrimination.

3.8.2 Discriminatory advertisements

By s. 29(1) of the 1976 Act it is unlawful to '. . . publish or to cause to be published an advertisement which indicates, or might reasonably be understood as indicating, an intention by a person to do an act of discrimination, whether the doing of that act by him would be lawful or, by virtue of Part II or III, unlawful . . .'. This section does not apply to an advertisement '. . . (a) if the intended act would be lawful by virtue of any of sections 5, 6, 7(3) and (4), 10(3), 26, 34(2)(b), 35 to 39 and 41; or (b) if the advertisement relates to the services of an employment agency (within the meaning of section 14(1)) and the intended act only concerns employment which the employer could by virtue of section 5, 6 or 7(3) or (4) lawfully refuse to offer to persons against whom the advertisement indicates an intention to discriminate'; nor to 'an advertisement which indicates that persons of any class defined otherwise than by reference to colour, race or ethnic or national origins are required for employment outside Great Britain' (ss. 29(2) and 29(3)).

The publisher of an advertisement made unlawful by subsection (1) shall not be subject to any liability under that subsection in respect of the publication of the advertisement if he proves (a) that the advertisement was published in reliance on a statement made to him by the person who caused it to be published to the effect that, by reason of the operation of subs. (2) or (3), the publication would not be unlawful; and (b) that it was reasonable for him to rely on the statement (s. 29(4)). However, by s. 29(5), a person who knowingly or recklessly makes a statement such as is mentioned in subs. (4)(a) which in a material respect is false or misleading commits an offence, and shall be liable on summary conviction to a fine not exceeding £400.

Proceedings in respect of discriminatory practices or discriminatory advertisements can only be brought by the Commission for Racial Equality, in accordance with ss. 58–62.

3.9 PROTECTION FROM DISCRIMINATION OUTSIDE THE 1976 ACT

Racial incidents ranging from harassment and abuse to physical violence are offences under the criminal law. Inciting racial hatred is also a criminal offence. Publishing and disseminating materials such as leaflets and newspapers that are likely to incite racial hatred is also a criminal offence. Complaints in respect of these sorts of matters should be reported to the police.

Racially offensive material in the media contravenes media codes of practice, and complaints can be made to the Press Complaints Commission or the Broadcasting Standards Authority. Complaints about advertisements should be made to the Advertising Standards Authority.

Chapter Four
Exceptions to the prohibition on discrimination by public authorities

4.1 INTRODUCTION

The 2000 Act incorporates several specific exceptions from the new section 19B prohibition on discrimination. Sections 34–42 of the 1976 Act also contain several general exceptions to Part III of the Act (into which the new s. 19B falls) which will continue to apply to the new s. 19B. The 2000 Act amends one of these general exceptions relating to discrimination on grounds of national security. This Chapter sets out the scope of each of these exceptions and the reasoning behind it.

SPECIFIC EXCEPTIONS TO THE APPLICABILITY OF THE NEW SECTION 19B

The following are the specific exceptions to the applicability of the new s. 19B. A summary of the Government's position in relation to each of these exceptions is set out on the Act's website, at www.homeoffice.gov.uk/raceact (frequently asked questions, question 3) and at Appendix 3 of the Home Secretary's Consultation Paper. The various Hansard debates also assist in understanding the rationale for the exceptions.

4.2 PARLIAMENTARY FUNCTIONS

Both Houses of Parliament and 'a person exercising functions in connection with proceedings in Parliament' are specifically excluded from the definition of 'public authority' for the purposes of the new s. 19B (new s. 19B(2)(3)(a) and (b)). Further, the new s. 19B does not apply to 'any act of, or relating to, making, confirming or approving any enactment or Order in Council or any instrument made by a Minister of the Crown under an enactment' (new s. 19C(2)). This exemption does not affect the existing applicability of the Act to both Houses of Parliament (for example, for employment purposes) but excludes both Houses and proceedings in Parliament from the applicability of the new s. 19B. The exemption is aimed at reflecting the sovereignty of Parliament and issues of Parliamentary privilege.

By the new s. 19C(5), 'Minister of the Crown' includes the National Assembly for Wales and a member of the Scottish Executive. The making of secondary and primary legislation and proceedings in the National Assembly for Wales and the Scottish Parliament are, therefore, also excluded from the application of s. 19B. Again, the Government's justification for this exception is that as Ministers are accountable to Parliament, and their legislative powers subject to Parliamentary scrutiny, to extend s. 19B to their functions would constitute an unjustified fetter on the legislation making powers of Ministers.

4.3 JUDICIAL FUNCTIONS

The new s. 19B does not apply to any 'any judicial act (whether done by a court, tribunal or other person)' or 'any act done on the instructions, or on behalf, of a person acting in a judicial capacity' (new s. 19C(1)(a) and (b)). The phrase 'judicial act' (as distinct from an 'administrative act') has been interpreted in the context of several statutes, although any cases under the similar exception in s. 9 of the Human Rights Act are likely to be of most relevance here (see further, Robin Allen QC, 'An overview of the Race Relations (Amendment) Act 2000 and its impact', Discrimination Law Association Briefings, Vol. 13, July 2001, p. 3). The rationale for the exemption is that permitting civil actions alleging race discrimination against judges would interfere with the concept of judicial immunity, which in turn is an important aspect of the independence of the judiciary. Such independence is a key feature of the constitution, and requires judges to be free from control by the legislature or the executive. The Government believes that the correct venue for challenging judicial decisions is through the normal appellate process.

There is, however, a concern that to the extent that judicial acts rely on and interact with the actions of other public authorities which are covered by s. 19B, the exception could frustrate the purpose of the Act. For example, in the criminal courts, a judge could make a decision on bail or custody largely influenced by an earlier police decision, take a decision on the use of handcuffs during a trial on the basis of information provided by the Prison Service and consider the suitability of a defendant for a community-based penalty on the basis of the views of the Probation Service. Care would be needed to ensure that insofar as any of these acts were unlawful acts by virtue of s. 19B, the judicial acts exception did not serve to perpetuate any earlier discrimination.

4.4 FUNCTIONS OF THE SECURITY SERVICES

The Security Service, the Secret Intelligence Service, the Government Communications Headquarters and any unit or part of a unit of any of the naval, military or air forces of the Crown which is for the time being required by the Secretary of State to assist the Government Communications Headquarters in carrying out its functions are also excluded from the definition of 'public authority' for the purposes of the new s. 19B (new s. 19B(1)(c)–(f)). Again, the existing application of the 1976 Act to the security services (for example, in relation to their employment purposes) is maintained, but they are not bound by the new s. 19B obligation to exercise their core functions without discrimination. The justification for not including the intelligence and security agencies within the new s. 19B is that it would have required specific changes to safeguard against claimants misusing certain provisions to undermine the agencies' operational effectiveness.

For example, a claimant could have used a s. 65 questionnaire to 'fish' for sensitive information. The Government view is that the necessary safeguards would have had, in practice, the same effect as excluding the agencies from the 2000 Act, and so it is more appropriate to make the exemption clear on the face of the Act.

4.5 DECISIONS NOT TO PROSECUTE OR TO DISCONTINUE CRIMINAL PROCEEDINGS

The new s. 19F provides that s. 19B does not apply to a decision not to institute criminal proceedings and, where such a decision has been made, any act done for the purpose of enabling the decision whether to institute criminal proceedings to be made (new s. 19F(a)). Further, where criminal proceedings are not continued as a result of a decision not to continue them, s. 19B does not apply to the decision. Where such a decision has been made, s. 19B does not apply to any act done for the purpose of enabling the decision whether to continue the proceedings to be made and any act done for the purpose of securing that the proceedings are not continued (new s. 19F(b)). In effect, therefore, both decisions not to prosecute and decisions to discontinue criminal proceedings are outwith the new s. 19B.

The justification for this exemption is the importance of preserving the role of the criminal courts as the sole forum for determining guilt. This was recognised by the Phillips Royal Commission in 1981 which said that 'publicly calling into question a decision not to prosecute could amount to a trial of the suspect without the safeguards which criminal proceedings are designed to provide'. The exception is also aimed at avoiding the risk that disclosure of reasons not to prosecute could prejudice any ongoing or future criminal investigation or proceedings to which the decision was relevant.

In the Parliamentary debates on the Bill, there was a certain amount of negative comment about this exception as the decision not to prosecute had, after all, been at the heart of the Stephen Lawrence scandal. This exception would of course mean that even under the 1976 Act as amended, the Lawrence family would not have been able to challenge the decision not to prosecute the alleged killers of their son under the Race Relations Act 1976. (See, for example, Lord Cope, Hansard HL, 14 December 1999, col. 139; Lord Dholakia, Hansard HL, 14 December 1999, col. 171). The Government did concede to its critics to the extent that it narrowed the exemption from 'acts leading up to' a decision to prosecute to 'acts done for the purpose of' making such a decision.

However, there is still a concern that the exception is too widely drawn on its face, given that the phrase 'any act done' for the purpose of enabling a decision to prosecute or to discontinue proceedings still appears rather broad. It is not hard to imagine that if the phrase is applied broadly to cover, for example, allegedly discriminatory acts by the police at the investigatory stage (insofar as they are such 'acts done'), the purpose of the Act would be frustrated. However, it is clear that this is not the purpose of the exemption. Lord Bassam said that it was meant to be '. . . no wider than it needs to be to preserve the role of the criminal courts as the sole forum for determining guilt . . .' (Hansard HL, 14 December 1999, col. 180; see also Hansard HL, 11 January 2000, col. 589). He later said that 'significant but remote acts' such as the initial arrest and, where appropriate, the gathering and assessment of evidence should be subject to the new s. 19B, so that the exemption should be much more focused on the decision to prosecute, and the immediate acts leading up to it (Hansard HL, 14 December 1999, col. 180; see also Hansard HL, 11 January 2000 col. 1698 and the discussions in the House of Commons Standing Committee D, 18 April 2000, parts 1–3). Practitioners may find that reference to those key Hansard statements assists in ensuring that a narrow rather than a broad interpretation is given to the exemption. It is also clear that the exemption does not extend to decisions *to* prosecute, which could previously only be challenged as an abuse of process. This opens up the possibility of challenging the application of such a discretion applied in a discriminatory way, without the 'hands off' approach to police decision-making, traditionally seen when the exercise of a discretion is challenged (see further, Matthew Ryder and James Laddie, 'Policing and the Race Relations Act', JUSTICE conference paper, 28 June 2001, p. 3).

4.6 CERTAIN IMMIGRATION AND NATIONALITY FUNCTIONS

4.6.1 Scope of the exemption

The new s. 19D(1) provides that s. 19B does not make it unlawful for a relevant person to discriminate against another person on grounds of nationality or ethnic or national origins in carrying out immigration and nationality functions, as defined.

A 'relevant person' means a Minister of the Crown acting personally or any other person acting in accordance with a relevant authorisation (new s. 19D(2)(a) and (b)). 'Immigration and nationality functions' means functions under any of the enactments mentioned in subsection (5), namely:

(a) the Immigration Acts (within the meaning of the Immigration and Asylum Act 1999 but excluding ss. 28A–28K of the Immigration Act 1971 so far as they relate to offences under Part III of that Act);
(b) the British Nationality Act 1981;
(c) the British Nationality (Falkland Islands) Act 1983;
(d) the British Nationality (Hong Kong) Act 1990;
(e) the Hong Kong (War Wives and Widows) Act 1996;
(f) the British Nationality (Hong Kong) Act 1997;
(g) the Special Immigration Appeals Commission Act 1997

and include any provision made under s. 2(2) of the European Communities Act 1972, or any provision of Community law, which relates to the subject-matter of any of these enactments (new ss. 19C(5), 19D(4) and (5)).

These functions include decisions to deport, exclusion directions, leave to enter or remain, the grant of asylum, exceptional leave to remain and naturalisation as a British citizen. At the Third Reading of the Bill in the House of Commons, the Government introduced an amendment to modify some aspects of the immigration exception. Dealing with certain immigration offences, it placed the immigration service on the same legal basis as the police in operating the Bill's provisions. Section 19B would therefore apply to searches and arrests made by immigration officers in relation to immigration offences. However, 'immigration service functions that support the removal or deportation of individuals from the United Kingdom' remain within the scope of the exemption' (Hansard HC, 30 October 2000, col. 535). Harry Cohen MP raised the issue of detention but no response was made by the Minister and it would seem that decisions on detention remain within the scope of the exemption, but that issues as to the conditions of immigration detention do fall within s. 19B. Entry Clearance Officers working outside the UK will also be subject to the Act.

Section 19C(4) states that s. 19B does not apply to any act of, or relating to, imposing a requirement, or giving an express authorisation, of a kind mentioned in s. 19D(3) in relation to the carrying out of immigration and nationality functions. A 'relevant authorisation' for the purposes of s. 19D(3) is a requirement imposed or express authorisation given with respect to a particular case or class of case, by a Minister of the Crown acting personally, (i) by any of the enactments mentioned in subsection (5); or (ii) by any instrument made under or by virtue of any of those enactments (new s. 19D(3)(a) and (b)).

The effect of the exception is therefore to provide a procedure by which a government Minister, immigration legislation or rules can authorise discrimination on grounds of *nationality* and *ethnic or national origin* in certain circumstances. Discrimination on grounds of *race or colour* in the exercise of any immigration functions or discrimination on grounds of nationality or ethnic or national origin *where there is no appropriate authorisation*, remains unlawful.

Complaints of racial discrimination in certain immigration decisions, namely in decisions relating to the right to enter or remain in Great Britain, will be heard (with human rights complaints) as part of a 'one-stop' immigration appeals system (see Chapter 8).

4.6.2 Justification of the exemption and criticisms of it

The Government's justification for the exemption was that the s. 41 exemption (see below), and the narrow construction which the courts had necessarily given to it, would be insufficient for immigration, nationality and asylum purposes in the light of the new Bill. A broader exemption was necessary to reflect the 'unique requirement' for immigration and entry clearance officers to discriminate on grounds of nationality and ethnic or national origin as set out in instructions, and to authorise special compassionate exercises where necessary for particular ethnic or national groups. The Government suggested that without such an exemption, for example, it would not have been possible to operate policies of the kind operated for Kosovar Albanians during the recent Balkan conflict. In introducing the exemption in the House of Lords, Lord Bassam stated that the exemption '. . . seeks to strike a sensible balance between prohibiting discriminatory behaviour we would all regard as abhorrent on the one hand, and allowing justified and necessary acts of discrimination to maintain the Government's immigration and nationality policies on the other' (Hansard HL, 14 December 1999, col. 130). The Act's website states that the exemption provides a 'good balance' between the needs of good government and the rights of individuals at www.homeoffice.gov.uk/raceact (frequently asked questions, question 3).

However, the exemption and the justification advanced for it provoked some of the most heated and — unusually, when compared with the passage of the rest of the Bill, unconstructive — Parliamentary debates. The Parekh Report had strongly recommended that the exemption be removed, on the grounds that it permits 'institutionalised discrimination on grounds of ethnicity or national origin, without the need to justify differential treatment . . .' (see *The Future of Multi-Ethnic Britain*, Runnymede Trust (Profile Books, October 2000), para. 15.30). It has also recently been the subject of detailed and reasoned criticism by the Immigration Law Practitioners' Association (see the report by Ann Dummett, *Ministerial Statements: The immigration exemption in the Race Relations (Amendment) Act 2000*), published by ILPA with the support of the CRE, April 2001). This report argues that while the general emphasis of the Bill is on extending powers to deal with racial discrimination and duties to promote equal opportunities, the Government's position on the immigration exemption was '. . . starkly different from its position on all other parts of the Bill . . .' in that the exemption is unduly restrictive and in some senses regressive, and the concessions made by the Government to its critics on this exemption were 'nugatory' (ILPA report, p. 3).

It is generally accepted that immigration laws should be able to discriminate on grounds of nationality (since states are permitted by international law to control the entry and stay of non-nationals while applying different standards to their own nationals). However, the first concern about the exemption is that it is questionable whether it should be permissible to discriminate on grounds of nationality in the treatment of asylum seekers, for example, when taking decisions as to detention, or the NASS voucher scheme, or the dispersal and status of people inside the country applying for one form or another of leave to remain, based on nationality rather than an individual's claim of persecution). Similar concerns arise in relation to the use of nationality to discriminate in the grant of British citizenship (by the exercise of the discretion to naturalise someone, to register a person who has renounced British citizenship for whatever reason or to register any minor, whether born inside or outside the UK) or in the grant of visas. There had been relatively little reference to these issues in the Parliamentary debates. The ILPA report argues that the Government offered no explanation in debate for the potential for the exemption to permit discrimination in these fields, and that no such rationale can be found. The concern is that '. . . like the rest of the exemption, it writes a hitherto unacceptable form of discrimination into statute law . . .' (ILPA report, pp. 3, 5, 9–10 and 12–13). As one writer has put it, the exemption overrides '. . . what were for many years accepted principles: first, that immigration officers must observe the law against racial bias, and second that ethnic groups must at all times be treated as individuals not as a collective . . .' (Hugo Young, 'Ministerial double-talk simply masks a racist law: The Race Relations (Amendment) Act offends against natural justice', *Guardian*, 24 April 2001).

Secondly, the concerns about the exemption focus on the fact that it extends beyond permitting discrimination on grounds of nationality and also permits discrimination on grounds of ethnic or national origin. Yet it is not obvious how the distinction is to be made between ethnic or national origin and race or colour. As Lord Lester forcefully argued at the Bill's Second Reading in the House of Lords, 'Unlike discrimination on grounds of nationality or place of residence, discrimination based on ethnic or national origins is as much racial discrimination as discrimination based on colour or race, as the definition in Article 1 of the United Nations Convention on the Elimination of All Forms of Discrimination

1966 makes clear. Such discrimination involves treating one individual less favourably than another for what is not chosen by them but for what is innate in them at birth — their genetic inheritance — whether as ethnic Jews, Roma gypsies or Hong Kong Indians. It is as invidious and unfair as is discrimination based on the colour of a person's skin. That is why the Race Relations Act 1976 forbids direct discrimination on any of those racial grounds, apart from a range of clearly defined exceptions' (Hansard HL, 14 December 1999, col. 144). Lord Cope had already pressed the Government for an explanation as to why the exemption had the potential to increase lawful discrimination into these areas (Hansard HL, 14 December 1999, col. 139); and at the Third Reading stage, Lord Lester unsuccessfully tabled an amendment which would confine the exemption to nationality (Hansard HL, 3 February 2000, cols. 356–358). At the Second Reading stage in the Commons, Fiona Mactaggart urged the Government to address the 'muddle-headedness' of this part of the Bill (Hansard HL, 9 March 2000, col. 1272).

However, this uncertainty about the ethnic or national origin/race or colour distinction remains even after lengthy Parliamentary debate. Uncertainty also remains despite the Ministerial statements that they wanted the matter to be 'crystal clear' so that Ministers would be able to authorise discrimination on the former grounds, quite lawfully, but would deal 'very firmly' with discrimination on the latter, which is unlawful (see, for example, Lord Bassam, Hansard HL, 11 January 2000, col. 584). The ILPA report gives the example of a Chinese person, lawfully discriminated against on the ground of his ethnic or national origin, who later claimed that he had been refused entry because of his race or colour. In these circumstances, how would his race or colour be distinguished from his ethnic or national origin? Lord Lester argued that in the absence of adequate judicial safeguards aimed at ensuring that the doing of a discriminatory act was justified by the Government's legitimate aims, the 'extraordinary power' afforded by the exemption would effectively authorise a 'future populist illiberal Home Secretary' or 'a prejudiced administration' to violate the various international human rights Conventions which the UK has signed. Of these, Article 3 of the Refugee Convention 1951 and the Conclusions of the UNHCR Executive Committee meant that decisions about refugee status should be made without discrimination as to ethnic or national origins. Consequently, there is a real concern that insofar as ethnic or national origin cannot be distinguished from colour or race, the exemption authorises discrimination in a way which is incompatible with the very principle of non-discrimination which the legislation intended to secure, which was not expressly permitted prior to the 2000 Act and which cannot therefore be justified (Hansard HL, 14 December 1999, cols. 145–6; ILPA report, pp. 4–8).

The Government's answer was that the powers in the Act will be subjected to very close safeguards in that both senior and junior staff will have to work within instructions from a Minister, and that if they go beyond what is expressly authorised, they will be dealt with 'very firmly'. Further, the Government has undertaken that the instructions will not go beyond what is 'justified' and 'necessary'. Lord Bassam also stated that the exemption would not do anything to *require* Ministers to do anything contrary to their international obligations, as the discretion which is given to Ministers still had to exercised bearing in mind the UK's international obligations (the Home Secretary, Jack Straw, Hansard HC, 9 March 2000, col. 1211; Lord Bassam, Hansard HL, 11 January 2000, col. 586;

ILPA report, pp. 4–8). However, the ILPA report argues that while Ministers might not be required to do anything contrary to their international organisations, the exemption would permit them to do so, and this statutory permission may constitute a breach of international obligations in itself (ILPA report, p. 14).

The example of the grant of exceptional leave to remain made to Kosovar Albanians during the recent Balkan conflict was repeatedly cited as a justification for the need for discrimination in asylum policy. Lord Lester argued that no such exception to the Race Relations Act was necessary if the Home Office wished to make such special arrangements aimed at providing protection to particular groups seeking shelter in the UK — the reason for affording them favourable treatment was not their ethnic or national origins, but their well-founded fear of persecution, the urgency of their humanitarian needs and the need for the UK to comply with its obligations under the Refugee Convention. In other words, if humanitarian provision is necessary, it can be done in a non-racist fashion if it is done on the basis of an 'objective assessment of the conditions in the country concerned' and not on the basis of nationality or ethnic or national origin. He therefore suggested that the immigration exception was '. . . not only unsightly but unnecessary . . .'. At the Committee stage, he proposed that if the exemption were to remain, it should be limited to acts done which constitute 'special treatment on humanitarian grounds' (Hansard HL, 11 January 2000, cols. 580–582). This suggestion had also been made by the CRE, and endorsed by the Northern Ireland Council for Ethnic Minorities (Hansard HL, 9 March 2000, col. 1253).

The Government also relied on the example of ethnic Chinese people arriving with Malaysian or Singaporean documents although they really came from the People's Republic. It was said that in order to combat criminal gangs who were organising economic migration from China, Chinese-looking applicants had to be singled out (Lord Bassam's letter to Lord Lester dated 26 January 2000, cited by Baroness Prashar, Hansard HL, 27 January 2000, col. 1691). When it was pointed out that there were also criminal gangs operating to bring in white economic migrants from Russia and eastern Europe and that immigration officials would not be able to distinguish them from any other white entrant from elsewhere in Europe, the Parliamentary Under-Secretary for the Home Office, Mike O'Brien, replied that in fact decisions as to stop and search were much more intelligence-led and relied less and less on immigration officers looking at people (Hansard HC Standing Committee D, 13 April 2000, part 9). The ILPA report suggests that this '. . . appears to undermine the Government's own case for taking ethnic or national origin into account . . .' (p. 9).

The principled criticisms of the exemption are apparently supported by the fact that while on their face, British immigration statutes are not racially discriminatory, there is evidence that the very wide discretion which they afford the Secretary of State has permitted such discrimination to be exercised in practice. A 1985 Commission for Racial Equality investigation, *Immigration Control Procedures*, for example, had shown that there was a bias against non-white applicants in terms of refusal or detention at port, admission under more restrictive conditions, delay in procedures for admitting spouses and arrangements for family reunion. It concluded that there should be a major change of emphasis in the procedures, and confirmed that if the full force of the 1976 Act had been applicable to immigration control, procedures would have had to be radically and fundamentally altered (ILPA report, pp. 3–4).

The ILPA report contains the text of all the relevant Ministerial statements and debates during the Bill's passage through Parliament, helpfully organised by theme (pp. 17–88).

4.6.3 The first Ministerial authorisation under the new section 19D(3)(a)

This was made on 27 March 2001 and came into force on 2 April 2001. It deals with discrimination on grounds of nationality only and not national or ethnic origin. It applies where there is 'statistical evidence' of a pattern or trend of breach of immigration laws by persons of the applicant's nationality, or if IND intelligence suggests that a significant number of persons of that nationality 'have breached or will attempt to breach' the immigration laws. It permits persons of that nationality to be subject to 'more rigorous examination' by immigration officers than other persons in the same circumstances. They may also be detained, refused permission to enter or remain pending a decision, or have restrictions imposed on their entry. The ILPA report is critical of the width of this authorisation when compared with the Ministerial assurances that the guidance would be clear and unjustified discrimination eliminated (p. 14 and Appendix E).

On 24 April 2001, permission was given to discriminate against people of Chinese ethnic origin with a Malaysian or Japanese passport or travel document; Kurds; Roma; Albanians; Tamils; Pontic Greeks; Somalis; and Afghans. JUSTICE, the human rights organisation, has recently announced that it is seeking counsel's advice as to the legality of the immigration exemption and the first Ministerial authorisation under it on the grounds that it contravenes Articles 2, 5 and 6 of the Convention on the Elimination of Racial Discrimination and Articles 2 and 26 of the International Covenant on Civil and Political Rights, as well as Article 3 of the 1951 UN Convention Relating to the Status of Refugees. JUSTICE is also concerned that the 'specific intelligence or information' on which IND officers can rely in invoking the exemption will not be available for objective scrutiny by courts and so cannot be tested or challenged. Others have also pointed out the apparent incompatibility of the exemption with the recent EU Race Directive, as well as with the Government's international human rights obligations (Colm O'Cinneide, 'The Race Relations (Amendment) Act 2000 [2001] P.L. Summer 220 at 228–9).

4.6.4 The new Race Monitor for the exemption

The new s. 19E(1) requires the Home Secretary to appoint a person who is not a member of his or her staff to act as a monitor of the exceptions in relation to immigration and nationality cases. This provision was introduced at a late stage in the Bill's progress, in response to a suggestion raised by Lord Lester that there be '. . . some machinery, some person, providing adequate safeguards against abuse of discretion within the system so that that might be built into the Government's thinking . . .' (Hansard HL, 3 February 2000, col. 360).

The Home Secretary must consult the Commission for Racial Equality before appointing any such monitor (new s. 19E(2)). The appointed person shall monitor, in such manner as the Secretary of State may determine, (a) the likely effect on the operation of the exception in s. 19D of any relevant authorisation relating to the carrying out of immigration and nationality functions which has been given by a Minister of the Crown acting personally, and (b) the operation of that exception in relation to acts which have been done by a person acting in accordance with such an authorisation (new s. 19E(3)). The Monitor will make an annual report on the discharge of his or her functions to the Home Secretary who is required to lay a copy of any report made to him or her in the Houses of Parliament (new ss. 19E(4) and (5)). The Secretary of State is obliged to pay to the Monitor such fees and allowances (if any) as he may determine (new s. 19E(6)).

According to the job description issued for the Race Monitor, it is expected that the work of the Monitor will occupy 40 days per year, and that he or she will have access to all relevant papers and will visit IND operational posts. The Monitor will not be an appellate authority and will not be concerned with recommendations in individual cases, but rather with the overall impact of the exemption. Concerns had been raised at the Third Reading of the Bill in the House of Commons by Harry Cohen MP about whether the Monitor might in fact be 'toothless' and therefore of little value (Hansard HC, 30 October 2000, col. 534). The post is comparable with the existing one of Entry Clearance Officer (Hansard HC, 30 October 2000, col. 544) (see further, ILPA report, p. 12 and Appendix D). Although the post has been advertised, no appointment has yet been announced. JUSTICE proposes to make representations about the immigration exemption to the Race Monitor when he or she is appointed (JUSTICE Bulletin, Summer 2001, p. 13).

GENERAL EXCEPTIONS

The following exceptions in the 1976 Act remain unaffected by the 2000 Act.

4.7 CERTAIN ACTS BY CHARITIES

There is a specific exception to s. 34 of the 1976 Act covering certain acts by charities. By s. 34(2) and (3), it is not unlawful for a charitable instrument to contain provision for conferring benefits on members of a racial group defined otherwise than by reference to colour. A charity can therefore act in accordance with a purpose which is to provide benefits to persons of a particular race (but not persons of a particular colour). Where, on the other hand, a charitable instrument does contain a provision for conferring benefits on a class of person defined by reference to colour, the provision has effect from 13 June 1977 as though it provided for conferring the benefits in question on the class of person which results if the colour restriction is disregarded, or, if the original class is defined by reference to colour only, on persons generally. The 'colour' aspect of the charitable instrument is thereby effectively removed.

4.8 SPECIAL PROVISIONS IN RELATION TO EDUCATION, TRAINING OR WELFARE AND TRADE UNION MEMBERSHIP — 'POSITIVE ACTION'

Although the 1976 Act does not allow positive discrimination or affirmative action, it does permit certain positive action to prevent discrimination or overcome past discrimination. The aim of positive action is to ensure that access to employment or services is on equal terms.

Section 35 of the 1976 Act permits acts to be done to enable the special needs of particular racial groups to be met as regards education, training or welfare or ancillary benefits. Access to facilities, services or benefits can be restricted, or be allocated first, to members of the particular racial group in question, provided it can be shown that members of that racial group have a special need with regard to their education, training, welfare or ancillary benefits, which is met by such a restriction or preferential allocation. Such a need is defined as one which must be attributable to and distinguished by a characteristic which is peculiar to the racial group in question. For example, an education provider can take positive action providing for special educational or training needs such as special classes in English as a second language. Similarly, a special health screening service for African Caribbeans to detect sickle cell anaemia would be lawful as it met the special welfare needs of that racial group.

Under s. 36 of the 1976 Act, there is a general exception for discrimination in affording access to facilities for education or training or ancillary benefits where the discrimination is for the benefit of a person who is not normally resident in Great Britain, and where it appears to the provider that the person in question does not intend to remain in Great Britain after his period of education or training here.

Section 37 provides that certain training bodies (the Manpower Services Commission, industrial training boards and other bodies specifically designated for the purpose by an order made by or on behalf of the Secretary of State) may discriminate in or in connection with limiting access to training to a racial group under-represented in a particular field, or may take steps to encourage members of that racial group to take advantage of opportunities for doing that work. It is therefore acceptable to only offer training to the under-represented racial group or to encourage people from that group to apply.

Similar provisions apply to employers under s. 38, so that it is lawful to encourage workers from an under-represented racial group to apply for promotion, or to print leaflets in relevant minority languages to encourage them to apply. Section 38 also provides an exception to allow trade unions, employers' or professional organisations etc to take positive action aimed at ensuring that members of all racial groups are fully represented at various levels in the organisation. These exceptions do not permit the organisations concerned, however, to discriminate in admitting people to membership or in appointing members to posts in the organisation.

For further information on positive action under the 1976 Act, see the CRE's *Guide to the Race Relations Act 1976*, www.cre.gov.uk/law/rra_action.html. For a thorough consideration of positive action generally, see Chapter 3 of A. McColgan, *Discrimination Law Cases and Materials* (Hart, 2000).

4.9 CERTAIN ACTS RELATED TO SPORT

Under s. 39 of the 1976 Act, there is a general exception for discrimination on the basis of nationality, place of birth or length of residence in any area or place if the discrimination occurs in selecting a person or team to represent a country, place or area, or any related association, in any sport or game, or is in pursuance of the rules of any competition relating to eligibility to compete in the sport or game in question.

4.10 ACTS DONE UNDER STATUTORY AUTHORITY

Section 41 of the 1976 Act provides a general exception for discrimination in pursuance of any statute, subordinate instrument or Order in Council; or in order to comply with a condition or requirement imposed by a Minister of the Crown by virtue of a statute (s. 41(1)). Also excepted from the Act is discrimination on the basis of nationality, place of ordinary residence or length of residence in or outside the UK or in an area within the UK, where the discrimination is in pursuance of arrangements made by, or with the approval of, or for the time being approved by, a Minister of the Crown, or in order to comply with a condition imposed by a Minister of the Crown (s. 41(2)). In *Hampson* v *Department of Education and Science* [1990] 2 All ER 513, the House of Lords held that s. 41 only authorises acts done in necessary performance of an express obligation contained in the instrument (see also the EAT in *General Medical Council* v *Goba* [1988] IRLR 425, [1988] ICR 885). The new s. 19C(3) specifically states that the new s. 19B does not apply to any act of, or relating to, making or approving arrangements, or imposing requirements or conditions, of a kind falling within s. 41 and so the exemption will apply to the new s. 19B.

4.11 NATIONAL SECURITY

Section 42 of the 1976 Act provides that an act of racial discrimination is not unlawful if done for the purposes of national security. Under s. 69(2), a Ministerial certificate was conclusive evidence that an act was done for that purpose. In *Tinnelly* v *UK*, *McElduff v UK* (1999) 27 EHRR 249, the European Court of Human Rights found that this provision was incompatible with the European Convention on Human Rights. The case concerned the issue of a Ministerial certificate under the provisions of the Fair Employment (Northern Ireland) Act 1976 similar to ss. 2 and 69 of the 1976 Act. The certificate had the effect of halting proceedings for discrimination on the ground of religious belief or political opinion. The European Court of Human Rights held that the issue of the certificate violated the applicants' right of access to a court inherent in their right to a fair hearing under Article 6 of the Convention. This was because the conclusive nature of the certificate had the effect of preventing a judicial determination of the merits of their underlying discrimination complaints.

The 2000 Act corrects this position by limiting the circumstances in which 'safeguarding national security' can be used to justify discrimination. It does this by s. 7(1) which, by amending s. 42, means that national security can only be used as a defence to discrimination 'if the doing of the act was justified by that purpose'. Section 7(2) also removes s. 69(2)(b), by which the Ministerial certificates which were the subject of *Tinnelly* could be conclusive proof of national security as a 'justification for discrimination'. The new s. 67A also inserts a new procedure by which national security issues can be determined at hearings from which the claimant may be excluded, but in which his or her interests can be protected by an advocate especially appointed for that purpose. As far as the Home Office can ascertain, the defence had only been used once in the 25 years that the provisions had been in place in any event (see www.homeoffice.gov.uk/raceact/concerin.htm).

Chapter Five
Vicarious and secondary liability under the Act

5.1 VICARIOUS LIABILITY UNDER THE ACT INCLUDING NEW VICARIOUS LIABILITY OF THE POLICE

5.1.1 Vicarious liability under the 1976 Act

By s. 32(1) of the 1976 Act, anything done by a person in the course of his employment is to be treated for the purposes of the Act (except as regards offences thereunder) as done by his employer as well as by him, whether or not it was done with the employer's knowledge or approval. By s. 32(2), anything done by a person as agent for another person with the authority (whether express or implied, and whether precedent or subsequent) of that other person is also to be treated for the purposes of the Act (except as regards offences thereunder) as done by that other person as well as by him. Therefore employers can be held to be vicariously liable for acts of racial discrimination by their employees, and principals for acts by their agents.

As far as employers are concerned, vicarious liability will only engage if the act was done during the 'course of employment'. In *Irving* v *Post Office* [1987] IRLR 289, CA, it had been held that although a postman's employment had afforded him the opportunity to vent his racist views (enabling him to write 'Go back to Jamaica, Sambo' on a neighbour's post), these were actions which were outside the scope of his employment and so the Post Office could not be vicariously liable. In *Jones* v *Tower Boot Co. Ltd* [1997] IRLR 168, CA, however, the Court of Appeal indicated that a purposive construction was required, so that s. 32 should be given a broad interpretation. On that basis, calling the appellant 'chimp', 'monkey' and 'baboon', whipping him across the legs with a piece of welt and burning his arm in a lasting machine could be considered as acts done 'in the course of employment'. Similarly, in *Chief Constable of Lincolnshire Police* v *Stubbs and others* [1999] IRLR 81, it was held that social gatherings involving employees either immediately after work or for an organised leaving party came within the 'course of employment'. (See also *Sidhu* v *Aerospace Technology Ltd* [2000] IRLR 602, CA and *Waters* v *Metropolitan Police Commissioner* [2000] IRLR 720.) The test of 'course of employment' is therefore significantly broader than the test for vicarious liability at common law.

5.1.2 The new sections 76A and 76B

However, s. 32 did not apply to police officers who were not 'employees' but 'office holders'. Chief constables were not vicariously liable for the acts of any of their officers and so it was only possible to sue individual officers under the 1976 Act (*Farah* v *Commissioner of Police for the Metropolis* [1998] 2 QB 65, CA). The Commission for Racial Equality's Third Review of the 1976 Act in 1998 recommended that this anomaly be removed. The Macpherson Report agreed, and urged the Government to ensure that 'Chief Officers of Police should be made vicariously liable for the acts and omissions of their officers' under the 1976 Act. Section 4 of the 2000 Act achieves this position, inserting a new s. 76A into the 1976 Act to make Chief Officers of Police liable for acts of discrimination by officers under their direction or control. The new s. 76A(3) provides that for the purposes of s. 32: (a) the holding of a relevant police office shall be treated as employment by the chief officer of police (and as not being employment by any other person); and (b) anything done by a person holding such an office in the performance, or purported performance, of his functions shall be treated as done in the course of that employment.

The new s. 76A(2) replicates s. 16 of the 1976 Act (which is repealed), to provide that for the purposes of Part II of the Act (the employment provisions), the holding of a relevant police office shall be treated as employment: (a) by the chief officer of police as respects any act done by him in relation to that office or a holder of it; or (b) by the police authority as respects any act done by it in relation to that office or a holder of it. 'Relevant police office' in both sections means the office of constable held as a member of a police force, on appointment as a special constable for a police area or on appointment as a police cadet to undergo training with a view to becoming a member of a police force (new s. 76A(1)).

The new s. 76A also makes provision for payment from the police fund of: (a) any compensation, costs or expenses awarded against a chief officer of police in any proceedings brought against him under this Act, and any costs or expenses incurred by him in any such proceedings so far as not recovered by him in the proceedings; and (b) any sum required by a chief officer of police for the settlement of any claim made against him under this Act if the settlement is approved by the police authority (new s. 76A(4)).

Further, by the new s. 76A(6), a police authority may, in such cases and to such extent as appear to it to be appropriate, pay out of the police fund: (a) any damages or costs awarded in proceedings under this Act against a person under the direction and control of the chief officer of police; (b) any costs incurred and not recovered by such a person in such proceedings; and (c) any sum required in connection with the settlement of a claim that has or might have given rise to such proceedings. These provisions are in line with the existing powers that Police Authorities have to make settlements in civil proceedings.

By the new s. 76A(5), any proceedings under this Act which, by virtue of this section, would lie against a chief officer of police shall be brought against: (a) the chief officer of police for the time being; or (b) in the case of a vacancy in that office, against the person for the time being performing the functions of that office, and references in subsection (4) to the chief officer of police shall be construed accordingly.

A new s. 76B sets out a list of other police bodies to whom the new s. 76A applies, namely the National Criminal Intelligence Service (NCIS), the National Crime Squad (NCS) and any other body of constables or cadets. Insofar as NCIS or NCS are concerned, the new s. 76A applies as it applies in relation to a police force but as if any reference:

(a) to the chief officer of police were to the Director General of NCIS or of the NCS, as the case may be;
(b) to the police authority were to the Service Authority for the NCIS or the Service Authority for the NCS, as the case may be;
(c) to the police fund were to the service fund established under s. 16 of the Police Act 1997 (NCIS service fund) or s. 61 of that Act (the NCS service fund), as the case may be (new s. 76B(1)).

For any other body of constables or cadets, the new s. 76A applies as it applies in relation to a police force but as if any reference:

(a) to the chief officer of police were to the officer or other person who has the direction and control of the body in question;
(b) to the police authority were to the authority by whom the members of the body are paid;
(c) to the police fund were to money provided by that authority (new s. 76B(2)).

Provision is also made to cover those officers who are not at a particular time under the direction and control of the chief officer of their own police force or for the police area in which they are appointed. It states that in those circumstances, references in s. 76A to the chief officer of police are references to the chief officer under whose direction and control they are at that particular time (new s. 76B(3)).

The new provisions do not affect the liability of individual police officers, so that if the officer commits an unlawful act, he or she will be liable, notwithstanding any potential liability of the chief officer. What the new sections do is to increase the accountability of chief officers by making them vicariously liable for the racially discriminatory acts of individual police officers. This brings them into line with both other organisations such as the Prison Service and Fire Service and with its own general practice. The practical effect of the new s. 76 is, therefore, that both the individual officer and the chief officer of police can be sued in a race discrimination claim.

5.1.3 The employer's defence under s. 32(3)

An employer may be able to rely on the statutory defence under s. 32(3), which provides that in proceedings brought under the Act against any person in respect of an act alleged to have been done by an employee of his, it is a defence for that person to prove that he took such steps as were 'reasonably practicable' to prevent the employee from doing that act, or from doing in the course of his employment acts of that description. A chief officer of police would be permitted to rely on the same defence of reasonable practicability under s. 32(3) as other employers. It has been held that whether an employer has made out the statutory defence should be approached in a commonsense and practical way and not in a technical and legalistic way, bearing in mind that reasonableness is not sufficient (*Julienne* v *The Post Office and another* (EAT, Judge C Smith presiding, 6 April 1998)). In the sex discrimination context, the following approach to the statutory defence has been recommended:

(a) to identify whether the defendant took any steps at all to prevent the employee, where it is vicariously liable, from doing the act or acts complained of in the course of his employment;

(b) having identified what steps, if any, the defendant took, to consider whether there were any further acts that it could have taken which were reasonably practicable (*Cunliffe* v *East Riding of Yorkshire Council* [2000] IRLR 555).

The Home Secretary's Consultation Paper suggests to Chief Officers that 'good governance' requires them to review the position within their forces to ensure that they have taken reasonable steps to ensure that officers under their direction and control do not discriminate racially. He also suggests that this position should be helped by the positive duty to promote race equality (para. 9.5). It has been pointed out that police forces may undergo much more training in equal opportunities than other employees, thereby raising the 'spectre' of the statutory defence being raised routinely in police discrimination claims. However, it is to be hoped that the courts take a rigorous approach to the defence so that the purpose of the Act is not frustrated (see Matthew Ryder and James Laddie, 'Policing and the Race Relations Act', JUSTICE conference paper, 28 June 2001, p. 6).

The Government's position in relation to vicarious liability of the police is set out on the Act's website, at www.homeoffice.gov.uk/raceact (frequently asked questions, questions 10–13) and at Chapter 9 of the Home Secretary's Consultation Paper.

5.2 SECONDARY LIABILITY

The 1976 Act includes several provisions by which those who incite or assist others into unlawful discrimination can be liable themselves. These provisions apply in the same manner to the forms of discrimination prohibited by the new s. 19B.

5.2.1 Instructions to discriminate

By s. 30, it is unlawful for a person: (a) who has authority over another person; or (b) in accordance with whose wishes that other person is accustomed to act, to instruct that person to do any act which is unlawful by virtue of Part II or III, or procure or attempt to procure the doing by him of any such act.

5.2.2 Pressure to discriminate

By s. 31(1) it is unlawful to '. . . induce, or attempt to induce, a person to do any act which contravenes Part II or III'. By s. 31(2), 'An attempted inducement is not prevented from falling within subsection (1) because it is not made directly to the person in question, if it is made in such a way that he is likely to hear of it'.

Legal proceedings for contraventions of ss. 30 or 31 can only be brought by the Commission for Racial Equality (ss. 58-63).

5.2.3 Aiding unlawful acts

By s. 33(1) of the 1976 Act, a person who knowingly aids another person to do an act which is unlawful under the 1976 Act shall be treated as himself doing a similar unlawful act. For the purposes of subsection (1) an employee or agent for whose act the employer or principal is liable under s. 32 (or would be so liable but for s. 33(3)) shall be deemed to aid the doing of the act by the employer or principal (s. 33(2)). However, by s. 33(3), a person does not under this section knowingly aid another to do an unlawful act if: (a) he acts in reliance on a statement made to him by that other person that, by reason of any provision of this Act, the act which he aids would not be unlawful; and (b) it is reasonable for him to rely on the statement. A person who knowingly or recklessly makes a statement such as is mentioned in subsection (3)(a) which in a material respect is false or misleading commits an offence, and is liable on summary conviction to a fine not exceeding £400 (s. 32(4)).

The scope of the concept of 'knowingly aids' as found in s. 33(1) has been significantly narrowed following the decisions of the Court of Appeal in *Anyanwu* v *South Bank Students' Union* [2000] ICR 221, CA, and *Hallam* v *Avery* [2000] ICR 583, CA. In *Anyanwu*, the majority (Laws LJ and Butler-Sloss LJ) endorsed a view of 'knowingly aids' which required it to be shown that the alleged aider had contributed towards bringing about a result desired by another. Laws LJ held that 'aid' means 'help' or 'assist'. In *Hallam* the appellant failed to show that the police had aided a council to discriminate against gypsies, on the ground that it would have to be proved, for the purposes of showing secondary liability under the statute, that the aider knew that the principal was treating, or about to treat or was contemplating treating someone less favourably on racial grounds. Furthermore, it had to be proved that with that knowledge or intention, aid was provided. It would therefore seem that where an employee is alleged to have aided his employer in a discriminatory act, it will have to be shown that the employee either wanted this to be the result, or knew that the employer would treat or was contemplating treating the victim in a discriminatory way.

5.2.4 Indirect access to benefits etc.

By s. 40(1) of the 1976 Act, any reference to 'the affording by any person of access to benefits, facilities or services' is not limited to benefits, facilities or services provided by that person himself, but includes any means by which it is in that person's power to facilitate access to benefits, facilities or services provided by any other person (the 'actual provider'). Where the affording of access to benefits, facilities or services in a discriminatory way is in certain circumstances prevented from being unlawful by any provision of the Act, the effect of the provision shall extend also to the liability under the Act of any actual provider (s. 40(2)).

5.2.5 Discriminatory terms in contracts

Under s. 72(2), where the inclusion of a term in a contract constitutes a contravention of the Act, or is in furtherance of, or provides for such a contravention, such a term is void and unenforceable. However, where the victim of the discrimination is a party to the contract, the term is not void, but it is unenforceable against him. The Act provides that any person with a concern in a contract which contains such a discriminatory term (i.e. one which is not void but is unenforceable) may seek an order from a designated county court or a sheriff court revising the contract so as to remove or modify the term.

By s. 72(3), a term in a contract is unenforceable by the person in whose favour it would otherwise operate where the term purports to exclude or limit any provision of the Act. However, under s. 72(4), there is an exception from this provision in respect of: (a) a contract settling a case under the Act before a designated county court or a sheriff court; or (b) a contract settling an industrial tribunal case under the Act where the contract has been made with the assistance of a conciliation officer. But a contract under (a) or (b) cannot affect a person's right to complain about any other alleged contravention of the Act. For example, if a person made a complaint that his employer had discriminated against him in selecting employees for a training course, and if one of the terms of the contract (made with the assistance of a conciliation officer) settling the complaint was that the person agreed not to complain again about the employer's selection procedure, that term could not be enforced against him.

Chapter Six
The new general and specific duties on public bodies to promote equality

6.1 INTRODUCTION

A central feature of the 2000 Act is the development of a broader 'general' duty and 'specific' duties on public bodies to eliminate discrimination and promote equality, and the introduction of mechanisms for the Commission for Racial Equality to give guidance as to the duties and to enforce them as necessary. This chapter outlines the positive duties under the 1976 Act, explains the changes made by the 2000 Act, details how the new general duty and specific duties will be enforced and summarises the existing enforcement powers available to the Commission.

Further information about the new positive duties can be found in Chapters 3–8 of the Consultation Paper, and the Commission for Racial Equality publications, *Strengthening the Race Relations Act* (December 2000) ('Commission Guide'), *The General Duty to Promote Racial Equality: Guidance for public authorities on their obligations under the Race Relations (Amendment) Act 2000* (April 2001) ('Commission Guidance') and their *Response to the Home Office consultation on proposals for implementation of the Race Relations (Amendment) Act 2000* (all available on the Commission's website, www.cre.gov.uk).

It is intended that the new positive duties will complement the prohibition on discrimination in the new s. 19B, with the combined effect of improving equality and good relations between people of different racial groups. The Government also acknowledges that preventing unlawful discrimination before it occurs avoids the costs of loss of reputation and loss of goodwill with ethnic minority communities which flow from discrimination claims, as well as avoids wasting talent and disenfranchising elements of the community (Consultation Paper, para. 3.8). The Commission for Racial Equality points out that although some public bodies have responded positively to the recommendation in the Macpherson Report and other government or departmental initiatives that they audit their functions for race implications and take measures to promote equality, many have not. The new general duty on public authorities to promote racial equality gives statutory force to the Macpherson Report's recommendation and '. . . makes compulsory what voluntary measures have been unable fully to achieve' (Commission Guidance, p. 6).

6.2 POSITIVE DUTIES UNDER THE 1976 ACT

Section 71 of the 1976 Act imposed a duty on all local authorities to make appropriate arrangements with a view to securing that their various functions were carried out with due regard to the need: (a) to eliminate unlawful racial discrimination; and (b) to promote equality of opportunity and good relations between persons of different racial groups. This duty was not enforceable and as a result compliance with it was extremely uneven and inconsistent (Commission Guide, p. 3). In its Third Review of the 1976 Act, the Commission had proposed that it be replaced with an enforceable legal duty on all public bodies in exercising their functions to promote equality of opportunity.

Section 19(1) of the 1976 Act also imposed a general duty on certain bodies responsible for educational establishments in the public sector (as defined by s. 19(6)) to ensure that facilities for education provided by them, and any ancillary benefits, were provided without racial discrimination. By s. 19(2), (3) and (5), this duty could be enforced by the powers available to the Secretary of State under s. 68 of the Education Act 1944 and s. 71 of the Education (Scotland) 1962 (to require duties in the Act to be exercised reasonably), s. 99 of the Education Act 1944 (to act where local education authorities etc are in default) and s. 68 of the Education (Scotland) 1962 (to cause a local inquiry to be held).

6.3 THE NEW GENERAL DUTY

6.3.1 Scope of the new duty

Section 2 of the 2000 Act repeals s. 71 of the 1976 Act and sch. 3 to the 2000 Act repeals s. 19. Section 2 replaces the old s. 71 with a broader duty in a new s. 71, and makes further provision by inserting new ss. 71A–71E.

The new s. 71(1) requires every public body or other person specified in sch. 1A to the Act or of a description falling within that schedule '. . . in carrying out its functions, to have due regard to the need — (a) to eliminate unlawful racial discrimination; and (b) to promote equality of opportunity and good relations between persons of different racial groups'. This is the new 'general' duty.

The duty under the new s. 71 is different to the one under the original s. 71 because it applies to a large number of listed public bodies (not merely to local authorities), and because it is a much clearer, stronger duty — rather than being obliged to 'make appropriate arrangements with a view to securing that their various functions are carried out' with due regard to the elimination of discrimination and the promotion of equality, public bodies are now *directed* to carry out their functions with that purpose. The element of discretion inherent in the wording of the old s. 71 is therefore reduced. Insofar as the new s. 71 replaces the old general duty on education authorities under s. 19, it is broader as they are obliged not merely to work towards the elimination of discrimination, but also actively to promote equality of opportunity and good relations between people of different ethnic groups. One very significant practical difference between the old and new s. 71 is that the specific duties under the new s. 71 are enforceable (see below).

The term 'functions' in the new s. 71(1) has a wide meaning and the expression 'are carried out' adds to that. The aim is clearly that the duty will apply not just when the employees of a specified public authority are performing its functions but also when an authority is carrying out the recruitment of staff. As the requirement is to have 'due regard', the general duty is proportionate. This means that public authorities need to give appropriate weight to the promotion of race equality when performing their functions, and recognises that some public functions (such as health and education service delivery) will lend themselves to a proactive approach more easily than others (such as air traffic control) (Consultation Paper, paras 3.9 and 3.10). In some instances, where racial equality has no direct relevance to a public authority's more technical functions, such as meteorological research or weather forecasting, a court may be satisfied that the general duty will not apply to its functions. The general duty may, however, apply to the way in which information about technical matters is provided to the public (Commission Guidance, p. 11).

For the avoidance of doubt, it is provided that where an entry in sch. 1A is limited to a person in a particular capacity, s. 71(1) does not apply to that person in any other capacity. Further, where an entry in sch. 1A is limited to particular functions of a person, s. 71(1) does not apply to that person in relation to any other functions (new ss. 71A(2) and (3)).

The requirement to have due regard for the need to eliminate unlawful racial discrimination, to promote equality of opportunity and good relations between persons of different racial groups includes three parts, which frequently overlap, depending on the nature of the function: promoting equality of opportunity may also eliminate racial discrimination and promote good race relations. If one measure does not fulfill all three parts of the requirement, separate measures may be required to satisfy each part. The Commission Guidance (p. 11) gives the following examples:

(i) Providing positive action training for a group that is under-represented in an authority may promote equality of opportunity but it would not tackle possible discrimination in the authority's recruitment procedures.

(ii) A local authority which failed to take account of information about recent racist incidents on a council estate before allocating accommodation there to an ethnic minority family would be failing to comply with the requirement in the general duty to promote race relations.

By the new s. 71(7), the new s. 71(1) is subject to the new s. 71A, which limits the scope of the general duty in immigration cases. Section 71A provides that in relation to the carrying out of immigration and nationality functions (within the meaning of s. 19D(1)), s. 71(1)(b) has effect with the omission of the words 'equality of opportunity and' (new s. 71A(1)). Immigration and nationality functions therefore only need to be carried out with due regard to eliminating unlawful racial discrimination and promoting good relations between persons of different racial groups.

6.3.2 Implications for bodies bound by the new general duty

Under the new general duty public bodies will be '. . . expected to consider the implications for racial equality of everything they do . . .', such as allocating council housing, closing or opening a hospital or school and managing prisons (Commission Guide, p. 3). As policy makers and service providers public authorities '. . . will need, for example, to ensure that they consult ethnic minority representatives, take account of the potential impact of policies on ethnic minorities, monitor the actual impact of policies and services and take remedial action when necessary to address any unexpected or unwarranted disparities'. In other words, they need '. . . to take steps to ensure that their policies are fair, and put things right when they are unfair or unlawful' (Home Office website, www.homeoffice.gov.uk/raceact — frequently asked questions, question 5; Home Office Guide, *New Laws . . . Race Equality*, p. 4). In the House of Commons debates on the issue, Simon Hughes MP said that to comply with the general duty, local authorities would need to introduce policies that meet the needs of the entire community, which meant consulting with the entire community about how best to do that. For example, in a social services department, areas in which policy will need to focus would be the kind of meals on wheels that are supplied to the entire community, and the variety of choice that there is, and the care of people from ethnic minority backgrounds in residential accommodation. These were difficult and complex areas, but it would be important for local authorities to consult about them, introduce policies and have ways of measuring those policies to ensure that people from ethnic minority backgrounds were taking full advantage of the services offered, and if not, why not (Hansard HC, 30 October 2000, col. 550).

As employers, public bodies '. . . will need, for example, to monitor their workforces and employment practices to ensure that the procedures and practices are fair so that the public sector can better reflect the society that it serves' (Home Office website, www.homeoffice.gov.uk/raceact — frequently asked questions, question 5; Home Office Guide, *New Laws . . . Race Equality*, p. 4). Public employers will need to 'equality proof' their employment policies, procedures and practice, and take all necessary steps to prevent discrimination (Commission Guidance, p. 11). It is also clear that where a public body has made arrangements for a private or voluntary body to carry out certain of its functions, these arrangements, for example, the terms of a contract and how it is to be monitored or enforced, should reflect its obligations under the general duty (www.cre.gov.uk/law/rra_duty.html). Further information on this aspect of the general duty can be found in the Commission Guidance (p. 14). The Guidance also explains how positive action can be used to comply with the general duty (pp. 16–17).

Section 3 of the Commission Guidance sets out a series of questions which public authorities should ask themselves and steps which can be taken by such authorities to ensure that they are complying with the general duty.

The new general duty builds on the legislation establishing the Greater London Authority, the Welsh Assembly and the Metropolitan Police Authority, all of which provided for a duty to promote racial equality. The Government believes that the imposition of the new general duty is '. . . a positive way of tackling the institutional problems highlighted by the Stephen Lawrence Inquiry . . . [it] enshrines in law an important principle to which the Government wishes public authorities to adhere' (Consultation paper, paras 3.2–3.3). The Commission also takes the view that 'In the long term, this duty may be the most significant aspect of the Race Relations Act, because it gives statutory force to the imperative of tackling racism' (Commission Guide, pp. 2–3). It is hoped that compliance with the new general duty will make public authorities 'more efficient, effective, transparent and accountable and will help them win the confidence and cooperation of the public they exist to serve, and on whom they depend for support' (Commission Guidance, p. 6).

6.4 THE NEW SPECIFIC DUTIES

6.4.1 Introduction

By the new s. 71(2), the Secretary of State may by order impose, on such persons falling within sch. 1A as he considers appropriate, such duties as he considers appropriate for the purpose of ensuring the better performance by those persons of their duties under subs. (1).

These are the new 'specific' duties. An order under subs. (2) may be made in relation to a particular person falling within sch. 1A, any description of persons falling within that schedule or every person falling within that schedule; and may make different provision for different purposes (in other words, there could be different types of duties for different types of authorities) (the new s. 71(3)(a) and (b)). The Secretary of State must consult the Commission before making an order under subs. (2) (new s. 71(4)).

The new s. 71B makes special provision for the statutory duties in Scotland and Wales. By the new s. 71B(1)), for the purposes of the Scotland Act 1998, subs. (2)–(4) of s. 71 (and ss. 71(6) and 74 so far as they apply to the power conferred by subs. (2) of s. 71) shall be taken to be pre-commencement enactments within the meaning of that Act. The effect of these provisions is that in relation to Scotland the power to impose specific duties remains in some cases with the Secretary of State and in other cases is transferred to Scottish Ministers in accordance with the principles underpinning the devolution settlement. Only the Secretary of State may make an Order in respect of a reserved body but Scottish Ministers will be competent to impose specific duties on bodies with devolved functions. Following the public consultation process currently under way and in advance of an Order being laid, formal consultation between the Secretary of State and Scottish Ministers will determine where the order-making power rests in respect of each body. It will be for the Scottish Ministers to determine how to exercise the powers in relation to devolved interests. The Secretary of State will impose specific duties in relation to Wales but the new s. 71B imposes certain limitations on his power to do so. By the new s. 71B(2), the Secretary of State cannot make a specific duties order under s. 71(2) in relation to functions exercisable in relation to Wales by a person who is not a Welsh public authority before consulting the National Assembly for Wales. Similarly, the Secretary of State can make no such order in relation to functions exercisable in relation to functions of a Welsh public authority except with the consent of the National Assembly for Wales (the new s. 71B(3)). In this section 'Welsh public authority' means any person whose functions are exercisable only in relation to Wales and includes the National Assembly for Wales (the new s. 71B(4)). Consultation will also take place between the Secretary of State and the National Assembly for Wales, in accordance with the Memorandum of Understanding between the Government and the devolved administrations and the Concordats.

The content of the specific duties to be imposed, and how they might apply to different types of authorities will be decided following the completion of the consultation exercise by the Home Secretary and the Scottish Executive which is currently underway. The Government is taking the specific duties that are already operating in Northern Ireland and those recommended by the Commission in its Third Review of the 1976 Act as its starting point. They form part of a 'seven pronged policy cycle' (Consultation Paper, paras 6.2–6.3). Although the Government believes that consistency with the Northern Ireland approach would be beneficial, it is currently consulting on whether it would be more helpful to encompass the proposed standards into fewer duties. It has stated that it believes it would not be appropriate to translate those arrangements wholesale to the mainland because of the significantly greater number of public authorities that would be involved. There is a concern to keep the new duties 'proportionate' to the size and functions of different public sector bodies. A distinction would be drawn, for example, between what central and local Government should be doing on the one hand and small rural schools on the other (Consultation Paper, para. 6.4; Home Office website, www.homeoffice.gov.uk/raceact — frequently asked questions, question 6). In seeking to keep burdens on public bodies proportional to the policy objective, the Government wishes to '. . . achieve a culture change in public bodies consistent with our overall approach of modernising Government. We do not want to create a system of ticking boxes, which will not benefit public bodies or ethnic minority communities . . .'. With that in mind, 'Public bodies are particularly encouraged to work within existing mechanisms as far as possible to avoid unnecessary burdens and duplication' (Consultation Paper, para. 5.8).

The specific duties that the Government has in mind for key central bodies in respect of policy development and implementation and service delivery are consistent with the concept of 'mainstreaming' race equality. This is defined by the Council of Europe as '. . . the organisation, improvement and evaluation of policy processes so that . . . equality perspective is incorporated in all policies at all levels and at all stages, by the actors normally involved in policy making'. Mainstreaming 'into the policy making process from the earliest stages' had been recommended to the Government by the Better Regulation Task Force in its review of anti-discrimination legislation in 1999 and by the Commission in its Third Review of the 1976 Act (Consultation Paper, paras 6.2–6.3). (For further discussion of the concept of 'mainstreaming', in the context of the positive duties already imposed on public bodies in Northern Ireland by s. 75 of the Northern Ireland Act 1999, and generally, see A. McColgan, *Discrimination Law Cases and Materials* (Hart, 2000) at pp. 2–3 and 332–338 respectively). The precise nature of the specific duties is currently the subject of consultation. Concern has been expressed, for example, by some of the consultees that the phrase 'set out its arrangements' which appears in many of the proposed duties is not strong enough, and that a duty would be nugatory if the only requirement was for bodies to indicate what arrangements they had made to promote equality, without being compelled to follow them.

6.4.2 Examples of proposed specific duties

The Home Secretary and the Commission expect that 'full cycle' of specific duties will be imposed on those key central bodies listed at Part 1 of Appendix 6 to the Consultation paper (set out at Appendix 3 of this book), and that these will include:

(a) a duty to prepare and publish a Racial Equality Scheme setting out how it intends to meet its obligations under the general duty and any other proposed specific duties to promote race equality which are relevant to it;
(b) a duty on all public employers to ethnically monitor staff in post and applicants for jobs, promotion and training;
(c) a duty on all public authorities to:

(i) assess which of its functions and policies are relevant to the general duty, with regular subsequent reviews, for example, three yearly;
(ii) make arrangements for assessing and consulting on the impact on the promotion of race equality of policies it is proposing for adoption;
(iii) make arrangements for monitoring for any adverse impact on the promotion of race equality of policies it has adopted or is proposing for adoption;
(iv) set out its arrangements for publishing the results of assessments, consultations and monitoring;
(v) set out its arrangements for ensuring that ethnic minorities have access to information and to services it provides;
(vi) set out its arrangements for training staff on issues relevant to the duty to promote race equality.

Insfoar as education is concerned, OFSTED, local education authorities and the Learning and Skills Council are amongst the public authorities which are made subject to the general duty to promote race equality on the face of the Act. (The Learning and Skills Council also has a duty under the Learning and Skills Act 2000 to promote equality of opportunity). In respect of schools which are subject to the general duty (those listed at Part 2 of Appendix 6 to the Consultation paper — see Appendix 3), the Government proposes that each school should have specific duties to:

(a) prepare a written policy on race equality;
(b) assess the impact of its policies on ethnic minority pupils, staff and parents, with the emphasis on the attainment of ethnic minority pupils;
(c) monitor levels of attainment of ethnic minority pupils and the impact of its race equality policy on pupils, staff and parents.

The Government is consulting on how best schools might use their existing planning systems to make information available about their policies to promote race equality. The Scottish Executive Ministers are also inviting views on the most appropriate approaches for schools, reflecting the Scottish context and the standards in the Scotland Schools etc (Scotland) Act 2000.

The Government proposes that higher and further education institutions which are subject to the general duty should have specific duties to:

(a) prepare a written policy on race equality;
(b) assess the impact of its policies on ethnic minority students and staff;
(c) monitor the recruitment and progress of ethnic minority students and staff;
(d) set out its arrangements for publishing its written policy, impact assessments and the monitoring required above.

Chapter 7 of the Consultation Paper sets out the specific duties which are proposed on certain public bodies in relation to their employment practices, which are drawn from the Commission for Racial Equality's *Racial Equality Means Quality: A Standard for Racial Equality for Employers*. These include:

(a) for all public employers subject to the general duty to promote race equality, a specific duty to ethnically monitor staff in post and applicants for jobs, promotion and training, in line with the lower tier set out in the Commission's standard;
(b) for all public bodies with 150 full-time employees, a specific duty to ethnically monitor and analyse grievances, disciplinary action, performance appraisal (when this results in benefits or sanctions), training and dismissals and other reasons for leaving, in line with the higher tier set out in the Commission's standard;
(c) for all public bodies made subject to these particular duties, a duty to publish annually the results of their ethnic monitoring. The Government would expect them to use existing annual reporting systems such as annual departmental reports, whenever possible rather than creating new reporting mechanisms;
(d) a duty on the Department for Education and Employment and the Scottish Executive Education Department to monitor the overall position for teaching staff in England and Wales and Scotland respectively drawing, where possible, on detailed data collected by local education authorities and to publish the results annually. These bodies would have responsibility for publishing data on the ethnicity of teaching staff rather than schools themselves;
(e) a duty on the Learning and Skills Council, the Scottish Further Education Funding Council and the National Council for Education and Training for Wales to monitor the overall position of teaching staff in their respective further education institutions and to publish the results annually.

Many of the arrangements which are already required or recommended by administrative or other standards, will, therefore, already be in place to varying degrees. These include:

(a) *Policy Appraisal for Equal Treatment* (guidance for central government);
(b) *Racial Equality Means Quality, the Commission for Racial Equality's Standard for Local Government*;
(c) the 2000/2001 Ministerial Priorities for the police (which included 'increasing trust and confidence in policing amongst ethnic minority communities');
(d) Community Race Relations Strategies which are worked from or being developed by 98% of police forces in England in Wales, to ensure that policy, strategic and operational decisions take account of race relations implications (see the 2000/01 thematic inspection on Police Community and Race Relations);
(e) *Without Prejudice*, the 2001 thematic inspection of police race relations in Scotland, which has established a baseline or benchmark of the current position of police forces and common police services in Scotland;
(f) s. 95 of the Criminal Justice Act 1991 (which requires monitoring of service delivery to ethnic minorities and others);
(g) the *Race Equality Agenda of the Department of Health* (January 2000), the *NHS Plan: A Plan for Investment, A Plan for Reform* (July 2000) and the *Equalities*

Framework for the NHS (April 2000) (setting racial equality standards in the NHS);

(h) *Learning for All, Standards for Racial Equality in Schools* (non-statutory guidance from the Commission for Racial Equality for schools in England and Wales);

(i) *Commission for Racial Equality Code of Practice (Scotland): for the Elimination of Racial Discrimination in Education 1991* (non-statutory guidance from the Commission for schools and further education colleges in Scotland).

The Equality Commission for Northern Ireland has also recently published a document, *Practical Guidance on Equality Impact Assessment*, aimed at assisting public authorities in discharging their duty under s. 75 of the Northern Ireland Act 1998 to review all their policies for potential adverse impact (see www.equalityni.org; see also the comments of Evelyn Collins, Chief Executive of the Equality Commission for Northern Ireland, at EOR, No. 95. January/February 2001, pp. 13–14).

The Government received 290 responses to its consultation process on the proposed specific duties — 30 per cent from local government bodies, 18 per cent from health bodies and 16 per cent from educational bodies. Eighty per cent of those who responded broadly agreed with the proposals and only 1 per cent were clearly against them (with 19 per cent not expressing a strong view either way). Many respondents offered suggestions for strengthening or 'fine-tuning' the proposed specific duties to provide greater clarity. At the time of writing, it was intended to lay the orders bringing the specific duties into effect as soon as possible after the Parliamentary Summer Recess, in October 2001 (see www.homeoffice.gov.uk/raceact). In any event, the Government has announced that it intends to keep the effectiveness and regulatory impact of the use of these new powers under review. As a result, there will be further opportunities to assess whether proportionality has been maintained in relation to the policy objective (Consultation Paper, para. 5.8).

6.5 PUBLIC BODIES BOUND BY THE NEW GENERAL AND SPECIFIC DUTIES

Schedule 1A to the Act lists those bodies who are currently bound by the general duty in s. 71(1) and who will be liable to the specific duties under s. 71(2). This finite list is different from the wider definition of 'public authority' which applies to the prohibition on discrimination under the new s. 19B. The reason for adopting the list approach is that it was felt that there is a need for greater clarity when duties are imposed requiring bodies to be proactive (Consultation Paper, para. 3.11). Schedule 1A currently includes:

(a) all ministers and central government departments;
(b) local authorities, regional development agencies and enterprise networks;
(c) police authorities;
(d) health authorities, health boards, NHS trusts and primary care trusts;
(e) governing bodies of maintained schools, colleges and universities;
(f) the Housing Corporation, Scottish Homes, housing action trusts.

The new s. 71(5) authorises the Secretary of State by order to amend sch. 1A by adding or deleting bodies (although no such order may extend the schedule unless the Secretary of State considers that the extension relates to a person who exercises functions of a public nature). This power is reserved to the Secretary of State as it is the Government's aim to ensure consistent application of the new general duty. The Government has, however, made clear during the passage of the 2000 Act through Parliament that it wishes to see the general duty given a wide application. In the consultation process which is currently under way, the Secretary of State has sought views on a list of over 300 bodies he proposes to add to schedule 1A. 78 of these are advisory Non-Departmental Public Bodies ('NDPB's') set up by statute or having some other legal status, 136 are executive NDPB's, 8 are Public Corporations, 6 are the public functions of nationalised industries and 74 concern regulatory or other bodies. Several advisory NDPB's are excluded as they do not have legal status. Judicial or quasi-judicial bodies are excluded as they are exempt from the prohibition on discrimination so as not to interfere with the concept of judicial independence, and the same consideration explains their absence from the general duty (Consultation paper, paras 4.1–4.7; the list of proposed bodies for inclusion in sch. 1A is set out at Appendix 5 of the Consultation Paper — see Appendix 3 of this book).

In its response to the consultation process, the Commission expressed the view that the general duty should apply to any public authority whose main functions come within any of the following criteria:

(a) delivers services to the public to which racial equality is relevant;
(b) creates policy that impacts on public services;
(c) commissions or disburses funding for the provision of public services to which racial equality is relevant;
(d) carries out law enforcement, regulatory or control functions that affect the public or sections of the public;
(e) monitors, inspects or reviews the performance of public authorities, including allocation of resources and implementation of policies;
(f) controls, regulates or accredits access to professions.

The omission of certain public authorities from both sch. 1A and Appendix 5 had been brought to the Commission's attention, and they have already asked the Home Office to consider whether these authorities should also be added to sch. 1A. They are aware that other organisations in responding to the consultation have also identified public authorities that they recommend for inclusion. By reference to the above criteria, the Commission submitted that there are bodies whose functions may, in part, be quasi-judicial, such as the different Ombudsmen, but who should be subject to the general duty having regard to their important monitoring, inspection and review functions. The CRE have expressed a wish to have a further opportunity to comment on the final list of authorities proposed for inclusion in sch. 1A. The Commission also anticipates that it will be necessary to keep sch. 1A under regular review, since future legislation is almost certain to create new public authorities and to re-name or remove the functions of existing public authorities.

The Commission also pointed out that for the general duty to be truly effective, it will be necessary not only for the listed public authorities to be aware of their obligations but also for the public, and in particular black and ethnic minority community organisations, to be able to know which authorities are subject to both general and specific duties. The Commission therefore recommend that there should be published a guide to the full range of the public authorities that are government departments for purposes of the general duty to promote racial equality.

At Part 3 of Appendix 6 to the Consultation paper (see Appendix 3), the Government has listed a large number of public bodies that carry out a mixture of public functions from astronomy research to the management of nuclear liabilities. It does not propose to apply specific duties to these bodies in respect of their policy and service functions (although specific duties are proposed in relation to their employment functions) on the basis that the general duty should suffice. The same is true of the advisory bodies listed at Part 4 of Appendix 6 to the Consultation paper (see Appendix 3), on the basis that these bodies provide advice to Ministers and Government Departments who themselves will be subject to the full range of specific duties (see, further, Home Office leaflet, *New Laws . . . Race Equality*, p. 4; Commission Guide, p. 4; Consultation Paper, paras 6.4–6.22 and Chapter 7).

The Secretary of State had indicated he proposed to lay the secondary legislation extending sch. 1A in July 2001, although this is now anticipated some time in October 2001.

6.6 COMMISSION FOR RACIAL EQUALITY CODES OF PRACTICE

Under s. 47 of the 1976 Act the Commission for Racial Equality could issue Codes of Practice containing practical guidance for the elimination of discrimination, and/or the promotion of equality of opportunity between persons of different racial groups in the employment field. The Codes issued under this section have given useful guidance on good practice to employers and provided employees complaining of discrimination with standards by which they can compare their own treatment in the tribunal (by virtue of s. 47(10) making such evidence admissible). The Commission also issued a similar statutory Code dealing with housing.

The new s. 71C(1) makes similar provision in relation to the broader functions of the public sector. It authorises the Commission to issue Codes of Practice containing such practical guidance as the Commission think fit in relation to the performance by persons of duties imposed on them by virtue of subs. (1) and (2) of s. 71. Without prejudice to subs. (1), a Code of Practice issued under this section may include such practical guidance as the Commission think fit as to what steps it is reasonably practicable for persons to take for the purpose of preventing their staff from doing acts in the course of their duties made unlawful by this Act (new s. 71C(12)). It is also intended that the Codes would include examples of best practice (Consultation Paper, para. 8.2).

The procedure by which the new Codes are to be issued is similar to that laid down in s. 47(3)–(9) of the 1976 Act for the employment Codes issued under that section. When the Commission proposes to issue a Code of Practice under the new s. 71C, it shall prepare and publish a draft of the Code and consider any representations made to it about the draft, and it may modify the draft accordingly (new s. 71C(2)(a)–(c)). Further, in the course of preparing any draft Code of Practice under this section the Commission must consult such organisations or bodies as appear to it to be appropriate having regard to the content of the draft Code (new s. 71C(3)). The Commission may revoke, or from time to time revise, the whole or any part of a Code of Practice issued under this section; and, where it revises the whole or any part of such a Code, it shall issue the revised Code, and the procedure in subs. (2)–(8) for Parliamentary approval of the Code (see below) shall apply (with appropriate modifications) to such a revised Code as it applies to the first issue of a Code (new s. 71C(8)).

If the Commission decides to proceed with a draft Code of Practice, it must transmit the draft to the Secretary of State who shall consult the Scottish Ministers and the National Assembly for Wales (new s. 71C(4)). After consulting the Scottish Ministers and the National Assembly for Wales, the Secretary of State shall, if he approves of the draft Code, lay it before both Houses of Parliament; and if he does not approve of it, publish details of his reasons for withholding approval (new s. 71C(5)). If, within the period of 40 days beginning with the day on which a copy of a draft Code of Practice is laid before each House of Parliament, or, if such copies are laid on different days, with the later of the two days, either House so resolves, no further proceedings shall be taken on the draft Code of Practice, but without prejudice to the laying before Parliament of a new draft (new s. 71C(6)). In reckoning the period of 40 days referred to in subs. (6), no account shall be taken of any period during which Parliament is dissolved or prorogued or during which both Houses are adjourned for more than four days (new s. 71C(7)). If no such resolution is passed as is referred to in subs. (6), the Commission shall issue the Code in the form of the draft and the Code shall come into effect on such day as the Secretary of State may, after consulting the Scottish Ministers and the National Assembly for Wales, by order appoint (new s. 71C(8)).

The relevance of the new Codes to an individual litigant is similar to that of the employment Codes under s. 47(10) of the 1976 Act. While a failure on the part of any person to observe any provision of a Code of Practice does not of itself render that person liable to any proceedings, any Code of Practice issued under the new s. 71C shall be admissible in evidence in any legal proceedings, and if any provision of such a Code appears to the court or tribunal concerned to be relevant to any question arising in the proceedings it shall be taken into account in determining that question (new s. 71C(11)). The new Codes will therefore effectively operate as the 'benchmarks' for good anti-discrimination and pro-equality practice by public authorities, deviation from which can assist an individual litigant in proving discrimination.

The Commission intends to issue Codes for central government departments, local government, education bodies, the police and the NHS, as well as a general Code for all other authorities. The Government has indicated that it expects the Commission to develop the Codes in consultation with practitioners on the ground and the Commission has indicated it will consult very widely before submitting the Codes to the Home Secretary. The Government has also indicated that the Codes should be practicable, proportionate, avoid duplication and work within existing arrangements wherever possible (Consultation Paper, para. 8.4; Commission Guide, p. 4).

If the Codes are to take account of the specific duties to promote race equality, public consultation on the Codes cannot begin until after the Order imposing the specific duties has been laid in Parliament. The Government has announced its intention to lay the Order imposing the specific duties as soon as possible after the public consultation but to allow a long lead-in time before they come into force. In the meantime the Commission would be free to consult on the Codes of Practice and seek approval for them so that their introduction broadly coincides with the specific duties coming into force. There will also need to be clearance with the Secretary of State and consultation with Scottish Executive Ministers and the National Assembly for Wales before the Codes are laid before Parliament. It was hoped that the Codes would be issued 'towards the end of 2001' (EOR No. 95, January/February 2001, p. 43), but early 2002 may be more realistic, given the delays with the specific duties orders.

6.7 ENFORCEMENT OF THE NEW DUTIES

6.7.1 The general duty

The new general duty to promote equality is different from the provisions outlawing race discrimination in that it is not meant to result in a particular outcome for an individual. Rather, its aim is to 'drive up standards from which individuals will benefit'. As a result no provision has been made in the Act for individuals to bring a challenge under the Act in the County or Sheriff court in respect of the general duty. Judicial review in the High Court or Court of Session would, however, still be available as a remedy (see Chapter 8). The intention is that all complaints should be channelled through the Commission for Racial Equality (Consultation Paper, para. 5.9).

6.7.2 The specific duties

A unique feature of the new specific duties compared with the old s. 71 duty is that they *are* enforceable. The Commission for Racial Equality has exclusive standing to enforce the specific duties imposed by an order under the new s. 71(2), and its powers are limited to the procedures set out in the new ss. 71D and 71E, although this is without prejudice to the enforcement under s. 57 or otherwise of any other provision of this Act (where the breach is also a contravention of that provision) (new s. 71E(4)). An individual is therefore precluded from bringing a claim alleging a breach of the specific duties. This reflects the Commission's exclusive powers to challenge discriminatory advertisements, instructions to discriminate, pressure to discriminate or aiding unlawful acts under ss. 28, 30, 31 and 33 of the 1976 Act. The means by which the Commission will enforce the new duties also builds on the powers it has had under ss. 48 to 51 of the 1976 Act to conduct formal investigations, including a power to serve notices compelling the body under investigation to provide information and, in default of compliance, to apply for an order from the county court to compel disclosure (see below).

By the new s. 71D(1), if the Commission is satisfied that a person has failed to comply with, or is failing to comply with, any duty imposed by an order under s. 71(2), it may serve on that person a notice ('a compliance notice'). A compliance notice shall require the person concerned — (a) to comply with the duty concerned; and (b) to inform the Commission, within 28 days of the date on which the notice is served, of the steps that the person has taken, or is taking, to comply with the duty (new s. 71D(2)). A compliance notice may also require the person concerned to furnish the Commission with such other written information as may be reasonably required by the notice in order to verify that the duty has been complied with (new s. 71D(3). The notice may specify:

(a) the time (no later than three months from the date on which the notice is served) at which any information is to be furnished to the Commission;
(b) the manner and form in which any such information is to be so furnished (new s. 71D(4)).

However, a compliance notice shall not require a person to furnish information which the person could not be compelled to furnish in evidence in civil proceedings before the High Court or the Court of Session (new s. 71D(5)).

By the new s. 71E(1), the Commission may apply to a designated county court or, in Scotland, a sheriff court for an order requiring a person falling within sch. 1A to furnish any information required by a compliance notice if:

(a) the person fails to furnish the information to the Commission in accordance with the notice; or
(b) the Commission has reasonable cause to believe that the person does not intend to furnish the information.

If the Commission considers that a person has not, within three months of the date on which a compliance notice was served on that person, complied with any requirement of the notice for that person to comply with a duty imposed by an order under s. 71(2), the Commission may apply to a designated county court or, in Scotland, a sheriff court for an order requiring the person to comply with the requirement of the notice (new s. 71E(2)). If the court is satisfied that the application is well-founded, it may grant the order in the terms applied for or in more limited terms (new s. 71E(3)).

Therefore if, for example, a hospital trust announces its decision to close a nursing home without having carried out its specific duties, the Commission can serve a compliance notice, and in default of that being complied with, can apply for an order from the county or sheriff court requiring the trust to comply with its specific duties.

The Government anticipates that the Commission will also initiate informal action in the light of complaints received from individuals or using their own general powers (Consultation paper, p.10). However, it is expected that the Commission will only use its powers at all if a partnership approach fails to work (Home Office website, www.homeoffice.gov.uk/raceact — frequently asked questions, question 7). In addition to enforcement by the Commission, compliance with the new duties could also be the subject of inspections and audits by, for example, OFSTED, Her Majesty's Inspectorate of Schools in Scotland, HM Inspectorate of Constabulary, HM Inspectorate of Constabulary in Scotland, HM Inspectorate of Prisons, the Audit Commission, the Accounts Commission, the National Audit Office and Audit Scotland (Commission Guide, p. 3; Commission Guidance, p. 17).

6.8 PREPARATION FOR THE NEW DUTIES

The Commission for Racial Equality has urged public authorities not to wait until the specific duties come into force before starting the following process:

(a) defining all their functions, including identifying by ethnicity and other relevant criteria, the people for whom they should be providing various services;

(b) consulting with their employees and other people affected by their policies, including people from ethnic minorities, as to their concerns, and their perceptions of the organisation's stand on racism and racial equality;

(c) setting up systems to monitor their workforce and the outcomes of their policies and practices;

(d) assessing the impact of their policies and practices and in particular, whether all ethnic groups are being treated fairly in terms of equal opportunities and equal access to benefits, facilities and services;

(e) where the evidence from monitoring shows unequal outcomes between different ethnic groups, considering what changes are needed and taking action to prevent direct or indirect discrimination and to promote greater equality;

(f) where there are already good policies on racial equality in place, ensuring that they are understood and put into practice at every level within the organisation, and that they are reinforced through staff appraisals and disciplinary procedures.

Similarly, the Home Secretary has urged public authorities to take action sooner rather than later:

> Good governance requires each public authority to make an assessment of its functions and policies which are relevant to the duty, and the extent of its compliance. This is a necessary precursor to taking appropriate action to address any unjustifiable differential impact on different groups that exists or may arise (Consultation Paper, para. 3.12).

6.9 EXISTING ENFORCEMENT POWERS OF THE COMMISSION

Section 43 of the 1976 Act which established the Commission set out its duties as follows:

(a) to work towards the elimination of discrimination;

(b) to promote equality of opportunity, and good relations, between persons of different racial groups generally; and

(c) to keep under review the working of this Act and, when they are so required by the Secretary of State or otherwise think it necessary, draw up and submit to the Secretary of State proposals for amending it.

The Commission has a general power to do anything requisite for the performance of its duties under s. 43(1), and also has the following specific enforcement mechanisms. These survive the 2000 Act and will be exercised by the Commission alongside the new powers with which they have been provided, with the new prohibitions on discrimination and new positive duties in mind.

6.9.1 Formal investigations

Under s. 48(1) of the 1976 Act, the Commission may if it thinks fit, and shall if required by the Secretary of State, conduct a formal investigation for any purpose connected with the carrying out of those duties. The Commission may, with the approval of the Secretary of State, appoint, on a full-time or part-time basis, one or more individuals as additional Commissioners for the purposes of a formal investigation (s. 48(2)). The Commission may nominate one or more Commissioners, with or without one or more additional Commissioners, to conduct a formal investigation on their behalf, and may delegate any of their functions in relation to the investigation to the persons so nominated (s. 48(3)). The terms of reference of the investigation must be drawn up by the Commission or, if the Commission were required by the Secretary of State to conduct the investigation, by the Secretary of State after consulting the Commission (s. 49(2)).

It is the duty of the Commission to give general notice of the holding of the investigation (for example, by taking space in a newspaper) unless the terms of reference confine it to activities of persons named in them, but in such a case the Commission shall in the prescribed manner give those persons notice of the holding of the investigation (s. 49(3)). Where the terms of reference of the investigation confine it to activities of persons named in them and the Commission in the course of it propose to investigate any act made unlawful by this Act which it believes that a person so named may have done, the Commission shall:

(a) inform that person of their belief and of their proposal to investigate the act in question; and

(b) offer him an opportunity of making oral or written representations with regard to it (or both oral and written representations if he thinks fit); and a person so named who avails himself of an opportunity under this subsection of making oral representations may be represented—

(i) by counsel or a solicitor; or

(ii) by some other person of his choice, not being a person to whom the Commission object on the ground that he is unsuitable (s. 49(4)).

There is a provision by which the terms of reference can from time to time be revised (s. 49(5)).

Section 50 of the 1976 Act gives the Commission the power to obtain information for the purposes of a formal investigation. Under s. 50(1), the Commission may, by a notice in the prescribed form in the prescribed manner:

(a) require any person to furnish such written information as may be described in the notice, and may specify the time at which, and the manner and form in which, the information is to be furnished; or

(b) require any person to attend at such time and place as is specified in the notice and give oral information about, and produce all documents in his possession or control relating to, any matter specified in the notice.

Except as provided by s. 60 (see below) a notice shall be served under subs. (1) only where:

(a) the Secretary of State has made an order authorising service of the notice; or

(b) the terms of reference of the investigation state that the Commission believe that the person named may have done or be doing acts of all or any of the following descriptions—

(i) unlawful discriminatory acts;
(ii) contraventions of s. 28; and
(iii) contraventions of ss. 29, 30 or 31,
and the investigation should be confined to those acts (s. 50(2)).

A notice under subs. (1) shall not require a person:

(a) to give information, or produce any documents, which he could not be compelled to give in evidence, or produce, in civil proceedings; or
(b) to attend at any place unless his expenses are paid (s. 50(3)).

If a person fails to comply with a notice served on him under subs. (1) or the Commission has reasonable cause to believe that he intends not to comply with it, the Commission may apply to a county court or, in Scotland, a sheriff court for an order requiring him to comply with it or with such directions for the like purpose as may be contained in the order (s. 50(4)). Section 84 of the County Courts Act 1959 (penalty for neglecting witness summons) shall apply to a failure without reasonable excuse to comply with an order of a county court under subs. (4) as it applies in the cases provided in s. 84; and para. 73 of sch. 1 to the Sheriff Courts (Scotland) Act 1907 (power of sheriff to grant second diligence for compelling the attendance of witnesses or havers) shall apply to an order of a sheriff court under subs. (4) as it applies in proceedings in the sheriff court (s. 50(5)). A person commits an offence if he:

(a) wilfully alters, suppresses, conceals or destroys a document which he has been required by a notice or order under this section to produce; or
(b) in complying with such a notice or order, knowingly or recklessly makes any statement which is false in a material particular,
and shall be liable on summary conviction to a fine not exceeding £400 (s. 50(6)).

Proceedings for an offence under subs. (6) may (without prejudice to any jurisdiction exercisable apart from this subsection) be instituted—

(a) against any person at any place at which he has an office or other place of business;
(b) against an individual at any place where he resides, or at which he is for the time being (s. 50(7)).

Section 51(1) permits the Commission to make recommendations as a result of formal investigations, providing that if in the light of any of its findings in a formal investigation it appears to the Commission necessary or expedient, whether during the course of the investigation or after its conclusion — (a) to make to any person, with a view to promoting equality of opportunity between persons of different racial groups who are affected by any of his activities, recommendations for changes in his policies or procedures, or as to any other matters; or (b) to make to the Secretary of State any recommendations, whether for changes in the law or otherwise, the Commission shall make those recommendations accordingly.

Section 51(2) requires the Commission to prepare a report of their findings in any formal investigation conducted by them. By s. 51(3)(a) and (b), if the formal investigation is one required by the Secretary of State, the Commission must deliver the report to the Secretary of State, and he or she shall ensure the report is published. If the formal investigation is not one required by the Secretary of State, the Commission shall either publish the report, or make it available so that any person shall be entitled, on payment of such fee (if any) as may be determined by the Commission to inspect the report during ordinary office hours and take copies of all or any part of the report; or to obtain from the Commission a copy, certified by the Commission to be correct, of the report (s. 51(4) and (5)(a) and (b)).

Section 52 restricts the disclosure of information given to the Commission by any person ('the informant') in connection with a formal investigation. Under s. 52(1) no such information shall be disclosed except:

(a) on the order of any court; or
(b) with the informant's consent; or
(c) in the form of a summary or other general statement published by the Commission which does not identify the informant or any other person to whom the information relates; or
(d) in a report of the investigation published by the Commission or made available for inspection under section 51(5); or
(e) to the Commissioners, additional Commissioners or employees of the Commission, or, so far as may be necessary for the proper performance of the functions of the Commission, to other persons; or
(f) for the purpose of any civil proceedings under this Act to which the Commission are a party, or any criminal proceedings.

Any person who discloses information in contravention of subs. (1) commits an offence and shall be liable on summary conviction to a fine not exceeding £400 (s. 52(2)). In preparing any report for publication or for inspection the Commission shall exclude, so far as is consistent with their duties and the object of the report, any matter which relates to the private affairs of any individual or the business interests of any person where the publication of that matter might, in the opinion of the Commission, prejudicially affect that individual or person (s. 52(3)).

The Commission has recently launched a formal investigation into racial discrimination in HM Prison Service. HMP Brixton will be under the spotlight after a recent damaging report by the prison's race relations advisor, and after the highly publicised and serious complaints of racial discrimination brought by Claude Johnson, a black officer serving at the prison. Feltham Young Offenders Institution will also be examined, with regard to the circumstances in which Zahid Mubarek, a young Asian man, was murdered by an openly racist cell mate in 2000. The privately run Parc Prison in South Wales, which has been criticised by the prison inspectorate, will also be investigated (see EOR No. 95, January/February 2001, pp. 3–4).

6.9.2 Non-discrimination notices

Sections 58–61 set out a procedure governing the Commission's power to issue non-discrimination notices if in the course of a formal investigation the Commission becomes satisfied that a person is committing, or has committed an unlawful discriminatory act or an act contravening ss. 28, 29, 30 or 31 (discriminatory practices, discriminatory advertisements, instructions or pressure to discriminate). The Commission may serve such a notice, whether or not proceedings have been brought in respect of the Act (s. 58(1) and (2)). The notice, which must be in the prescribed form and served in the prescribed manner can require the recipient (a) not to commit any such acts; and (b) where compliance with paragraph (a) involves changes in any of his practices or other arrangements — (i) to inform the Commission that he has effected those changes and what those changes are; and (ii) to take such steps as may be reasonably required by the notice for the purpose of affording that information to other persons concerned (s. 58(2)). It may also require the person on whom it is served to furnish the Commission with such other information as may be reasonably required by the notice in order to verify that the notice has been complied with (s. 58(3)); and may specify the time at which, and the manner and form in which, any information is to be furnished to the Commission, but the time at which any information is to be furnished in compliance with the notice shall not be later than five years after the notice has become final (s. 58(4)).

Before serving a non-discrimination notice, the Commission must ensure that they have: (a) given the recipient notice that they are minded to issue a non-discrimination notice in his case, specifying the grounds on which they contemplate doing so; and (b) offered him an opportunity of making oral or written representations in the matter (or both oral and written representations if he thinks fit) within a period of not less than 28 days specified in the notice; and (c) taken account of any representations so made by him (s. 57(5)). By s. 58(7), the ability of the Commission to apply to a county court or sheriff court for an order for compliance or directions shall apply to requirements under subs. (2)(b), (3) and (4) contained in a non-discrimination notice which has become final as it applies to requirements in a notice served under s. 50(1) (a notice requiring the furnishing of information).

The significance of a non-discrimination notice is that, when final, it renders the recipient liable for the next five years to further action for persistent discrimination should he or she continue to commit unlawful acts (see 6.7.3 below).

Under s. 59(1), not later than six weeks after a non-discrimination notice is served on any person he may appeal against any requirement of the notice: (a) to an employment tribunal, so far as the requirement relates to acts which are within the jurisdiction of the tribunal; or (b) to a designated county court or a sheriff court, so far as the requirement relates to acts which are within the jurisdiction of the court and are not within the jurisdiction of an employment tribunal. Where the tribunal or court considers a requirement in respect of which an appeal is brought under subs. (1) to be unreasonable because it is based on an incorrect finding of fact or for any other reason, the tribunal or court shall quash the requirement (s. 59(2)). On quashing a requirement under subs. (2) the tribunal or court may direct that the non-discrimination notice shall be treated as if, in place of the requirement quashed, it had contained a requirement in terms specified in the direction (s. 59(3)).

By s. 60(1), if (a) the terms of reference of a formal investigation state that its purpose is to determine whether any requirements of a non-discrimination notice are being or have been carried out, but s. 50(2)(b) does not apply; and (b) s. 49(3) is complied with in relation to the investigation on a date ('the commencement date') not later than the expiration of the period of five years beginning when the non-discrimination notice became final, the Commission may within the period referred to in subs. (2) serve notices under s. 50(1) for the purposes of the investigation without needing to obtain the consent of the Secretary of State. The period in subs. (2) is the period which begins on the commencement date and ends on the later of the following dates — (a) the date on which the period of five years mentioned in subs. (1)(b) expires; (b) the date two years after the commencement date.

Under s. 61(1), the Commission must establish and maintain a register of non-discrimination notices which have become final. Any person is entitled, on payment of such fee (if any) as may be determined by the Commission — (a) to inspect the register (or a copy of it, if the Commission think so fit) during ordinary office hours and take copies of any entry; or (b) to obtain from the Commission a copy, certified by the Commission to be correct, of any entry in the register (s. 61(2) and (3)). The Commission must give general notice of the place or places where, and the times when, the register or a copy of it may be inspected (s. 61(4)).

The Commission has recently issued a non-discrimination notice on the London Borough of Hackney, following what it sees as the Council's failure to implement agreed equality measures. It is the first time in over five years that the Commission has resorted to issuing such a notice (see EOR No. 95, January/February 2001, p. 4).

6.9.3 Persistent discrimination

Section 62 enables the Commission to monitor persistent discrimination. It provides that if, during the period of five years beginning on the date on which (a) a non-discrimination notice was served on a recipient; (b) a finding was made by a tribunal or court under s. 54 or 57 that a respondent had done an unlawful discriminatory act; or (c) a finding was made by a court in proceedings under s. 19 or 20 of the Race Relations Act 1968 that he had done an act which was unlawful by virtue of any provision of Part I of that Act, it appears to the Commission that unless restrained the person is likely to do one or more acts falling within paragraph (b), or contravening s. 28 (engaging in discriminatory practices), the Commission may apply to a designated county court for an injunction, or to a sheriff court for an order, restraining him from doing so; and the court, if satisfied that the application is well-founded, may grant the injunction or order in the terms applied for or in more limited terms. In proceedings under this section the Commission shall not allege that the person to whom the proceedings relate has done an act falling within subs. (1)(b) or contravening s. 28 which is within the jurisdiction of an employment tribunal unless a finding by an employment tribunal that he did that act has become final (s. 62(2)).

6.9.4 Discriminatory practices, discriminatory advertisements, instructions or pressure to discriminate

Chapter 5 explains the provisions of ss. 29–31 which prohibit discriminatory practices, discriminatory advertisements, instructions or pressure to discriminate.

By s. 63(1), proceedings in respect of a contravention of s. 29, 30 or 31 can only be brought by the Commission. They can only be brought by an application for a decision as to whether the alleged contravention occurred (s. 63(2)(a)) or an application under subs. (4) (s. 63(2)(b)) or both.

An application under subs. (2)(a) shall be made:

(a) in a case based on any provision of Part II, to an industrial tribunal; and
(b) in any other case, to a designated county court or a sheriff court (s. 63(3)).

By s. 68(4), the employment tribunal, county court or sheriff court cannot hear a claim under s. 63(2)(a) unless it is made before the end of the period of six months beginning when the act to which it relates was done.

An application under subs. (4) arises where it appears to the Commission — (a) that a person has done an act which by virtue of s. 29, 30 or 31 was unlawful; and (b) that unless restrained he is likely to do further acts which by virtue of that section are unlawful, in which case the Commission may apply to a designated county court for an injunction, or to a sheriff court for an order, restraining him from doing such acts; and the court, if satisfied that the application is well-founded, may grant the injunction or order in the terms applied for or more limited terms. Again, in proceedings under subs. (4) the Commission shall not allege that the person to whom the proceedings relate has done an act which is unlawful under this Act and within the jurisdiction of an employment tribunal unless a finding by an employment tribunal that he did that act has become final (s. 63(5)). By s. 68(4), a county court or sheriff court shall not consider an application under s. 63(4) unless it is made before the end of the period of five years so beginning.

6.9.5 Providing assistance to organisations

Under s. 44(1), the Commission may give financial or other assistance to any organisation appearing to the Commission to be concerned with the promotion of equality of opportunity, and good relations, between persons of different racial groups, but shall not give any such financial assistance out of money provided (through the Secretary of State) by Parliament except with the approval of the Secretary of State given with the consent of the Treasury. Section 44(2) sets out the general procedure under which the Commission is to exercise this power, namely by a committee of the Commission consisting of at least three but not more than five Commissioners, of whom one shall be the deputy chairman or one of the deputy chairmen of the Commission.

6.9.6 Research and education

Under s. 45(1), the Commission may undertake or assist (financially or otherwise) the undertaking by other persons of any research, and any educational activities, which appear to the Commission necessary or expedient for the purposes of s. 43(1). The Commission may make charges for educational or other facilities or services made available by them (s. 43(2)).

6.9.7 Annual reports

Under s. 46(1), the Commission is obliged to make to the Secretary of State a report on their activities during the year as soon as practicable after the end of each calendar year. This must include a general survey of developments, during the period to which it relates, in respect of matters falling within the scope of the Commission's functions, and is to be laid before each House of Parliament and published (s. 46(2) and (3)).

For further commentary on the various enforcement powers of the Commission, see A. McColgan, *Discrimination Law Cases and Materials* (Hart, 2000) at pp. 293–319 and R. Townshend-Smith, *Discrimination Law: Text, Cases and Materials* (Cavendish, 1998) at pp. 524–536.

Chapter Seven
Discrimination in public appointments

By s. 76 of the 1976 Act, where Ministers of the Crown or government departments made appointments to offices or posts which do not constitute employment for the purposes of the Act, or made arrangements for determining who should be offered the office or post, they were under a general obligation not to act in a way which would constitute unlawful discrimination if the offices or posts were in fact such employment (s. 76(1) and (2)).

Evidence of continued inequality in access to public life was one of the driving forces behind the Act (Consultation Paper, para. 1.14), and there was a concern that the protection against discrimination in public appointments in s. 76 of the 1976 Act did not go far enough.

Section 3 of the 2000 Act therefore extends s. 76 by inserting new s. 76(3)–(15) into the 1976 Act, to cover recommendations or approvals for Crown appointments, as well as the making of the appointments themselves and to the conferring of honours and dignities (such as peerages). It also addresses an anomaly regarding the terms and conditions, or termination, of such appointments, and discrimination in these areas is now covered. The new s. 76 will apply to any new arrangements for appointing members of the House of Lords.

The first new prohibition on discrimination can be found in the new s. 76(5) which provides that in making a recommendation, or giving approval, and in making arrangements for determining who should be recommended or approved, the Minister of the Crown or government department shall not do an act which would be unlawful under s. 4 of the 1976 Act if the recommendation or approval were an offer of employment and the Crown were the employer for the purposes of this Act. The new s. 76(5) extends to any recommendation made by a Minister of the Crown or government department in relation to an appointment to an office or post where s. 4 does not apply in relation to the appointment; any approval given by such a Minister or department in relation to any such appointment; any recommendation made by a Minister of the Crown or government department in relation to a conferment by the Crown of a dignity or honour; and any approval given by such a Minister or department in relation to any such conferment (new s. 76(3) and (4)).

Subsections (3) to (5) do not apply in relation to the making of negative recommendations (new s. 76(6)) which are dealt with by the new s. 76(9). This provides that in making a negative recommendation or in refusing to make a recommendation or give an approval, and in making the arrangements for determining whether to make such a recommendation or refusal, the Minister of the Crown or government department shall not do an act which would be unlawful under s. 4 if the recommendation or refusal were a refusal to offer the person concerned employment and the Crown were the employer for the purposes of this Act (new s. 76(7) and (8)).

By the new s. 76(11), a Minister of the Crown or government department shall not do an act in connection with the terms of the appointment; access for the person appointed to opportunities for promotion, transfer or training, or to any other benefits, facilities or services; or the termination of the appointment, or subjecting the person appointed to any other detriment which would be unlawful under s. 4 if the Crown were the employer for the purposes of this Act. The new s. 76(11) applies in relation to any appointment to an office or post where s. 4 does not apply and the appointment is made by a Minister of the Crown or government department or the office or post is an office or post in relation to which a Minister of the Crown or government department has made a recommendation (other than a negative recommendation) or given an approval.

Throughout the new extended s. 76(6), references to refusal include references to deliberate omission; references to Ministers of the Crown and government departments include references to the National Assembly for Wales and any part of the Scottish Administration; and references to Ministers of the Crown and government departments (insofar as they relate to the making of a recommendation or a refusal to make a recommendation, or the giving or refusal of an approval, in relation to a conferment of a peerage for life under s. 1 of the Life Peerages Act 1958) include references to any body established by a Minister of the Crown to make such a recommendation to the Prime Minister or to determine whether to give such an approval (new s. 76(15)).

The means of challenging discrimination under this section is by way of an application for judicial review in the High Court or in Scotland, the Court of Session. On such an application, the High Court may make a declaration to the effect that a Minister of the Crown or government department has contravened subs. (5), subs. (9) or, in relation to an appointment falling within subs. (10)(b), subs. (11), and may award damages in respect of the contravention (new s. 76(12)). In Scotland, the Court of Session may grant declarator to the like effect and may award damages in respect of the contravention (new s. 76(13)).

Chapter Eight
Procedure for challenging unlawful discrimination under the Act

8.1 INTRODUCTION

The provisions of the 1976 Act are enforced by the strategic functions of the Commission for Racial Equality to enforce the law in the public interest together with the ability of individuals to bring proceedings alleging unlawful discrimination under the Act. The enforcement mechanisms of the new provisions of the 2000 Act, broadly speaking, follow the same pattern. The Commission's main functions in relation to the 2000 Act are as set out in Chapter 6, namely the issuing of new codes of practice and the enforcement of the specific duties to promote equality, in addition to exercising their existing statutory powers with the new provisions in mind. This Chapter explains the procedure open to an individual under the 2000 Act to challenge discrimination by a public body contrary to the new s. 19B. A failure by a public body to comply with its general duty to promote racial equality under the new s. 71 or unlawful discrimination in public appointments contrary to the expanded s. 76 should be challenged by way of judicial review to the High Court or the Court of Session in Scotland. If an individual has a concern that a public authority is not complying with one of its specific duties, reference should be made to the Commission for Racial Equality.

8.2 COMMENCING PROCEEDINGS IN THE COUNTY COURT OR SHERIFF COURT

The new s. 19B fits into Part III of the 1976 Act, the enforcement of which is governed by s. 57 (ss. 54–56 provide for enforcement in the employment field). Section 57 and the additional provisions which apply to it govern claims under the new s. 19B, with modifications in those cases where there is an ongoing criminal investigation and in immigration cases (see below). By s. 57(1)(a) an individual ('the claimant') alleging that another person ('the respondent') has committed an act of discrimination against the claimant which is unlawful by virtue of Part III is entitled to bring civil proceedings in like manner as any other claim in tort or (in Scotland) in reparation for breach of statutory duty. The same applies in relation to a respondent who is to be treated by virtue of ss. 32 or 33 (the vicarious and secondary liability provisions — see Chapter 5) as having committed such an act of discrimination against the claimant (s. 57(1)(b)).

A claim under s. 57(1) must be brought in a designated county court in England and Wales, or in a sheriff court in Scotland (s. 57(2)(a) and (b)). Under s. 67(1), for the purposes of the Act a 'designated' county court is one designated for the time being for those purposes by an order made by the Lord Chancellor. Such an order shall assign to that court as its district for those purposes any county court district or two or more county court districts (s. 67(2)). A designated county court or a sheriff court shall have jurisdiction to entertain proceedings under the Act with respect to an act done on a ship, aircraft or hovercraft outside its district, including such an act done outside Great Britain (s. 67(3)). The appropriate court is usually the court for the district in which either:

(a) the respondent resides or carries on its functions, or
(b) the unlawful discrimination in question wholly or in part occurred.

These provisions are subject to the special provisions for claims arising out of immigration and asylum cases (see 8.11 below).

Proceedings are instituted in England and Wales by sending or delivering to the office of the appropriate county court a claim form giving details of the parties and two copies of particulars of the claim (which is a simple statement of the nature of the complaint and of the relief sought), together with the prescribed fee. In Scotland there is a similar procedure. In the employment context, it has been held that an originating application need only be in writing and contain information which is sufficient to identify who is making the complaint, against whom, and information sufficient to show what sort of complaint it is (*Dodd* v *British Telecom plc* [1988] IRLR 16, [1988] ICR 116). The usual Civil Procedure Rules on statements of case apply.

When he has instituted proceedings in a designated county court the claimant must forthwith write to the Commission for Racial Equality, giving notice that he has done so; he must also send a copy of the letter to the court office. It is advisable to use the recorded delivery service for sending the letter to the Commission and the copy to the court office. In the case of proceedings which have been instituted in a sheriff court the claimant must send a copy of the summons or initial writ initiating the action to the Commission as soon as possible and by recorded delivery.

Insofar as the claim under the Race Relations Act 1976 can also be construed as unlawful discrimination contrary to the Human Rights Act 1998, any such argument can be made as a supplementary basis of the application (under the HRA 1998, s. 7(1)(b)). Before commencing proceedings under the new provisions in a criminal justice related case, practitioners may need to consider how such a claim will interact with other claims such as those in false imprisonment or malicious prosecution. There can be, for example, different tribunals of fact (experienced race relations assessors and a jury) in relation to the two sorts of claim, and it is not clear how this will be accommodated where both claims arise out of the same facts and are therefore joined.

8.3 THE QUESTIONNAIRE PROCEDURE

Section 65 sets out a useful questionnaire procedure by which an individual who believes he or she has been discriminated against can obtain information from the potential respondent, so as to decide whether to institute proceedings and if so, to formulate and present the claim in the most effective manner. Section 65(1) provides that, for those purposes, the Secretary of State shall by order prescribe:

(a) forms by which the person aggrieved may question the respondent on his reasons for doing any relevant act, or on any other matter which is or may be relevant; and

(b) forms by which the respondent may if he so wishes reply to any questions.

The exchange of questions and answers should focus attention on what would have to be shown in order to prove unlawful discrimination, but the main purpose is to establish as far as possible both the facts of the grievance and, in particular, the reasons why the respondent took the action complained of. In some cases the exchange of information may show the complaint to have been groundless, or based on a misunderstanding. In others it may result in a settlement so that legal proceedings are unnecessary. Where proceedings are instituted, it should help to simplify them by identifying in advance what is agreed and what is in dispute between the parties. For the purposes of the questionnaire procedure, the exchange of questions and answers between the parties does not have to be conducted on the prescribed forms; it may be done by other means (e.g. by letter). There are, however, certain practical advantages in using the forms because the questions and answers they contain are designed to make it easier for both parties to focus on the relevant issues, i.e. whether there has been discrimination which is unlawful under the Act. The standard questionnaire to be completed by the potential claimant is generally known as 'form RR65'. A new version of form RR65 and guidance on how to use it has been produced to take into account the changes made to the 1976 Act by the 2000 Act. This can be found at Appendix 4.

Section 65(2) provides that where the person aggrieved questions the respondent (whether in accordance with an order under subs. (1) or not):

(a) the question, and any reply by the respondent (whether in accordance with such an order or not) shall, subject to the following provisions of the section, be admissible as evidence in the proceedings;

(b) if it appears to the court or tribunal that the respondent deliberately, and without reasonable excuse, omitted to reply within a reasonable period or that his reply is evasive or equivocal, it may draw any inference from that fact that it considers it just and equitable to draw, including an inference that he committed an unlawful act.

There are certain limitations on the inferences which can be drawn in discrimination claims arising out of criminal proceedings (see 8.10 below).

By s. 65(3), the Secretary of State may by order:

(a) prescribe the period within which questions must be duly served in order to be admissible under subsection (2)(a); and

(b) prescribe the manner in which a question, and any reply by the respondent, may be duly served.

This order (the Racc Relations (Questions and Replies) Order 1977, SI 1977, No. 842) specifies the following periods:

(a) Where legal proceedings in respect of the alleged discrimination have not been brought, the period for serving questions is the period within which proceedings in respect of the alleged discrimination may be brought (disregarding the discretion of an industrial tribunal, a designated county court or a sheriff court to entertain the complaints out of time);
(b) Where a complaint in respect of the alleged discrimination has been presented to an industrial tribunal, the period for serving questions is either:

(i) 21 days beginning on the date on which the complaint was presented, or
(ii) if the 21-day period has expired (in which case the leave of the tribunal to serve the questions must be obtained), such period as the tribunal may specify;

(c) Where a claim in respect of the alleged discrimination has been made to a designated county court or a sheriff court (in which case the leave of the court to serve the questions must be obtained) the period is such a period as the court may specify.

Rules may enable the court entertaining a claim under s. 57 to determine, before the date fixed for the hearing of the claim, whether a question or reply is admissible under this section or not (s. 65(4)). Section 65 is without prejudice to any other enactment or rule of law regulating interlocutory and preliminary matters in proceedings before a county court, sheriff court or industrial tribunal, and has effect subject to any enactment or rule of law regulating the admissibility of evidence in such proceedings.

8.4 PUBLIC FUNDING FOR DISCRIMINATION CLAIMS

Funding is available to people who are financially eligible, in that their income and/or assets fall below certain levels, and whose cases pass the Legal Services Commission's Funding Code. The Code sets out general conditions which must be met in order for cases to be supported by funding from the Commission. However, the Home Office has indicated that cases brought under the new prohibition on discrimination will count as claims against public authorities under Part 8 of the Funding Code and in these instances, the general terms are not applied as strictly. For example, the availability of 'no win, no fee' arrangements will not have to be considered first, before funding can be granted (see the Act's website, at www.homeoffice.gov.uk/raceact (frequently asked questions, question 19).

8.5 ASSISTANCE BY THE COMMISSION FOR RACIAL EQUALITY

Section 66(2) makes provision for the Commission to assist an individual who is an actual or prospective complainant or claimant by:

(a) giving advice;
(b) procuring or attempting to procure the settlement of any matter in dispute;
(c) arranging for the giving of advice or assistance by a solicitor or counsel;
(d) arranging for representation by any person, including all such assistance as is usually given by a solicitor or counsel in the steps preliminary or incidental to any proceedings, or in arriving at or giving effect to a compromise to avoid or bring to an end any proceedings;
(e) any other form of assistance which the Commission may consider appropriate.

Under s. 66(1), the Commission must consider requests for assistance and may grant assistance if they think fit to do so:

(a) on the ground that the case raises a question of principle; or
(b) on the ground that it is unreasonable, having regard to the complexity of the case, or to the applicant's position in relation to the respondent or another person involved, or to any other matter, to expect the applicant to deal with the case unaided; or
(c) by reason of any other special consideration.

Within two months of receiving a written request for assistance, the Commission shall:

(a) consider the application after making such enquiries as they think fit;
(b) decide whether or not to grant it; and
(c) inform the applicant of their decision, stating whether or not assistance under this section is to be provided by the Commission and, if so, what form it will take (s. 66(3)).

There is provision for the Commission to extend the period during which they must determine an application for assistance provided they serve the applicant within the two months with a notice indicating that in his or her case, the period the Commission need is to be extended to three months. This has the effect of giving the Commission the additional month they need, and extends the time limit for lodging a complaint to the county court under s. 68(3) accordingly (s. 66(4)).

Section 66(5) provides that the recovery of expenses incurred by the Commission in providing the applicant with assistance (as taxed or assessed in such manner as may be prescribed by rules or regulations) shall constitute a first charge for the benefit of the Commission:

(a) on any costs or expenses which (whether by virtue of a judgment or order of a court or tribunal or an agreement or otherwise) are payable to the applicant by any other person in respect of the matter in connection with which the assistance is given; and
(b) so far as relates to any costs or expenses, on his rights under any compromise or settlement arrived at in connection with that matter to avoid or bring to an end any proceedings.

The charge conferred by this subsection is subject to any charge under the Legal Aid Act 1974, or any charge or obligation for payment in priority to other debts under the Legal Aid and Advice (Scotland) Acts 1967 and 1972, and is subject to any provision in any of those Acts for payment of any sum into the legal aid fund (s. 66(6)).

Section 66 is also extended to allow the Commission to assist people in immigration appeal proceedings.

8.6 TIME LIMIT FOR COMMENCING PROCEEDINGS

By s. 68(2)(a) a county court or a sheriff court may not consider a claim under s. 57 unless proceedings in respect of the claim are instituted within six months of the act complained of. However, by s. 68(3), where in relation to proceedings or prospective proceedings by way of a claim under s. 57, an application for assistance under s. 66 is made to the Commission before the end of the period of six months, the period shall be extended by two months (s. 68(3)). If the Commission has served a notice indicating that it requires a further month to determine the application for assistance, the time limit for commencing proceedings is extended by a further month (s. 66(4)). (Section 68(2)(b) and s. 66 also made provision for a further extension of time in education cases by two months, to allow for the period of notification to the Secretary of State which has now been repealed — see below.)

Section 68(7) makes the following provisions for the purposes of calculating time:

(a) when the inclusion of any term in a contract renders the making of the contract an unlawful act, that act shall be treated as extending throughout the duration of the contract (s. 68(7)(a));

(b) any act extending over a period shall be treated as done at the end of that period (s. 68(7)(b)); and

(c) a deliberate omission shall be treated as done when the person in question decided upon it (and in the absence of evidence establishing the contrary a person shall be taken for the purposes of this section to decide upon an omission when he does an act inconsistent with doing the omitted act or, if he has done no such inconsistent act, when the period expires within which he might reasonably have been expected to do the omitted act if it was to be done) (s. 68(7)(c)).

Insofar as s. 68(7)(b) is concerned the courts have been at pains to distinguish 'continuing acts' from 'continuing consequences' (see *Sougrin* v *Haringey Health Authority* [1992] IRLR 416, CA; *Owusu* v *London Fire and Civil Defence Authority* [1995] IRLR 574 and *Cast* v *Croydon College* [1998] IRLR 319). It is only 'continuing acts' which will fall within s. 68(7)(b), and what is meant by this is 'some policy, rule or practice, in accordance with which decisions are taken from time to time' (per Mummery LJ in *Owusu*).

By s. 68(6), a court or tribunal may nevertheless consider any such complaint, claim or application which is out of time if, in all the circumstances of the case, it considers that it is 'just and equitable' to do so. In the employment context, the tribunal can consider 'anything which it judges to be relevant' in determining whether it is 'just and equitable to extend time' (*Hutchison* v *Westward Television* [1977] IRLR 69). The court will have to consider the prejudice which would result to each party as a result of granting or refusing the extension, and to have regard to the length of and reasons for the delay, the extent to which the cogency of the evidence is likely to be affected by the delay, the extent to which the party sued has co-operated with any requests for information, the promptness with which the claimant acted once he or she knew of the facts giving rise to the cause of action, and the steps taken by the claimant to obtain appropriate professional advice once he or she knew of the possibility of taking action (see *Hutchison*, *British Coal Corporation* v *Keeble* [1997] IRLR 336, EAT and *Berry* v *Ravensbourne National Health Service Trust* [1993] IRLR 871, EAT). The fact that the claim is additional to, and overlaps with, a timeous complaint which has not yet been heard, the fact that the delay in commencing proceedings is due to reliance on incorrect legal advice, and the fact that the claimant has invoked an internal grievance procedure *may*, by analogy with employment cases, justify an extension of time (see *Berry*; *Aniagwu* v *London Borough of Hackney* [1999] IRLR 303, EAT and *Robinson* v *Post Office* [2000] IRLR 804, EAT).

Acts which occurred before the time limit can, in any event, generally be used as evidence of racial discrimination in subsequent proceedings based upon some later act of discrimination (*Din (Ghulam)* v *Carrington Viyella Ltd (Jersey Kapwood Ltd)* [1982] IRLR 281, [1982] ICR 256 EAT: *Kingston* v *British Railways Board* [1982] IRLR 274, [1982] ICR 392, EAT).

8.7 RACE RELATIONS ASSESSORS TO ASSIST THE JUDGE OR SHERIFF

In any proceedings under the Act in a designated county court or a sheriff court the judge or sheriff shall, unless the parties consent, be assisted by two assessors appointed from a list of persons prepared and maintained by the Secretary of State, being persons appearing to the Secretary of State to have special knowledge and experience of problems connected with relations between persons of different racial groups (s. 67(4)). The assessors are remunerated at such rate as may, with the approval of the Minister for the Civil Service, be determined by the Lord Chancellor (for proceedings in England and Wales) or the Lord President of the Court of Session (for proceedings in Scotland) (s. 67(5)). A Practice Direction in the county court states that only appropriately experienced County Court judges should sit in indirect discrimination cases.

8.8 BURDEN OF PROOF

In a case involving direct discrimination, the claimant has, in the first instance, to provide sufficient evidence to show that he or she has been treated less favourably than another person was or would have been treated, in circumstances suggesting that the reason for the treatment was his or her (or someone else's) colour, race, nationality or ethnic or national origins. It is then for the respondent to seek to rebut this evidence. Although it is for the applicant to make out his or her case, tribunals and courts are fully aware of the difficulties faced by applicants in proving direct discrimination, in that it is rare that a discriminator will admit that any less favourable treatment was by reason of the complainant's race. It is therefore incumbent on the tribunal or court to decide whether it can infer discrimination from all the evidence in the case. It may well do so in cases where the respondent can put forward no explanation for discrimination or puts forward one which the court considers inadequate or unsatisfactory (see *King* v *Great Britain China Centre* [1992] ICR 516 and *Glasgow City Council* v *Zafar* [1998] ICR 120). A tribunal which seeks to rely on *King* must not be too hasty in concluding that discrimination has occurred once it has held that an explanation put forward by an employer for adverse treatment towards an employee is unsatisfactory. Before so ruling, a tribunal must be satisfied that the employer would have treated others of a different race more favourably.

Information, especially statistical evidence, obtained in the questionnaire procedure, can be used to invite a tribunal to infer discrimination. A failure on the part of an employer to take steps to counter racial discrimination is evidence from which unlawful prejudice may be inferred, but it is going too far to suggest that such an inference will always be warranted (see, for example, *Qureshi* v *London Borough of Newham* [1991] IRLR 264). Individuals alleging contraventions of the new s. 19B can also pray in aid any evidence that there has been non-compliance with the new Commission for Racial Equality Codes of Practice, and with the general or a specific duty to promote equality (see Chapter 6).

Having heard all the evidence made available at the hearing, the court will decide the case on the balance of probabilities. Where a court has found for the complainant, it will proceed to consider what remedies to award.

The implementation of the new European Race Directive into domestic law will require a change in the law to shift the burden of proof in race discrimination claims (see Chapter 9), though the practical effect of this, given the *King* approach, may not be great. For further cases and commentary on proving direct discrimination, see R. Townshend-Smith, *Discrimination Law: Text, Cases and Materials* (Cavendish, 1998) at pp. 159–172).

8.9 REMEDIES, COSTS AND APPEALS

All remedies as would be obtainable in the High Court or the Court of Session are available in proceedings under the 1976 Act (s. 57(2)). Where a designated county court or a sheriff court finds in favour of the complainant, it may therefore award any of the following remedies:

(a) an order declaring the rights of the parties;
(b) an injunction or order;
(c) damages.

The court also has power in appropriate cases to remove or modify a discriminatory term in a contract.

Insofar as damages are concerned, the tribunal is not obliged to make an order for compensation if it does not consider it just and equitable to do so; but, having decided to make such an order, it must adopt the usual measure of damages: there is no jurisdiction to award only such as the tribunal considers just and equitable in the circumstances (*Hurley* v *Mustoe (No. 2)* [1983] ICR 422, EAT). Having regard to the strict rules of causation, however, losses must be attributable to specific acts of discrimination complained of, not background findings (*Chapman* v *Simon* [1994] IRLR 124).

An award of damages may consist of damages for any expenses or other loss sustained by the claimant for which it is possible to make substantially precise calculations (e.g. for loss of earnings) and also any damages for any loss which cannot be precisely calculated. The limit on damages which applies to discrimination cases under the employment provisions in Part II of the 1976 Act does not apply to claims under Part III.

For the avoidance of doubt, s. 57(4) makes clear that damages in respect of an unlawful act of discrimination may include compensation for injury to feelings whether or not they include compensation under any other head. Personal injury damages for psychiatric (or, presumably, physical) injury arising from acts of discrimination, such as harassment, are also recoverable. Indeed, it has been held in the employment sphere that once such a claim has been dealt with in the discrimination claim by the tribunal or settled, it is issue estopped elsewhere (*Sheriff* v *Klyne Tugs (Lowestoft) Ltd* [1999] IRLR 481).

However, no award of damages can be made for discrimination falling within s. 1(1)(b) (indirect race discrimination) of the 1976 Act if the respondent proves that the requirement or condition in question was not applied with the intention of treating the claimant unfavourably on racial grounds (s. 57(3) — although this may change in the future — see Chapter 9). The rule that exemplary damages could not be awarded in respect of a finding of race discrimination (*Deane* v *London Borough of Ealing* [1993] IRLR 209, EAT) has effectively been overturned by *Kuddus* v *Chief Constable of Leicestershire Constabulary* [2001] 2 WLR 1789. Aggravated damages are also payable, when it is thought appropriate to award compensation for damage to the claimant's feelings of dignity and pride, although these factors may be subsumed in a global injury to feelings award.

It is hard to predict the level of damages which are likely to be awarded for discrimination under the new s. 19B, although in *Alexander* v *Home Office* [1988] IRLR 190, [1988] ICR 685, the Court of Appeal gave some general guidance on awards in race discrimination claims:

> Awards should not be minimal, because this would tend to trivialise or diminish respect for the public policy to which the Act gives effect. On the other hand, just because it is impossible to assess the monetary value of injured feelings, awards should be restrained. To award sums which are generally felt to be excessive does almost as much harm to the policy and the results which it seeks to achieve as do nominal awards. Further, injury to feelings, which is likely to be of a relatively short duration, is less serious than physical injury to the body or mind which may persist for months, in many cases for life.

If a case has the potential for a very large award of damages, there is a need for carefully managed remedies hearings, with directions, statements and schedules of loss akin to personal injury cases (*Buxton* v *Equinox Designs Ltd* [1999] IRLR 158, EAT).

The EAT, Judge Peter Clark presiding, has recently held in *Tchoula* v *ICTS (UK) Ltd* [2000] ICR 1191 that it will only review an award for injury to feelings on the ground that it is excessive if it is satisfied that the facts of the case, taken overall, mean that it should be categorised as falling within a 'lower' (i.e. less serious) category of discrimination. If this is so, then a manifestly high award for injury to feelings (£27,000 in *Tchoula*, including £5,000 aggravated damages) will be overturned. In deciding whether it is faced with a 'lower' or 'higher' category of discrimination, it will be important for a tribunal to know whether the discrimination formed part of a campaign of harassment over a long period, and also what actual loss was attributable to the discrimination suffered (e.g. depression, marriage breakdown). It is also clear that damages for injury to feelings should bear some relationship to personal injury awards for psychiatric harm. Following *Tchoula*, such awards may also be 'globally' assessed for several acts of discrimination.

In the employment field, there is often scope for very high awards in cases where discrimination has been not only bad in itself, but has persisted over a long period of time. In *Yeboah* v *Crofton and London Borough of Hackney*, Case Numbers 56617/94, 69479/94, 23230/95, 70911/95 and 7093/96/S, for example, Hackney Borough paid, by consent, the sum of £380,000 (including £40,000 in respect of injury to feelings) to a senior employee who had been the victim of a campaign of racial discrimination which had disastrous effects on his well-being and health. It may be that similarly substantial awards will be made under the new s. 19B if the discrimination by the public body is of a comparable nature. However, awards in non-employment discrimination cases in the county court have generally been much lower. The average level of an award is £1,000 and the average settlement is approximately £2,000 (although the Commission achieve negotiated settlements of approximately £6,000 on average) (the Parliamentary Secretary for the Privy Council Office, Mr Paddy Tipping, Hansard HC, 13 April 2000, Standing Committee D, part 5). The Commission for Racial Equality's annual report also provides examples of quantum which may assist practitioners.

There are certain limitations on the remedies available in discrimination claims arising out of criminal proceedings (see 8.10.1 below).

Interest is payable on awards. The usual costs provisions of the CPR will apply to discrimination claims under the new s. 19B. There is a right of appeal to the Court of Appeal against a decision of a designated county court, and to the Court of Session against a decision of a sheriff court.

8.10 SPECIAL PROVISIONS FOR CLAIMS ARISING OUT OF CRIMINAL PROCEEDINGS

8.10.1 Limitation on remedies

Section 5 of the new Act imposes certain procedural limitations on claims arising out of criminal investigations. It does this by inserting new ss. 57(4A)–(4D) and 65(4A)–(4D) into the 1976 Act.

By the new s. 57(4A), no remedy other than (a) damages, or (b) a declaration or, in Scotland, a declarator, shall be obtainable unless the court is satisfied that the remedy concerned would not prejudice a criminal investigation, a decision to institute criminal proceedings or any criminal proceedings where the act which is alleged to constitute discrimination contrary to the new s. 19B was an act done by a person in carrying out public investigator functions or functions as a public prosecutor. The new s. 57(4B) defines 'criminal investigation' as:

> (a) any investigation which a person in carrying out functions to which section 19B applies has a duty to conduct with a view to it being ascertained whether a person should be charged with, or in Scotland prosecuted for, an offence, or whether a person charged with or prosecuted for an offence is guilty of it;
> (b) any investigation which is conducted by a person in carrying out functions to which section 19B applies and which in the circumstances may lead to a decision by that person to institute criminal proceedings which the person has power to conduct; or
> (c) any investigation which is conducted by a person in carrying out functions to which section 19B applies and which in the circumstances may lead to a decision by that person to make a report to the procurator fiscal for the purpose of enabling him to determine whether criminal proceedings should be instituted.

'Public investigator functions' are defined as functions of conducting criminal investigations or charging offenders; and 'offence' as any offence under the Army Act 1955, the Air Force Act 1955 or the Naval Discipline Act 1957 (and 'offender' shall be construed accordingly). This provision therefore effectively creates a presumption against ordering any remedy other than damages or a declaration if there is a risk of prejudice to a criminal investigation. Damages and a declaration are, however, often the most significant remedies in any event. Lord Lester spoke out against this part of the Act and proposed an amendment to make the test one of 'serious' prejudice (Hansard HL, 13 January 2000, col. 755), but the text remains unchanged.

8.10.2 Adjournments while criminal proceedings are pending

By the new s. 57(4C) and 57(4D), where a party to proceedings under s. 19B has applied for a stay or sist of those proceedings on the grounds of prejudice to:

(a) particular criminal proceedings;
(b) a criminal investigation; or
(c) a decision to institute criminal proceedings,

the court *shall* grant the stay or sist unless it is satisfied that the continuance of the proceedings under subs. (1) would not result in the prejudice alleged. The justification for this provision is to ensure that criminal trials are not unduly delayed for victims and witnesses pending the outcome of civil proceedings (Lord Bassam, Hansard HL, 14 December 1999, col. 132). There is therefore a clear presumption in favour of adjourning claims under the new s. 19B where there are like criminal proceedings.

8.10.3 Limitations on the questionnaire procedure

By the new s. 65(4A) and (4B), s. 65(2)(b) (the provision by which just and equitable inferences can be drawn from the fact that a respondent to a questionnaire deliberately, and without reasonable excuse, omitted to reply within a reasonable period or that his reply is evasive or equivocal) does not apply in relation to a failure to reply, or a particular reply if:

(a) at the time of doing any relevant act, the respondent was carrying out public investigator functions or was a public prosecutor; and

(b) he reasonably believes that a reply or (as the case may be) a different reply would be likely to prejudice any criminal investigation, any decision to institute criminal proceedings or any criminal proceedings or would reveal the reasons behind a decision not to institute, or a decision not to continue, criminal proceedings.

There is therefore a limitation on the nature of the inferences which can be drawn against respondents for their questionnaire replies which impinge on criminal proceedings.

(See further, the discussions in the House of Commons Standing Committee D, 18 April 2000, parts 3–5.)

8.11 SPECIAL PROVISIONS FOR CLAIMS ARISING OUT OF IMMIGRATION AND ASYLUM CASES

Section 6 of the 2000 Act imposes a different procedure for claims arising out of immigration and asylum cases, so that complaints of racial discrimination in certain immigration decisions, namely in decisions relating to the right to enter or remain in Great Britain, will be heard (with human rights complaints) by the Immigration Appellate Authorities as part of the 'one-stop' immigration appeals procedure established by the Immigration and Asylum Act 1999 ('the 1999 Act'). Cases with a national security element are appeals to the Special Immigration Appeals Commission. The new one-stop procedure for appeals was aimed at ensuring that by April 2001, the majority of asylum applications would be resolved within an average of two months, and appeals against a refusal within a further four months (Lord Bassam, Hansard HL, 14 December 1999, col. 130).

Section 6 achieves this by inserting a new s. 57A into the 1976 Act. The new s. 57A(1) provides that no proceedings may be brought by a claimant under s. 57(1) in respect of an immigration claim if:

(a) the act to which the claim relates was done in the taking by an immigration authority of a relevant decision and the question whether that act was unlawful by virtue of s. 19B has been or could be raised in proceedings on an appeal which is pending, or could be brought, under the Special Immigration Appeals Commission Act 1997 ('the 1997 Act') or Part IV of the 1999 Act (disregarding any power to grant leave to appeal out of time — new s. 57A(5)); or

(b) it has been decided in relevant immigration proceedings that that act was not unlawful by virtue of that section.

An 'immigration claim' is a claim that a person:

(a) has committed a relevant act of discrimination against the claimant which is unlawful by virtue of s. 19B; or

(b) is by virtue of s. 32 or 33 to be treated as having committed such an act of discrimination against the claimant (new s. 57A(2)).

An 'immigration authority' means an authority within the meaning of s. 65 of the 1999 Act (human rights and racial discrimination cases); a 'relevant decision' means:

(a) in relation to an immigration authority, any decision under the Immigration Acts relating to the entitlement of the claimant to enter or remain in the UK; and

(b) in relation to an immigration appellate body, any decision on an appeal under the 1997 Act or Part IV of the 1999 Act in relation to a decision falling within para. (a);

'relevant immigration proceedings' means proceedings on an appeal under the 1997 Act or Part IV of the 1999 Act; and 'relevant act of discrimination' means an act of discrimination done by an immigration authority in taking any relevant decision (new s. 57A(5)).

A claimant who substantiates his or her claim will then be able to apply to a county or sheriff court for damages.

Claims of race discrimination against immigration authorities which are unrelated to a decision on entitlement to enter or remain in the UK can proceed directly to the county or sheriff court. This is achieved by the new s. 7A(3) which provides that where it has been decided in relevant immigration proceedings that an act to which an immigration claim relates was unlawful by virtue of s. 19B, any court hearing that claim under s. 57 shall treat that act as an act which is unlawful by virtue of s. 19B for the purposes of the proceedings before it. Once a finding of unlawful discrimination has been made in the 'one-stop' procedure, the claimant is therefore entitled to rely on that finding in the county court, to where he or she must apply for a remedy. A finding of unlawful race discrimination does not vitiate the immigration decision itself: as by the new s. 57A(4), no relevant decision of an immigration authority involving an act to which an immigration claim relates and no relevant decision of an immigration appellate body in relation to such a decision shall be subject to challenge or otherwise affected by virtue of a decision of a court hearing the immigration claim under s. 57.

A person making a claim to the immigration appellate authorities will, under sch. 2 to the 1976 Act, be denied access to the questionnaire procedure under s. 65. This will, according to the Parliamentary Under-Secretary for the Home Office, Mike O'Brien, 'keep the administrative processes efficient in terms of obtaining and maintaining a faster system' (Hansard HC Standing Committee D, 18 April 2000, part 6).

Judicial review will also be available under the 'one-stop' procedure, and the Commission for Racial Equality now has the power to make a formal investigation and to issue a non-discrimination notice on immigration and asylum issues as on others. It is likely that in both situations, everything will turn on the interpretation of the distinctions between 'ethnic or national origin' and 'race or colour' (see Ann Dummett, *Ministerial Statements: The immigration exemption in the Race Relations (Amendment) Act 2000)*, published by ILPA with the support of the CRE, April 2001, at p. 11).

The national security exemption, which may be especially relevant for immigration cases, is explained in Chapter 4.

(See further, the discussions in the House of Commons Standing Committee D, 18 April 2000, parts 5–9.)

8.12 SPECIAL PROVISIONS FOR EDUCATION CASES

Under the 1976 Act, there were special arrangements for the enforcement of ss. 17 and 19 against establishments and bodies in the public sector of education (i.e. educational establishments maintained by a local education authority, special schools which are not maintained by a local education authority (or an education authority in Scotland) certain independent polytechnics in London, certain establishments which receive grants from the Department of Education and Science and grant-aided schools and central institutions and colleges of education in Scotland). Although complaints by individuals about discrimination by these bodies could be made to a designated county court or, in Scotland, the sheriff court, complaints relating to the public sector of education first had to be referred to the appropriate Education Minister. The Education Minister would have the complaints investigated and, where appropriate, would deal with the matter complained of under his statutory powers. By s. 57(5), a complaint in respect of a body subject to the Education Minister's powers could be brought before the courts in the normal way two months after the complaint had been notified by the complainant to the appropriate Education Minister, or before the end of the two months if he had informed the complainant that he did not require further time to consider it. If the Education Minister had not reached a conclusion in two months he would, without prejudice to the complainant's right to bring proceedings in the courts, continue his consideration of the complaint and notify his decision as soon as possible. This two month delay was seen as a 'cooling off' period, as well as giving the Secretary of State the opportunity to seek to resolve the dispute or to use powers of direction under the education legislation to avoid resort to the courts. In practice it was not as effective as originally envisaged and, more often than not, only served to delay a claimant's action. It was an inconsistency which only applied to educational bodies.

The Commission for Racial Equality recommended in its Third Review of the 1976 Act that this requirement should be removed. The 2000 Act does this, by allowing complaints of racial discrimination in education to be brought directly before county and sheriff courts without the two month period of notification to the appropriate Education Minister. This is achieved by sch. 3 to the Act which partially repeals s. 57(5). The relevant Secretary of State must still be informed of the claim before it can be brought, but there is no need to await the expiry of the two month period.

8.13 FINDINGS UNDER SECTION 19 OR 20 TO BE CONCLUSIVE

Section 69(1) of the 1976 Act provides that any finding by a court under s. 19 or 20 of the Race Relations Act 1968, or by a court or industrial tribunal under the 1976 Act, in respect of any act shall, if it has become final, be treated as conclusive in any proceedings under the 1976 Act. (Section 69(2) provided that where s. 42 was relied on (national security) to justify discrimination, a Ministerial certificate was conclusive evidence that the act was done for the purposes of national security. This has now been removed by s. 7(2) of the 2000 Act — see Chapter 4.)

Chapter Nine
Conclusion

9.1 EXPECTATIONS OF THE ACT

It is fair to say that the Race Relations (Amendment) Act 2000 has had a mixed reception, coming into force as it did with a General Election looming and issues of race firmly on the political agenda.

The website for the Act states that:

> The Government wants to transform Britain into a society that is inclusive and prosperous, where equality of opportunity is a reality for all. It is working to create the right legislative and administrative framework to remove barriers and improve the position of groups facing disadvantage and discrimination in employment, public life and public service delivery. It wants the public sector to set the pace in the drive for equality, to lead by example. The Race Relations (Amendment) Act 2000 is a key part of that drive. . . . The Act . . . impacts on the implementation of Government policies and services across the board (see www.homeoffice.gov.uk/raceact/welcome.htm and www.homeoffice.gov.uk/raceact/bilingen.htm).

The Commission for Racial Equality press release announcing the coming into force of the Act was, unsurprisingly, also full of optimism for the new Act. Gurbux Singh, the Chairman of the Commission, said that by the 2000 Act,

> Britain . . . moves into a new gear on racial equality. . . . Areas of discrimination that were immune from the Race Relations Act but which could have a devastating impact on people's lives have now been brought within its scope and individuals will be able to take cases to the courts. The public sector has not lived up to the justified expectation that it should deliver racial equality. It now has no option but to do so. Parliament, united with the agreement of all parties on this historical step, has put racial equality at the heart of responsibilities of public bodies. They will now need to look at what they do, who they serve and who they employ, and make sure that they provide equality of opportunity across all their activities. This will end the waste of talent that discrimination imposes,

> improve the quality of individual lives and lay the basis for a new and positive relationship between public authorities such as the police and all members of Britain's diverse communities.

Speaking in the context of the summer 2001 race related violence in Burnley, Bradford and Oldham, Chris Myant of the Commission expressed his hope that the Codes of Practice will 'concentrate minds wonderfully in a way that the law has not' (Penny Lewis, 'Time to read the riot act on race', *The Independent*, 24 July 2001).

Concern has, however, been expressed about the general ethos of the Act. Some would argue that it is misconceived to rely on the law to bring about improvements in the social position of ethnic minority groups. Passing legislation may create the false impression that the problem of discrimination and disadvantage has been tackled and perhaps even solved, as people often assume that laws necessarily achieve their purpose. This fails to take adequate account of the symbolic function of the law, but the strength of the argument lies in the recognition that law can only ever be one strand in what is, effectively, a political campaign concerning the allocation of resources (see, further, R. Townshend-Smith, *Discrimination Law: Text, Cases and Materials* (Cavendish, 1998) at pp. 82–86).

Some commentators see the Act, along with other campaigns by the Commission for Racial Equality, as actually likely to exaggerate tensions and sensitivities between ethnic groups (Michael Gove, 'This pledge is an insult to everyone in Britain', *The Times*, 24 April 2001). Some argue that the Act has a role to play, but really only when seen in the context of other relevant legal frameworks and efforts to improve the social conditions which often permit racism to flourish (Penny Lewis, *op cit*).

There has also been widespread concern expressed about the implications for immigration, asylum and nationality law of the immigration exemption as explained in Chapter 4. The report by Ann Dummett, published by the Immigration Law Practitioners' Association with the support of the Commission for Racial Equality in April 2001, expressed a concern that the immigration exemption received no mention either in the long title and stated purposes of the Bill, that newspaper reports concentrated on the implementation of the Bill as a response to the McPherson report and that organisations and individuals concerned with immigration were not alerted to the exemption (p. 5). A leading immigration lawyer, Frances Webber, has also commented that 'It is ironic that a law brought in to counter institutional racism ends up — so far as immigration is concerned at least — by rationalising and instututionalising it' ('The last frontier: immigration controls and racism', journal number 56 of the Campaign Against Racism and Facism, quoted by Harry Cohen MP at the Third Reading of the Bill in the House of Commons, Hansard HC, 30 October 2000, col. 532). Because of the immigration exemption, the Act has been described as '. . . the bluntest piece of state-sponsored ethnic discrimination in the 35 years since British parliaments started legislating in the field. . . . What Jack Straw, famous for his anti-racism, has done is write into statute a law of national and ethnic and racial discrimination . . .' (Hugo Young, 'Ministerial double-talk simply masks a racist law: The Race Relations (Amendment) Act offends against natural justice', *The Guardian*, 24 April 2001).

9.2 ADMINISTRATIVE SUPPORT FOR THE ACT

The Government believes that in addition to legislation, an appropriate administrative framework is necessary to create improvements in racial equality (Consultation Paper, para. 1.19). This administrative action will take the form of:

(a) Guidance — the Commission for Racial Equality will provide statutory codes of practice giving guidance to public authorities on how to fulfill their obligations under the general and specific duties. This will cover, for example, policy development and implementation, service delivery, employment and performance management. These statutory Codes will be admissible as evidence in respect of an alleged breach of the Act. These Codes are to be seen alongside the statutory Codes of Practice on employment and housing and the non-statutory guidance, for example in race equality standards for local authorities and schools, also provided by the CRE.
(b) Performance indicators — where appropriate, these will be linked to progress against the CRE statutory Codes of Practice or other guidance, and other performance indicators linked to Central Government Public Service Agreements and Service Delivery Agreements.
(c) Audit and reporting — this covers monitoring and reporting by public bodies, the Audit Commission in local authorities, the National Audit Office, Audit Scotland, the police, fire and probation inspectorates and so on.
(d) Measuring progress — indicators for measuring progress on racial equality in the public sector are published in Race Equality in Public Services.

A Race Equality Bill Team was established to advise and support Ministers in relation to the Act as it passed through Parliament. As well as conducting ongoing work on the Act, the Team is now taking forward implementation of the Act, including public consultation on the positive duties to promote racial equality. The Team is also responsible for taking forward other regulatory commitments arising from the CRE's Third Review of the 1976 Act as soon as parliamentary time permits. The Team is headed by Callton Young, assisted by Sally Edmunds and Ian Cheeseman. They can be contacted by writing to The Race Equality Bill Team, 12th Floor, Home Office, 58 Queen Anne's Gate, London SW1H 9AT, by fax to 020 7273 3400 or by email to BTRE2@homeoffice.gsi.gov.uk.

9.3 EUROPEAN DEVELOPMENTS

Motivation for further reform of domestic discrimination law is also coming from the European Community. In 1997, the Treaty of Amsterdam amended the Treaty of Rome so that Article 13 provided that:

> Without prejudice to the other provisions of this Treaty, and within the limits of the powers conferred by it upon the Community, the Council, acting unanimously on a proposal from the Commission, and after consulting the European Parliament, may take appropriate action to combat discrimination based on sex, racial or ethnic origin, religion or belief, disability, age or sexual orientation.

Article 13 therefore makes anti-discrimination a basic founding principle of the European Union and confers jurisdiction on the Council to take steps in the area of discrimination. The general principles of Article 13 are not themselves legally binding. To give effect to Article 13, in 2000 the Council of Ministers approved an Employment Framework Directive, a Race Directive and an Action Programme to support practical efforts in the member states to combat discrimination.

The Employment Framework Directive (Com (2000) 328(01)) requires member states to make discrimination unlawful on grounds of religion or belief, disability, age or sexual orientation in the areas of employment and training. The Race Directive covers employment, self-employment, working conditions, access to vocational training and work experience, membership of workers', employers' or professional organisations, education, social protection, including social security and health care, 'social advantages' such as concessionary fares and subsidised meals and access to goods and services which are available to the public, including housing. The directive specifically excludes protection against discrimination on grounds of nationality, which is dealt with separately in the Treaty.

Both directives set out clear definitions of direct and indirect discrimination. The definition of direct discrimination is very similar to that in UK legislation. However, the test for indirect discrimination is whether 'an apparently neutral provision, criterion or practice . . . would put persons of a racial or ethnic origin at a particular disadvantage compared with other persons'. The directives provide that indirect discrimination will be unlawful unless the provision, criterion or practice 'is objectively justified by a legitimate aim and the means of achieving that aim are appropriate and necessary'. This is therefore a broader definition of indirect discrimination than the one in current UK law as it encompasses 'practices' as well as provisions or criteria, and it will look at situations which 'would put' people at a particular disadvantage so that discrimination does not have to have occurred if it can be established that there is a real likelihood of it occurring. (It is also similar to the definition which the Commission for Racial Equality proposed in its proposals for reform of the Race Relations Act.) Harassment, defined as 'unwanted conduct related to any of the grounds covered by the directives, or conduct which is intended, or has the effect of, violating an individual's dignity and creating a humiliating, intimidating or hostile environment', is to be regarded as a form of discrimination. Both directives include protection against victimisation as a consequence of complaining of discrimination, or bringing or taking part in discrimination proceedings.

In line with Directive 97/80 on the burden of proof in cases of discrimination based on sex, both directives also shift the burden of proof in recognition of the fact that it is often very difficult for complainants to obtain evidence in discrimination cases. They state that when a complainant establishes before a court or tribunal 'facts from which it may be presumed that there has been direct or indirect discrimination,' it is for the respondent to prove that discrimination has not occurred. Current domestic law specifically does not go as far as reversing the burden of proof in direct discrimination claims, although it does assist complainants in permitting inferences of discrimination to be drawn from evidence establishing a prima facie case (see *King* v *Great Britain China Centre* [1992] ICR 561 and *Glasgow City Council* v *Zafar* [1998] ICR 120). Domestic law is largely compliant in respect of indirect discrimination claims in that once adverse impact is shown, it is for the respondent to show justification.

Both directives also enable organisations with an interest in combatting discrimination, including non-governmental organisations (NGOs), to support complainants or to bring proceedings on their behalf (with their approval). Both directives permit member states to take positive action measures to 'prevent or compensate for' situations of inequality. In the Race Directive, there is an obligation on each member state to designate a body to promote racial equality, which should have powers to assist victims of discrimination to pursue their complaints, conduct independent surveys concerning discrimination, and publish independent reports with recommendations relating to such discrimination. This role will be performed in the UK by the Commission for Racial Equality. There is an obligation on member states to publicise widely their existing laws on equal treatment and non-discrimination, in the areas within each of the directives, and any new measures they adopt to bring their laws in line with the directives.

The Action Programme will allocate 100 million euros over 2001–06 to fund practical action by member states to promote racial equality in all the areas covered by the two directives. The scheme aims to promote 'transnational co-operation' between organisations in the 15 member states in tackling discrimination throughout the European Union, and to encourage the exchange of ideas and information. The European Commission will administer the scheme, in conjunction with an advisory committee made up of representatives from all the member states.

The aim of these measures is to set minimum standards of legal protection against discrimination across all 15 member states of the European Union, whereas previously the scope and enforceability of discrimination measures in each Member State varied considerably. (Member states are free to introduce greater degrees of protection, in accordance with their individual histories and traditions: where higher levels of protection already exist in national law, the member state will be required to uphold these).

9.4 FUTURE DISCRIMINATION LEGISLATION

Both European directives referred to above require member states to introduce or amend their laws and procedures to comply with the directives. From the date for compliance, member states will also be expected to ensure that their laws, regulations and administrative provisions, as well as employment contracts and collective agreements, are non-discriminatory.

The Race Directive must be complied with by 19 July 2003. This is likely to mean further legislation to incorporate the new, wider definition of indirect discrimination and the shift in the burden of proof once a *prima facie* case is established. It will also mean legislation in areas within the scope of the directive that are not covered by the 1976 Act, for example access to self-employment or occupation, and the full ambit of 'social protection' and 'social advantages' (to the extent that the 2000 Act does not address these issues). Legislation will also be necessary to remove any exceptions that are not permitted in the directive, or define more restrictively the exceptions which in the directives are permitted in very limited, specific circumstances only, and to permit organisations to bring proceedings on behalf of individual complainants. It will be necessary to ensure that the sanctions for unlawful discrimination that are available to courts and tribunals are 'effective, proportional and dissuasive', which may include changes in the compensation arrangements for indirect race discrimination, in line with those which have been made for indirect sex discrimination. Any laws and regulations that are contrary to the principle of equal treatment will have to be abolished and any provisions contrary to this principle in individual or collective contracts, internal rules for public and private organisations, and rules of trade unions and professional organisations will be declared null and void.

The Employment Framework Directive means that in the UK, new legislation will be required to cover equal treatment on grounds of age or sexual orientation; and in Great Britain, on grounds of religion or belief. (Northern Ireland has had legislation prohibiting discrimination in employment on grounds of religious belief or political opinion since its Fair Employment Acts 1976 and 1989. The Fair Employment and Treatment (Northern Ireland) Order 1998 extended the reach of these Acts beyond the employment sphere). This will have to be in force by December 2003 in the case of sexual orientation and religion and belief and by December 2006 in the case of age discrimination. Religious discrimination was the subject matter of two reports recently commissioned by the Government. The first, *Religious Discrimination in England and Wales*, examines the history and background of British multi-faith society, and the second, *Tackling Religious Discrimination: practical implications for policy-makers and legislators*, considers the legal options open to the Government in responding to religious discrimination. These reports were published as consultation documents on 23 February 2001. The Home Office has indicated that there is to be discussion with faith communities and others about the practical steps that can be taken to tackle and overcome religious discrimination. The major impact in the UK of this part of the Directive will be to increase protection for the Muslim community.

For further information on these European developments and their effect on domestic race relations legislation, see the 'Law' section of the Commission for Racial Equality's website at www.cre.gov.uk; and EOR No. 95, January/February 2001, at pp. 32–6.

Article 21 of the recently adopted European Union's Charter of Fundamental Rights also contains a broad prohibition of discrimination on any ground, including race, colour, ethnic or social origin or membership of any national minority.

In its Equality Statement of 30 November 1999, the Government also indicated that it would, when legislative time permits, extend the prohibitions on discrimination in the Sex Discrimination Act 1975 and the Disability Discrimination Act 1995 to all public bodies in the same way that the Race Relations Act 1976 has now been extended (Equality Statement, point 6 — Cabinet Office Press Release 274/99, 30 November 1999; Consultation Paper, Appendix 1). The Commission for Racial Equality's Third Review of the Race Relations Act 1976).

Protocol 12 to the European Convention on Human Rights creates a free-standing protection from discrimination on any ground, including racial grounds. The significance of the Protocol right is that it does not require proof of discrimination in the enjoyment of another Convention right. The Protocol was opened for signature on 4 November 2000. The present Government has indicated its unwillingness to sign this Protocol, despite the fact that it was heavily involved in the discussions on its drafting, and despite a recommendation to that effect in the Joint Submission by NGO's to the UN Committee on the Elimination of all Forms of Racial Discrimination (published by Liberty and the 1990 Trust, August 2000).

This Submission also urged the Government to make a declaration under Article 14 of the Convention on the Elimination of all Forms of Racial Discrimination to allow individuals the right to petition the Committee; to extend the powers of the Commission for Racial Equality to enable it to bring legal action in its own name and/or class actions on behalf of victims of racism and give similar rights to other non-governmental organisations; and to consider legislating for an overarching principle of equality by which all legislation should be interpreted. There was recurring debate in the passage of this Act through Parliament as to whether or not there should be a single Equality Act (rather than the piecemeal position generated by there being separate discrimination statutes for race, sex and disability) (see, for example, Lord Lester, Hansard HL, 14 December 1999, col. 140). The current Government has, however, set its face firm against increasing pressure for such root-and-branch reform of the law.

9.5 CONCLUSION

It is hard to predict how much litigation will follow under the Act, especially in the field of indirect discrimination, although it is likely that, in some fields, the ability to challenge discriminatory behaviour by public bodies will be a powerful tool. It may well be that one of the most significant aspects of the Act will be the imposition of the positive duties on public bodies. In the rapidly changing landscape of discrimination law, however, the 2000 Act is a very significant development, which does have the potential to improve the quality of access to public services by the large number of ethnic minority groups in Great Britain. For that alone, it is to be welcomed.

Appendix 1

A. The Race Relations Act 1976, as amended

CHAPTER 74
ARRANGEMENT OF SECTIONS

PART I
DISCRIMINATION TO WHICH ACT APPLIES

PART II
DISCRIMINATION IN THE EMPLOYMENT FIELD

Discrimination by employers

Discrimination by other bodies

PART III
DISCRIMINATION IN OTHER FIELDS

Education

17A. Meaning of pupil in section 17.
18. Other discrimination by local education authorities.
18A. Discrimination by Further Education and Higher Education Funding Councils.
18B. Discrimination by Scottish Further and Higher Education Funding Councils.
18C. . . .
18D. Discrimination by Teacher Training Agency.
19. . . .
19ZA. . . .

Planning

19A. Discrimination by planning authorities.

Public authorities

19B. Discrimination by public authorities.
19C. Exceptions or further exceptions from section 19B for judicial and legislative acts etc.
19D. Exception from section 19B for certain acts in immigration and nationality cases.
19E. Monitoring of exception in relation to immigration and nationality cases.
19F. Exceptions from section 19B for decisions not to prosecute etc.

Goods, facilities, services and premises

20. Discrimination in provision of goods, facilities or services.
21. Discrimination in disposal or management of premises.
22. Exception from ss. 20(1) and 21: small dwellings.
23. Further exceptions from ss. 20(1) and 21.
24. Discrimination: consent for assignment or sub-letting.
25. Discrimination: associations not within s. 11.
26. Exception from s. 25 for certain associations.

Barristers

26A. Discrimination by, or in relation to, barristers.
26B. Discrimination by, or in relation to, advocates.

Extent

27. Extent of Part III.

PART IV
OTHER UNLAWFUL ACTS

28. Discriminatory practices.
29. Discriminatory advertisements.
30. Instructions to discriminate.
31. Pressure to discriminate.
32. Liability of employers and principals.
33. Aiding unlawful acts.

PART V
CHARITIES

34. Charities.

PART VI
GENERAL EXCEPTIONS FROM PARTS II TO IV

35. Special needs of racial groups in regard to education, training or welfare.

PART VII
THE COMMISSION FOR RACIAL EQUALITY

General

Section

Codes of practice

Investigations

PART VIII
ENFORCEMENT

General

Enforcement in employment field

Enforcement of Part III

Non-discrimination notices

Other enforcement by Commission

An Act to make fresh provision with respect to discrimination on racial grounds and relations between people of different racial groups; and to make in the Sex Discrimination Act 1975 amendments for bringing provisions in that Act relating to its administration and enforcement into conformity with the corresponding provisions in this Act.

[22nd November 1976]

BE IT ENACTED by the Queen's most Excellent Majesty, by and with the advice and consent of the Lords Spiritual and Temporal, and Commons, in this present Parliament assembled, and by the authority of the same, as follows:—

PART I
DISCRIMINATION TO WHICH ACT APPLIES

1. Racial discrimination

(1) A person discriminates against another in any circumstances relevant for the purposes of any provision of this Act if—

(a) on racial grounds he treats that other less favourably than he treats or would treat other persons; or

(b) he applies to that other a requirement or condition which he applies or would apply equally to persons not of the same racial group as that other but—

(i) which is such that the proportion of persons of the same racial group as that other who can comply with it is considerably smaller than the proportion of persons not of that racial group who can comply with it; and

(ii) which he cannot show to be justifiable irrespective of the colour, race, nationality or ethnic or national origins of the person to whom it is applied; and

(iii) which is to the detriment of that other because he cannot comply with it.

(2) It is hereby declared that, for the purposes of this Act, segregating a person from other persons on racial grounds is treating him less favourably than they are treated.

2. Discrimination by way of victimisation

(1) A person ('the discriminator') discriminates against another person ('the person victimised') in any circumstances relevant for the purposes of any provision of this Act if he treats the person victimised less favourably than in those circumstances he treats or would treat other persons, and does so by reason that the person victimised has—

(a) brought proceedings against the discriminator or any other person under this Act; or

(b) given evidence or information in connection with proceedings brought by any person against the discriminator or any other person under this Act; or

(c) otherwise done anything under or by reference to this Act in relation to the discriminator or any other person; or

(d) alleged that the discriminator or any other person has committed an act which (whether or not the allegation so states) would amount to a contravention of this Act,

or by reason that the discriminator knows that the person victimised intends to do any of those things, or suspects that the person victimised has done, or intends to do, any of them.

(2) Subsection (1) does not apply to treatment of a person by reason of any allegation made by him if the allegation was false and not made in good faith.

3. Meaning of 'racial grounds' 'racial group', etc

(1) In this Act, unless the context otherwise requires—

'racial grounds' means any of the following grounds, namely colour, race, nationality or ethnic or national origins;

'racial group' means a group of persons defined by reference to colour, race, nationality or ethnic or national origins, and references to a person's racial group refer to any racial group into which he falls.

(2) The fact that a racial group comprises two or more distinct racial groups does not prevent it from constituting a particular racial group for the purposes of this Act.

(3) In this Act—

(a) references to discrimination refer to any discrimination falling within section 1 or 2; and

(b) references to racial discrimination refer to any discrimination falling within section 1, and related expressions shall be construed accordingly.

(4) A comparison of the case of a person of a particular racial group with that of a person not of that group under section 1(1) must be such that the relevant circumstances in the one case are the same, or not materially different, in the other.

PART II
DISCRIMINATION IN THE EMPLOYMENT FIELD

Discrimination by employers

4. Discrimination against applicants and employees

(1) It is unlawful for a person, in relation to employment by him at an establishment in Great Britain, to discriminate against another—

(a) in the arrangements he makes for the purpose of determining who should be offered that employment; or

(b) in the terms on which he offers him that employment; or

(c) by refusing or deliberately omitting to offer him that employment.

(2) It is unlawful for a person, in the case of a person employed by him at an establishment in Great Britain, to discriminate against that employee—

(a) in the terms of employment which he affords him; or

(b) in the way he affords him access to opportunities for promotion, transfer or training, or to any other benefits, facilities or services, or by refusing or deliberately omitting to afford him access to them; or

(c) by dismissing him, or subjecting him to any other detriment.

(3) Except in relation to discrimination falling within section 2, subsections (1) and (2) do not apply to employment for the purposes of a private household.

(4) Subsection (2) does not apply to benefits, facilities or services of any description if the employer is concerned with the provision (for payment or not) of benefits, facilities or services of that description to the public, or to a section of the public comprising the employee in question, unless—

(a) that provision differs in a material respect from the provision of the benefits, facilities or services by the employer to his employees; or

(b) the provision of the benefits, facilities or services to the employee in question is regulated by his contract of employment; or

(c) the benefits, facilities or services relate to training.

5. Exceptions for genuine occupational qualifications

(1) In relation to racial discrimination—

(a) section 4(1)(a) or (c) does not apply to any employment where being of a particular racial group is a genuine occupational qualification for the job; and

(b) section 4(2)(b) does not apply to opportunities for promotion or transfer to, or training for, such employment.

(2) Being of a particular racial group is a genuine occupational qualification for a job only where—

(a) the job involves participation in a dramatic performance or other entertainment in a capacity for which a person of that racial group is required for reasons of authenticity; or

(b) the job involves participation as an artist's or photographic model in the production of a work of art, visual image or sequence of visual images for which a person of that racial group is required for reasons of authenticity; or

(c) the job involves working in a place where food or drink is (for payment or not) provided to and consumed by members of the public or a section of the public in a particular setting for which, in that job, a person of that racial group is required for reasons of authenticity; or

(d) the holder of the job provides persons of that racial group with personal services promoting their welfare, and those services can most effectively be provided by a person of that racial group.

(3) Subsection (2) applies where some only of the duties of the job fall within paragraph (a), (b) (c) or (d) as well as where all of them do.

(4) Paragraph (a), (b), (c) or (d) of subsection (2) does not apply relation to the filling of a vacancy at a time when the employer already has employees of the racial group in question—

(a) who are capable of carrying out the duties falling within that paragraph; and

(b) whom it would be reasonable to employ on those duties; and

(c) whose numbers are sufficient to meet the employer's likely requirements in respect of those duties without undue inconvenience.

6. Exception for employment intended to provide training in skills to be exercised outside Great Britain

Nothing in section 4 shall render unlawful any act done by an employer for the benefit of a person not ordinarily resident in Great Britain in or in connection with employing him at an, establishment in Great Britain, where the purpose of that employment is to provide him with training in skills which he appears to the employer to intend to exercise wholly outside Great Britain.

7. Discrimination against contract workers

(1) This section applies to any work for a person ('the principal') which is available for doing by individuals ('contract workers') who are employed not by the principal himself but by another person, who supplies them under a contract made with the principal.

(2) It is unlawful for the principal, in relation to work to which this section applies, to discriminate against a contract worker—

(a) in the terms on which he allows him to do that work; or

(b) by not allowing him to do it or continue to do it; or

(c) in the way he affords him access to any benefits, facilities or services or by refusing or deliberately omitting to afford him access to them; or

(d) by subjecting him to any other detriment.

(3) The principal does not contravene subsection (2)(b) by doing any act in relation to a person not of a particular racial group at a time when, if the work were to be done by a person taken into the principal's employment, being of that racial group would be a genuine occupational qualification for the job.

(4) Nothing in this section shall render unlawful any act done by the principal for the benefit of a contract worker not ordinarily resident in Great Britain in or in connection with allowing him to do work to which this section applies, where the purpose of his being allowed to do that work is to provide him with training in skills which he appears to the principal to intend to exercise wholly outside Great Britain.

(5) Subsection (2)(c) does not apply to benefits, facilities or services of any description if the principal is concerned with the provision (for payment or not) of benefits, facilities or services of that description to the public, or to a section of the public to which the contract worker in question belongs, unless that provision differs in a material respect from the provision of the benefits, facilities or services by the principal to his contract workers.

8. Meaning of employment at establishment in Great Britain

(1) For the purposes of this Part ('the relevant purposes'), employment is to be regarded as being at an establishment in Great Britain unless the employee does his work wholly . . . outside Great Britain.

(2) . . .

(3) In the case of employment on board a ship registered at a port of registry in Great Britain (except where the employee does his work wholly outside Great Britain) the ship shall for the relevant purposes be deemed to be the establishment.

(4) Where work is not done at an establishment it shall be treated for the relevant purposes as done at the establishment from which it is done or (where it is not done from any establishment) at the establishment with which it has the closest connection.

(5) In relation to employment concerned with exploration of the sea bed or subsoil or the exploitation of their natural resources, Her Majesty may by Order in Council provide that subsections (1) to (3) shall have effect as if in both subsection (1) and subsection (3) the last reference to Great Britain included any area for the time being designated under section 1(7) of the Continental Shelf Act 1964, except an area or part of an area in which the law of Northern Ireland applies.

(6) An Order in Council under subsection (5) may provide that, in relation to employment to which the Order applies, this Part is to have effect with such modifications as are specified in the Order.

(7) An Order in Council under subsection (5) shall be of no effect unless a draft of the Order has been laid before and approved by resolution of each House of Parliament.

9. Exception for seamen recruited abroad

(1) Nothing in section 4 shall render unlawful any act done by an employer in or in connection with employment by him on any ship in the case of a person who applied or was engaged for that employment outside Great Britain.

(2) Nothing in section 7 shall, as regards work to which that section applies, render unlawful any act done by the principal in or in connection with such work on any ship in the case of a contract worker who was engaged outside Great Britain by the person by whom he is supplied.

(3) Subsections (1) and (2) do not apply to employment or work concerned with [any activity falling within section 23(2) of the Oil and Gas (Enterprise) Act 1982] in any area for the time being designated under section 1(7) of the Continental Shelf Act 1964 [or specified under section 22(5) of the Oil and Gas (Enterprise) Act 1982], not being an area or part of an area in which the law of Northern Ireland applies.

(4) For the purposes of subsection (1) a person brought to Great Britain with a view to his entering into an agreement in Great Britain to be employed on any ship shall be treated as having applied for the employment outside Great Britain.

Discrimination by other bodies

10. Partnerships

(1) It is unlawful for a firm consisting of six or more partners, in relation to a position as partner in the firm, to discriminate against a person—

(a) in the arrangements they make for the purpose of determining who should be offered that position; or

(b) in the terms on which they offer him that position; or

(c) by refusing or deliberately omitting to offer him that position; or

(d) in a case where the person already holds that position—

(i) in the way they afford him access to any benefits, facilities or services, or by refusing or deliberately omitting to afford him access to them; or

(ii) by expelling him from that position, or subjecting him to any other detriment.

(2) Subsection (1) shall apply in relation to persons proposing to form themselves into a partnership as it applies in relation to a firm.

(3) Subsection (1)(a) and (c) do not apply to a position as partner where, if it were employment, being of a particular racial group would be a genuine occupational qualification for the job.

(4) In the case of a limited partnership references in this section to a partner shall be construed as references to a general partner as defined in section 3 of the Limited Partnerships Act 1907.

[(5) This section applies to a limited liability partnership as it applies to a firm; and in its application to a limited liability partnership, references to a partner in the firm are references to a member of the limited liability partnership.]

11. Trade unions etc.

(1) This section applies to an organisation of workers, an organisation of employers, or any other organisation whose members carry on a particular profession or trade for the purposes of which the organisation exists.

(2) It is unlawful for an organisation to which this section applies, in the case of a person who is not a member of the organisation, to discriminate against him—

(a) in the terms on which it is prepared to admit him to membership; or

(b) by refusing, or deliberately omitting to accept, his application for membership.

(3) It is unlawful for an organisation to which this section applies, in the case of a person who is a member of the organisation, to discriminate against him—

(a) in the way it affords him access to any benefits, facilities or services, or by refusing or deliberately omitting to afford him access to them; or

(b) by depriving him of membership, or varying the terms on which he is a member; or

(c) by subjecting him to any other detriment.

12. Qualifying bodies

(1) It is unlawful for an authority or body which can confer an authorisation or qualification which is needed for, or facilitates, engagement in a particular profession or trade to discriminate against a person—

(a) in the terms on which it is prepared to confer on him that authorisation or qualification; or

(b) by refusing, or deliberately omitting to grant, his application for it; or

(c) by withdrawing it from him or varying the terms on which he holds it.

(2) In this section—

(a) 'authorisation or qualification' includes recognition, registration, enrolment, approval and certification;

(b) 'confer' includes renew or extend.

(3) Subsection (1) does not apply to discrimination which is rendered unlawful by section 17 or 18.

[13. Persons concerned with provision of vocational training

(1) It is unlawful, in the case of an individual seeking or undergoing training which would help fit him for any employment, for any person who provides, or makes arrangements for the provision of, facilities for such training to discriminate against him—

(a) in the terms on which that person affords him access to any training course or other facilities concerned with such training; or

(b) by refusing or deliberately omitting to afford him such access; or

(c) by terminating his training; or

(d) by subjecting him to any detriment during the course of his training.

(2) Subsection (1) does not apply to—

(a) discrimination which is rendered unlawful by section 4(1) or (2) or section 17 or 18; or

(b) discrimination which would be rendered unlawful by any of those provisions but for the operation of any provision of this Act.]

14. Employment agencies

(1) It is unlawful for an employment agency to discriminate against a person—

(a) in the terms on which the agency offers to provide any of its services; or

(b) by refusing or deliberately omitting to provide any of its services; or

(c) in the way it provides any of its services.

[(2) It is unlawful for a local education authority or education authority or any other person to do any act in providing services in pursuance of arrangements made, or a direction given, under section 10 of the Employment and Training Act 1973 which constitutes discrimination.]

(3) References in subsection (1) to the services of an employment agency include guidance on careers and any other services related to employment.

(4) This section does not apply if the discrimination only concerns employment which the employer could lawfully refuse to offer the person in question.

(5) An employment agency or local education authority [, education authority or other person] shall not be subject to any liability under this section if it proves—

(a) that it acted in reliance on a statement made to it by the employer to the effect that, by reason of the operation of subsection (4), its action would not be unlawful; and

(b) that it was reasonable for it to rely on the statement.

(6) A person who knowingly or recklessly makes a statement such as is referred to in subsection (5)(a) which in a material respect is false or misleading commits an offence, and shall be liable on summary conviction to a fine not exceeding [level 5 on the standard scale].

15. Manpower Services Commission etc.

[(1) It is unlawful for the [Secretary of State . . .] to discriminate in the provision of facilities or services under section 2 of the Employment and Training Act 1973.]

(2) This section does not apply in a case where—

(a) section 13 applies; or

(b) the [Secretary of State] is acting as an employment agency.

. . .

16. . . .

PART III
DISCRIMINATION IN OTHER FIELDS

Education

17. Discrimination by bodies in charge of educational establishments

It is unlawful, in relation to an educational establishment falling within column 1 of the following table, for a person indicated in relation to the establishment in column 2 (the 'responsible body') to discriminate against a person—

(a) in the terms on which it offers to admit him to the establishment as a pupil; or

(b) by refusing or deliberately omitting to accept an application for his admission to the establishment as a pupil; or

(c) where he is a pupil of the establishment—

(i) in the way it affords him access to any benefits, facilities or services, or by refusing or deliberately omitting to afford him access to them; or

(ii) by excluding him from the establishment or subjecting him to any other detriment.

TABLE
ENGLAND AND WALES

Establishment	*Responsible body*
1. Educational establishment maintained by a local education authority.	Local education authority or . . . [governing body], according to which of them has the function in question.
2. Independent school not being a special school.	Proprietor.

3. Special school not maintained by a local education authority.	Proprietor.
[3A. . . .]	
[3B. Institution within the further education sector (within the meaning of section 91(3) of the Further and Higher Education Act 1992).	Governing body.]
4. University.	Governing body.
[4A. Institution, other than a university, within the higher education sector (within the meaning of section 91(5) of the Further and Higher Education Act 1992).	Governing body.]
5. Establishment (not falling within paragraphs 1 [to 4A]) providing full-time or part-time education, being an establishment designated under section 24(1) of the Sex Discrimination Act 1975 for the purposes of paragraph 5 of the corresponding table in section 22 of that Act.	Governing body.

SCOTLAND

Establishment	*Responsible body*
6. Educational establishment managed by an education authority.	Education authority.
7. Educational establishment in respect of which the managers are for the time being receiving grants under section [73(d)] of the Education (Scotland) Act 1962.	Managers of the educational establishment.
[7AA. A grant-aided school, within the meaning of section 135 of the Education (Scotland) Act 1980.	The managers of the school.]
7B. College of further education within the meaning of section 36(1) of the Further and Higher Education (Scotland) Act 1992 under the management of a board of management.	Board of management
7C. Designated institution within the meaning of Part II of the Further and Higher Education (Scotland) Act 1992.	Governing body.
8. University.	Governing body.
9. Independent school.	Proprietor.
10. Any other educational establishment (not falling within paragraphs 6, 7 and 9) providing full or part-time school education or further education.	Managers of the educational establishment.

[17A. Meaning of pupil in section 17
For the purposes of section 17, 'pupil' includes, in England and Wales, any person who receives education at a school or institution to which that section applies.]

18. Other discrimination by local education authorities
(1) It is unlawful for a local education authority, in carrying out such of its functions under [the Education Acts] as do not fall under section 17, to do any act which constitutes racial discrimination.
(2) It is unlawful for an education authority, in carrying out such of its functions under the Education (Scotland) Acts 1939 to 1974 as do not fall under section 17, to do any act which constitutes racial discrimination.

[18A. Discrimination by Further Education and Higher Education Funding Councils
It is unlawful for the [Learning and Skills Council for England, the National Council for Education and Training for Wales,] the Higher Education Funding Council for England or the Higher Education Funding Council for Wales in carrying out their functions under the Education Acts [and the Learning and Skills Act 2000], to do any act which constitutes racial discrimination.]

[18B. Discrimination by Scottish Further and Higher Education Funding Councils
It is unlawful for the Scottish Further Education Funding Council or the Scottish Higher Education Funding Council in carrying out any of their functions to do any act which constitutes racial discrimination.]

[18C. . . .]

[18D. Discrimination by Teacher Training Agency
It is unlawful for the Teacher Training Agency in carrying out their functions under Part I of the Education Act 1994 to do any act which constitutes racial discrimination.]

19. . . .

19ZA. . . .

[*Planning*

19A. Discrimination by planning authorities
(1) It is unlawful for a planning authority to discriminate against a person in carrying out their planning functions.
(2) In this section 'planning authority' means—
(a) in England and Wales, a county, [county borough,] district or London borough council, [the Broads Authority] [a National Part authority or] a joint planning board, . . ., and
(b) in Scotland, a planning authority or regional planning authority;
and includes an urban development corporation and a body having functions (whether as an enterprise zone authority or a body invited to prepare a scheme) under Schedule 32 to the Local Government, Planning and Land Act 1980.
(3) In this section 'planning functions' means—
(a) in England and Wales, functions under [the Town and Country Planning Act 1990, the Planning (Listed Buildings and Conservation Areas) Act 1990 and the Planning (Hazardous Substances) Act 1990], and such other functions as may be prescribed, and
(b) in Scotland, functions under [the Town and Country Planning (Scotland) Act 1997, the Planning (Listed Buildings and Conservation Areas) (Scotland) Act 1997 and the Planning (Hazardous Substances) (Scotland) Act 1997], and such other functions as may be prescribed,
and includes, in relation to an urban development corporation, planning functions under Part XVI of the Local Government, Planning and Land Act 1980 and, in relation to an enterprise zone authority or body invited to prepare an enterprise zone scheme, functions under Part XVIII of that Act.]

[*Public authorities*

19B. Discrimination by public authorities

(1) It is unlawful for a public authority in carrying out any functions of the authority to do any act which constitutes discrimination.

(2) In this section 'public authority'—

(a) includes any person certain of whose functions are functions of a public nature; but

(b) does not include any person mentioned in subsection (3).

(3) The persons mentioned in this subsection are—

(a) either House of Parliament;

(b) a person exercising functions in connection with proceedings in Parliament;

(c) the Security Service;

(d) the Secret Intelligence Service;

(e) the Government Communications Headquarters; and

(f) any unit or part of a unit of any of the naval, military or air forces of the Crown which is for the time being required by the Secretary of State to assist the Government Communications Headquarters in carrying out its functions.

(4) In relation to a particular act, a person is not a public authority by virtue only of subsection (2)(a) if the nature of the act is private.

(5) This section is subject to sections 19C to 19F.

(6) Nothing in this section makes unlawful any act of discrimination which—

(a) is made unlawful by virtue of any other provision of this Act; or

(b) would be so made but for any provision made by or under this Act.

19C. Exceptions or further exceptions from section 19B for judicial and legislative acts etc.

(1) Section 19B does not apply to—

(a) any judicial act (whether done by a court, tribunal or other person); or

(b) any act done on the instructions, or on behalf, of a person acting in a judicial capacity.

(2) Section 19B does not apply to any act of, or relating to, making, confirming or approving any enactment or Order in Council or any instrument made by a Minister of the Crown under an enactment.

(3) Section 19B does not apply to any act of, or relating to, making or approving arrangements, or imposing requirements or conditions, of a kind falling within section 41.

(4) Section 19B does not apply to any act of, or relating to, imposing a requirement, or giving an express authorisation, of a kind mentioned in section 19D(3) in relation to the carrying out of immigration and nationality functions.

(5) In this section—

'immigration and nationality functions' has the meaning given in section 19D; and

'Minister of the Crown' includes the National Assembly for Wales and a member of the Scottish Executive.

19D. Exception from section 19B for certain acts in immigration and nationality cases

(1) Section 19B does not make it unlawful for a relevant person to discriminate against another person on grounds of nationality or ethnic or national origins in carrying out immigration and nationality functions.

(2) For the purposes of subsection (1), 'relevant person' means—

(a) a Minister of the Crown acting personally; or

(b) any other person acting in accordance with a relevant authorisation.

(3) In subsection (2), 'relevant authorisation' means a requirement imposed or express authorisation given—

(a) with respect to a particular case or class of case, by a Minister of the Crown acting personally;

(b) with respect to a particular class of case—

(i) by any of the enactments mentioned in subsection (5); or
(ii) by any instrument made under or by virtue of any of those enactments.

(4) For the purposes of subsection (1), 'immigration and nationality functions' means functions exercisable by virtue of any of the enactments mentioned in subsection (5).

(5) Those enactments are—

(a) the Immigration Acts (within the meaning of the Immigration and Asylum Act 1999 but excluding sections 28A to 28K of the Immigration Act 1971 so far as they relate to offences under Part III of that Act);
(b) the British Nationality Act 1981;
(c) the British Nationality (Falkland Islands) Act 1983;
(d) the British Nationality (Hong Kong) Act 1990;
(e) the Hong Kong (War Wives and Widows) Act 1996;
(f) the British Nationality (Hong Kong) Act 1997; and
(g) the Special Immigration Appeals Commission Act 1997;

and include any provision made under section 2(2) of the European Communities Act 1972, or any provision of Community law, which relates to the subject-matter of any of the enactments mentioned above.

19E. Monitoring of exception in relation to immigration and nationality cases

(1) The Secretary of State shall appoint a person who is not a member of his staff to act as a monitor.

(2) Before appointing any such person, the Secretary of State shall consult the Commission.

(3) The person so appointed shall monitor, in such manner as the Secretary of State may determine—

(a) the likely effect on the operation of the exception in section 19D of any relevant authorisation relating to the carrying out of immigration and nationality functions which has been given by a Minister of the Crown acting personally; and

(b) the operation of that exception in relation to acts which have been done by a person acting in accordance with such an authorisation.

(4) The monitor shall make an annual report on the discharge of his functions to the Secretary of State.

(5) The Secretary of State shall lay a copy of any report made to him under subsection (4) before each House of Parliament.

(6) The Secretary of State shall pay to the monitor such fees and allowances (if any) as he may determine.

(7) In this section 'immigration and nationality functions' and relevant authorisation' have the meanings given to them in section 19D.

19F. Exceptions from section 19B for decisions not to prosecute etc.

Section 19B does not apply to—

(a) a decision not to institute criminal proceedings and, where such a decision has been made, any act done for the purpose of enabling the decision whether to institute criminal proceedings to be made;

(b) where criminal proceedings are not continued as a result of a decision not to continue them, the decision and, where such a decision has been made—

(i) any act done for the purpose of enabling the decision whether to continue the proceedings to be made; and

(ii) any act done for the purpose of securing that the proceedings are not continued.]

Goods, facilities, services and premises

20. Discrimination in provision of goods, facilities or services

(1) It is unlawful for any person concerned with the provision (for payment or not) of goods, facilities or services to the public or a section of the public to discriminate against a person who seeks to obtain or use those goods, facilities or services—

(a) by refusing or deliberately omitting to provide him with any of them; or

(b) by refusing or deliberately omitting to provide him with goods, facilities or services of the like quality, in the like manner and on the like terms as are normal in the first-mentioned person's case in relation to other members of the public or (where the person so seeking belongs to a section of the public) to other members of that section.

(2) The following are examples of the facilities and services mentioned in subsection (1)—

(a) access to and use of any place which members of the public are permitted to enter;

(b) accommodation in a hotel, boarding house or other similar establishment;

(c) facilities by way of banking or insurance or for grants, loans, credit or finance;

(d) facilities for education;

(e) facilities for entertainment, recreation or refreshment;

(f) facilities for transport or travel;

(g) the services of any profession or trade, or any local or other public authority.

21. Discrimination in disposal or management of premises

(1) It is unlawful for a person, in relation to premises in Great Britain of which he has power to dispose, to discriminate against another—

(a) in the terms on which he offers him those premises; or

(b) by refusing his application for those premises; or

(c) in his treatment of him in relation to any list of persons in need of premises of that description.

(2) It is unlawful for a person, in relation to premises managed by him, to discriminate against a person occupying the premises—

(a) in the way he affords him access to any benefits or facilities, or by refusing or deliberately omitting to afford him access to them; or

(b) by evicting him, or subjecting him to any other detriment.

(3) Subsection (1) does not apply to a person who owns an estate or interest in the premises and wholly occupies them unless he uses the services of an estate agent for the purposes of the disposal of the premises, or publishes or causes to be published an advertisement in connection with the disposal.

22. Exception from ss. 20(1) and 21: small dwellings

(1) Sections 20(1) and 21 do not apply to the provision by a person of accommodation in any premises, or the disposal of premises by him, if—

(a) that person or a near relative of his ('the relevant occupier') resides, and intends to continue to reside, on the premises; and

(b) there is on the premises, in addition to the accommodation occupied by the relevant occupier, accommodation (not being storage accommodation or means of access) shared by the relevant occupier with other persons residing on the premises who are not members of his household; and

(c) the premises are small premises.

(2) Premises shall be treated for the purposes of this section as small premises if—

(a) in the case of premises comprising residential accommodation for one or more households (under separate letting or similar agreements) in addition to the accommodation occupied by the relevant occupier, there is not normally residential accommodation for more than two such households and only the relevant occupier and any member of his household reside in the accommodation occupied by him;

(b) in the case of premises not falling within paragraph (a), there is not normally residential accommodation on the premises for more than six persons in addition to the relevant occupier and any members of his household.

23. Further exceptions from ss. 20(1) and 21

(1) Sections 20(1) and 21 do not apply—

(a) to discrimination which is rendered unlawful by any provision of Part II or section 17 or 18; or

(b) to discrimination which would be rendered unlawful by any provision of Part II but for any of the following provisions, namely sections 4(3), 5(1)(b), 6, 7(4), 9 and 14(4).

(2) Section 20(1) does not apply to anything done by a person as a participant in arrangements under which he (for reward or not) takes into his home, and treats as if they were members of his family, children, elderly persons, or persons requiring a special degree of care and attention.

24. Discrimination: consent for assignment or sub-letting

(1) Where the licence or consent of the landlord or of any other person is required for the disposal to any person of premises in Great Britain comprised in a tenancy, it is unlawful for the landlord or other person to discriminate against a person by withholding the licence or consent for disposal of the premises to him.

(2) Subsection (1) does not apply if—

(a) the person withholding a licence or consent, or a near relative of his ('the relevant occupier') resides, and intends to continue to reside, on the premises; and

(b) there is on the premises, in addition to the accommodation occupied by the relevant occupier, accommodation (not being storage accommodation or means of access) shared by the relevant occupier with other persons residing on the premises who are not members of his household; and

(c) the premises are small premises.

(3) Section 22(2) (meaning of 'small premises') shall apply for the purposes of this as well as of that section.

(4) In this section 'tenancy' means a tenancy created by a lease or sub-lease, by an agreement for a lease or sub-lease or by a tenancy agreement or in pursuance of any enactment; and 'disposal', in relation to premises comprised in a tenancy, includes assignment or assignation of the tenancy and sub-letting or parting with possession of the premises or any part of the premises.

(5) This section applies to tenancies created before the passing of this Act, as well as to others.

25. Discrimination: associations not within s. 11

(1) This section applies to any association of persons (however described, whether corporate or unincorporate, and whether or not its activities are carried on for profit) if—

(a) it has twenty-five or more members; and

(b) admission to membership is regulated by its constitution and is so conducted that the members do not constitute a section of the public within the meaning of section 20(1); and

(c) it is not an organisation to which section 11 applies.

(2) It is unlawful for an association to which this section applies, in the case of a person who is not a member of the association, to discriminate against him—

(a) in the terms on which it is prepared to admit him to membership; or

(b) by refusing or deliberately omitting to accept his application for membership.

(3) It is unlawful for an association to which this section applies, in the case of a person who is a member or associate of the association, to discriminate against him—

(a) in the way it affords him access to any benefits, facilities or services, or by refusing or deliberately omitting to afford him access to them; or

(b) in the case of a member, by depriving him of membership, or varying the terms on which he is a member; or

(c) in the case of an associate, by depriving him of his rights as an associate, or varying those rights; or

(d) in either case, by subjecting him to any other detriment.

(4) For the purposes of this section—

(a) a person is a member of an association if he belongs to it by virtue of his admission to any sort of membership provided for by its constitution (and is not merely a person with certain rights under its constitution by virtue of his membership of some other association), and references to membership of an association shall be construed accordingly;

(b) a person is an associate of an association to which this section applies if, not being a member of it, he has under its constitution some or all of the rights enjoyed by members (or would have apart from any provision in its constitution authorising the refusal of those rights in particular cases).

26. Exception from s. 25 for certain associations

(1) An association to which section 25 applies is within this subsection if the main object of the association is to enable the benefits of membership (whatever they may be) to be enjoyed by persons of a particular racial group defined otherwise than by reference to colour; and in determining whether that is the main object of an association regard shall be had to the essential character of the association and to all relevant circumstances including, in particular, the extent to which the affairs of the association are so conducted that the persons primarily enjoying the benefits of membership are of the racial group in question.

(2) In the case of an association within subsection (1), nothing in section 25 shall render unlawful any act not involving discrimination on the ground of colour.

[*Barristers*

26A. Discrimination by, or in relation to, barristers

(1) It is unlawful for a barrister or barrister's clerk, in relation to any offer of a pupillage or tenancy, to discriminate against a person—

(a) in the arrangements which are made for the purpose of determining to whom it should be offered;

(b) in respect of any terms on which it is offered: or

(c) by refusing, or deliberately omitting, to offer it to him.

(2) It is unlawful for a barrister or barrister's clerk, in relation to a pupil or tenant in the chambers in question, to discriminate against him—

(a) in respect of any terms applicable to him as a pupil or tenant;

(b) in the opportunities for training, or gaining experience which are afforded or denied to him;

(c) in the benefits, facilities or services which are afforded or denied to him; or

(d) by terminating his pupillage or by subjecting him to any pressure to leave the chambers or other detriment.

(3) It is unlawful for any person, in relation to the giving, withholding or acceptance or instructions to a barrister, to discriminate against any person.

(4) In this section—

'barrister's clerk' includes any person carrying out any of the functions of a barrister's clerk; and

'pupil', 'pupillage', 'tenancy' and 'tenant' have the meanings commonly associated with their use in the context of a set of barristers' chambers.

(5) This section does not apply to Scotland].

[*Advocates*

26B. Discrimination by, or in relation to, advocates

(1) It is unlawful for an advocate, in relation to taking any person as his pupil, to discriminate against a person—

(a) in the arrangements which he makes for the purpose of determining whom he will take as his pupil;

(b) in respect of any terms on which he offers to take any person as his pupil; or

(c) by refusing, or deliberately omitting, to take a person as his pupil.

(2) It is unlawful for an advocate, in relation to a person who is a pupil, to discriminate against him—

(a) in respect of any terms applicable to him as a pupil;

(b) in the opportunities for training, or gaining experience, which are afforded or denied to him;

(c) in the benefits, facilities or services which are afforded or denied to him; or

(d) by terminating the relationship or by subjecting him to any pressure to terminate the relationship or other detriment.

(3) It is unlawful for any person, in relation to the giving, withholding or acceptance of instructions to an advocate, to discriminate against any person.

(4) In this section—

'advocate' means a member of the Faculty of Advocates practising as such; and

'pupil' has the meaning commonly associated with its use in the context of a person training to be an advocate.

(5) This section does not apply to England and Wales.]

Extent

27. Extent of Part III

(1) Sections 17 to [18D] do not apply to benefits, facilities or services outside Great Britain except—

(a) travel in a ship registered at a port of registry in Great Britain; and

(b) benefits, facilities or services provided on a ship so registered.

[(1A) In its application in relation to granting entry clearance (within the meaning of the Immigration Act 1971) section 19B applies in relation to acts done outside the United Kingdom, as well as those done within Great Britain.]

(2) Section 20(1)—

(a) does not apply to goods, facilities or services outside Great Britain except as provided in subsections (3) and (4); and

(b) does not apply to facilities by way of banking or insurance or for grants, loans, credit or finance, where the facilities are for a purpose to be carried out, or in connection with risks wholly or mainly arising, outside Great Britain.

(3) Section 20(1) applies to the provision of facilities for travel outside Great Britain where the refusal or omission occurs in Great Britain or on a ship, aircraft or hovercraft within subsection (4).

(4) Section 20(1) applies on and in relation to—

(a) any ship registered at a port of registry in Great Britain; and

(b) any aircraft or hovercraft registered in the United Kingdom and operated by a person who has his principal place of business, or is ordinarily resident, in Great Britain, even if the ship, aircraft or hovercraft is outside Great Britain.

(5) This section shall not render unlawful an act done in or over a country outside the United Kingdom, or in or over that country's territorial waters, for the purpose of complying with the laws of that country.

PART IV
OTHER UNLAWFUL ACTS

28. Discriminatory practices

(1) In this section 'discriminatory practice' means the application of a requirement or condition which results in an act of discrimination which is unlawful by virtue of any provision of Part II or III taken with section 1(1)(b), or which would be likely to result in such an act of discrimination if the persons to whom it is applied included persons of any particular racial group as regards which there has been no occasion for applying it.

(2) A person acts in contravention of this section if and so long as—

(a) he applies a discriminatory practice; or

(b) he operates practices or other arrangements which in any circumstances would call for the application by him of a discriminatory practice.

(3) Proceedings in respect of a contravention of this section shall be brought only by the Commission in accordance with sections 58 to 62.

29. Discriminatory advertisements

(1) It is unlawful to publish or to cause to be published an advertisement which indicates, or might reasonably be understood as indicating, an intention by a person to do an act of discrimination, whether the doing of that act by him would be lawful or, by virtue of Part II or III, unlawful.

(2) Subsection (1) does not apply to an advertisement—

(a) if the intended act would be lawful by virtue of any of sections 5, 6, 7(3) and (4), 10(3), 26, 34(2)(b), 35 to 39 and 41; or

(b) if the advertisement relates to the services of an employment agency (within the meaning of section 14(1)) and the intended act only concerns employment which the employer could by virtue of section 5, 6 or 7(3) or (4) lawfully refuse to offer to persons against whom the advertisement indicates an intention to discriminate.

(3) Subsection (1) does not apply to an advertisement which indicates that persons of any class defined otherwise than by reference to colour, race or ethnic or national origins are required for employment outside Great Britain.

(4) The publisher of an advertisement made unlawful by subsection (1) shall not be subject to any liability under that subsection in respect of the publication of the advertisement if he proves—

(a) that the advertisement was published in reliance on a statement made to him by the person who caused it to be published to the effect that, by reason of the operation of subsection (2) or (3), the publication would not be unlawful; and

(b) that it was reasonable for him to rely on the statement.

(5) A person who knowingly or recklessly makes a statement such as is mentioned in subsection (4)(a) which in a material respect is false or misleading commits an offence, and shall be liable on summary conviction to a fine not exceeding [level 5 on the standard scale].

30. Instructions to discriminate

It is unlawful for a person—

(a) who has authority over another person; or

(b) in accordance with whose wishes that other person is accustomed to act,

to instruct him to do any act which is unlawful by virtue of Part II or III, or procure or attempt to procure the doing by him of any such act.

31. Pressure to discriminate

(1) It is unlawful to induce, or attempt to induce, a person to do any act which contravenes Part II or III.

(2) An attempted inducement is not prevented from falling within subsection (1) because it is not made directly to the person in question, if it is made in such a way that he is likely to hear of it.

32. Liability of employers and principals

(1) Anything done by a person in the course of his employment shall be treated for the purposes of this Act (except as regards offences thereunder) as done by his employer as well as by him, whether or not it was done with the employer's knowledge or approval.

(2) Anything done by a person as agent for another person with the authority (whether express or implied, and whether precedent or subsequent) of that other person shall be treated for the purposes of this Act (except as regards offences thereunder) as done by that other person as well as by him.

(3) In proceedings brought under this Act against any person in respect of an act alleged to have been done by an employee of his it shall be a defence for that person to prove that he took such steps as were reasonably practicable to prevent the employee from doing that act, or from doing in the course of his employment acts of that description.

33. Aiding unlawful acts

(1) A person who knowingly aids another person to do an act made unlawful by this Act shall be treated for the purposes of this Act as himself doing an unlawful act of the like description.

(2) For the purposes of subsection (1) an employee or agent for whose act the employer or principal is liable under section 32 (or would be so liable but for section 32(3)) shall be deemed to aid the doing of the act by the employer or principal.

(3) A person does not under this section knowingly aid another to do an unlawful act if—

(a) he acts in reliance on a statement made to him by that other person that, by reason of any provision of this Act, the act which he aids would not be unlawful; and

(b) it is reasonable for him to rely on the statement.

(4) A person who knowingly or recklessly makes a statement such as is mentioned in subsection (3)(a) which in a material respect is false or misleading commits an offence, and shall be liable on summary conviction to a fine not exceeding [level 5 on the standard scale].

PART V
CHARITIES

34. Charities

(1) A provision which is contained in a charitable instrument (whenever that instrument took or takes effect) and which provides for conferring benefits on persons of a class defined by reference to colour shall have effect for all purposes as if it provided for conferring the like benefits—

(a) on persons of the class which results if the restriction by reference to colour is disregarded; or

(b) where the original class is defined by reference to colour only, on persons generally; but nothing in this subsection shall be taken to alter the effect of any provision as regards any time before the coming into operation of this subsection.

(2) Nothing in Parts II to IV shall—

(a) be construed as affecting a provision to which this subsection applies; or

(b) render unlawful an act which is done in order to give effect to such a provision.

(3) Subsection (2) applies to any provision which is contained in a charitable instrument (whenever that instrument took or takes effect) and which provides for conferring benefits on persons of a class defined otherwise than by reference to colour (including a class resulting from the operation of subsection (1)).

(4) In this section 'charitable instrument' means an enactment or other instrument passed or made for charitable purposes, or an enactment or other instrument so far as it relates to charitable purposes, and in Scotland includes the governing instrument of an endowment or of an educational endowment as those expressions are defined in section 135(1) of the Education (Scotland) Act 1962.

In the application of this section to England and Wales, 'charitable purposes' means purposes which are exclusively charitable according to the law of England and Wales.

PART VI
GENERAL EXCEPTIONS FROM PARTS II TO IV

35. Special needs of racial groups in regard to education, training or welfare

Nothing in Parts II to IV shall render unlawful any act done in affording persons of a particular racial group access to facilities or services to meet the special needs of persons of that group in regard to their education, training or welfare, or any ancillary benefits.

36. Provision of education or training for persons not ordinarily resident in Great Britain

Nothing in Parts II to IV shall render unlawful any act done by a person for the benefit of persons not ordinarily resident in Great Britain in affording them access to facilities for education or training or any ancillary benefits, where it appears to him that the persons in question do not intend to remain in Great Britain after their period of education or training there.

37. Discriminatory training by certain bodies

(1) Nothing in Parts II to IV shall render unlawful any act done in relation to particular work by [any person] in or in connection with—

(a) affording only persons of a particular racial group access to facilities for training which would help to fit them for that work; or

(b) encouraging only persons of a particular racial group to take advantage of opportunities for doing that work,

where it [reasonably appears to that person] that at any time within the twelve months immediately preceding the doing of the act—

(i) there were no persons of that group among those doing that work in Great Britain; or

(ii) the proportion of persons of that group among those doing that work in Great Britain was small in comparison with the proportion of persons of that group among the population of Great Britain.

(2) Where in relation to particular work it [reasonably appears to any person] that although the condition for the operation of subsection (1) is not met for the whole of Great Britain it is met for an area within Great Britain, nothing in Parts II to IV shall render unlawful any act done by [that person] in or in connection with—

(a) affording persons who are of the racial group in question, and who appear likely to take up that work in that area, access to facilities for training which would help to fit them for that work; or

(b) encouraging persons of that group to take advantage of opportunities in the area for doing that work.

[(3) The preceding provisions of this section shall not apply to any discrimination which is rendered unlawful by section 4(1) or (2).]

38. Other discriminatory training etc.

(1) Nothing in Parts II to IV shall render unlawful any act done by an employer in relation to particular work in his employment at a particular establishment in Great Britain, being an act done in or in connection with—

(a) affording only those of his employees working at that establishment who are of a particular racial group access to facilities for training which would help to fit them for that work; or

(b) encouraging only persons of a particular racial group to take advantage of opportunities for doing that work at that establishment,

where any of the conditions in subsection (2) was satisfied at any time within the twelve months immediately preceding the doing of the act.

(2) Those conditions are—

(a) that there are no persons of the racial group in question among those doing that work at that establishment; or

(b) that the proportion of persons of that group among those doing that work at that establishment is small in comparison with the proportion of persons of that group—

(i) among all those employed by that employer there; or

(ii) among the population of the area from which that employer normally recruits persons for work in his employment at that establishment.

(3) Nothing in section 11 shall render unlawful any act done by an organisation to which that section applies in or in connection with—

(a) affording only members of the organisation who are of a particular racial group access to facilities for training which would help to fit them for holding a post of any kind in the organisation; or

(b) encouraging only members of the organisation who are of a particular racial group to take advantage of opportunities for holding such posts in the organisation,

where either of the conditions in subsection (4) was satisfied at any time within the twelve months immediately preceding the doing of the act.

(4) Those conditions are—

(a) that there are no persons of the racial group in question among persons holding such posts in that organisation; or

(b) that the proportion of persons of that group among those holding such posts in that organisation is small in comparison with the proportion of persons of that group among the members of the organisation.

(5) Nothing in Parts II to IV shall render unlawful any act done by an organisation to which section 11 applies in or in connection with encouraging only persons of a particular racial group to become members of the organisation where at any time within the twelve months immediately preceding the doing of the act—

(a) no persons of that group were members of the organisation; or

(b) the proportion of persons of that group among members of the organisation was small in comparison with the proportion of persons of that group among those eligible for membership of the organisation.

(6) Section 8 (meaning of employment at establishment in Great Britain) shall apply for the purposes of this section as if this section were contained in Part II.

39. Sports and competitions

Nothing in Parts II to IV shall render unlawful any act whereby a person discriminates against another on the basis of that other's nationality or place of birth or the length of time for which he has been resident in a particular area or place, if the act is done—

(a) in selecting one or more persons to represent a country, place or area, or any related association, in any sport or game; or

(b) in pursuance of the rules of any competition so far as they relate to eligibility to compete in any sport or game.

40. Indirect access to benefits etc.

(1) References in this Act to the affording by any person of access to benefits, facilities or services are not limited to benefits, facilities or services provided by that person himself, but include any means by which it is in that person's power to facilitate access to benefits, facilities or services provided by any other person (the 'actual provider').

(2) Where by any provision of this Act the affording by any person of access to benefits, facilities or services in a discriminatory way is in certain circumstances prevented from being unlawful, the effect of the provision shall extend also to the liability under this Act of any actual provider.

41. Acts done under statutory authority etc.

(1) Nothing in Parts II to IV shall render unlawful any act of discrimination done—

(a) in pursuance of any enactment or Order in Council; or

(b) in pursuance of any instrument made under any enactment by a Minister of the Crown; or

(c) in order to comply with any condition or requirement imposed by a Minister of the Crown (whether before or after the passing of this Act) by virtue of any enactment.

References in this subsection to an enactment, Order in Council or instrument include an enactment, Order in Council or instrument passed or made after the passing of this Act.

(2) Nothing in Parts II to IV shall render unlawful any act whereby a person discriminates against another on the basis of that other's nationality or place of ordinary residence or the length of time for which he has been present or resident in or outside the United Kingdom or an area within the United Kingdom, if that act is done—

(a) in pursuance of any arrangements made (whether before or after the passing of this Act) by or with the approval of, or for the time being approved by, a Minister of the Crown; or

(b) in order to comply with any condition imposed (whether before or after the passing of this Act) by a Minister of the Crown.

42. Acts safeguarding national security
Nothing in Parts II to IV shall render unlawful an act done for the purpose of safeguarding national security [if the doing of the act was justified by that purpose].

PART VII
THE COMMISSION FOR RACIAL EQUALITY

General

43. Establishment and duties of Commission
(1) There shall be a body of Commissioners named the Commission for Racial Equality consisting of at least eight but not more than fifteen individuals each appointed by the Secretary of State on a full-time or part-time basis, which shall have the following duties—

(a) to work towards the elimination of discrimination;

(b) to promote equality of opportunity, and good relations, between persons of different racial groups generally; and

(c) to keep under review the working of this Act and, when they are so required by the Secretary of State or otherwise think it necessary, draw up and submit to the Secretary of State proposals for amending it.

(2) The Secretary of State shall appoint—

(a) one of the Commissioners to be chairman of the Commission; and

(b) either one or more of the Commissioners (as the Secretary of State thinks fit) to be deputy chairman or deputy chairmen of the Commission.

(3) The Secretary of State may by order amend subsection (1) so far as it regulates the number of Commissioners.

(4) Schedule 1 shall have effect with respect to the Commission.

(5) The Race Relations Board and the Community Relations Commissioner are hereby abolished.

44. Assistance to organisations
(1) The Commission may give financial or other assistance to any organisation appearing to the Commission to be concerned with the promotion of equality of opportunity, and good relations, between persons of different racial groups, but shall not give any such financial assistance out of money provided (through the Secretary of State) by Parliament except with the approval of the Secretary of State given with the consent of the Treasury.

(2) Except in so far as other arrangements for their discharge are made and approved under paragraph 13 of Schedule 1—

(a) the Commission's functions under subsection (1); and

(b) other functions of the Commission in relation to matters connected with the giving of such financial or other assistance as is mentioned in that subsection,

shall be discharged under the general direction of the Commission by a committee of the Commission consisting of at least three but not more than five Commissioners, of whom one shall be the deputy chairman or one of the deputy chairmen of the Commission.

45. Research and education

(1) The Commission may undertake or assist (financially or otherwise) the undertaking by other persons of any research, and any educational activities, which appear to the Commission necessary or expedient for the purposes of section 43(1).

(2) The Commission may make charges for educational or other facilities or services made available by them.

46. Annual reports

(1) As soon as practicable after the end of each calendar year the Commission shall make to the Secretary of State a report on their activities during the year (an 'annual report').

(2) Each annual report shall include a general survey of developments, during the period to which it relates, in respect of matters falling within the scope of the Commission's functions.

(3) The Secretary of State shall lay a copy of every annual report before each House of Parliament, and shall cause the report to be published.

Codes of practice

47. Codes of practice

(1) The Commission may issue codes of practice containing such practical guidance as the Commission think fit for [all or any] of the following purposes, namely—

(a) the elimination of discrimination in the field of employment;

(b) the promotion of equality of opportunity in that field between persons of different racial groups;

[(c) the elimination of discrimination in the field of housing . . .;

(d) the promotion of equality of opportunity in the field of . . . housing between persons of different racial groups.]

(2) When the Commission propose to issue a code of practice, they shall prepare and publish a draft of that code, shall consider any representations made to them about the draft and may modify the draft accordingly.

(3) In the course of preparing any draft code of practice relating to the field of employment for eventual publication under subsection (2) the Commission shall consult with—

(a) such organisations or associations of organisations representative of employers or of workers; and

(b) such other organisations, or bodies,

as appear to the Commission to be appropriate.

[(3A) In the course of preparing any draft code of practice relating to the field of . . . housing for eventual publication under subsection (2) the Commission shall consult with such organisations or bodies as appear to the Commission to be appropriate having regard to the content of the draft code.]

(4) If the Commission determine to proceed with [a draft code of practice], they shall transmit the draft to the Secretary of State who shall—

(a) if he approves of it, lay it before both Houses of Parliament; and

(b) if he does not approve of it, publish details of his reasons for withholding approval.

(5) If, within the period of forty days beginning with the day on which a copy of a draft code of practice is laid before each House of Parliament, or, if such copies are laid on different days, with the later of the two days, either House so resolves, no further proceedings shall be taken thereon, but without prejudice to the laying before Parliament of a new draft.

(6) In reckoning the period of forty days referred to in subsection (5), no account shall be taken of any period during which Parliament is dissolved or prorogued or during which both Houses are adjourned for more than four days.

(7) If no such resolution is passed as is referred to in subsection (5), the Commission shall issue the code in the form of the draft and the code shall come into effect on such day as the Secretary of State may by order appoint.

(8) Without prejudice to section 74(3), an order under subsection (7) may contain such transitional provisions or savings as appear to the Secretary of State to be necessary or expedient in connection with the code of practice thereby brought into operation.

(9) The Commission may from time to time revise the whole or any part of a code of practice issued under this section and issue that revised code, and subsections (2) to (8) shall apply (with appropriate modifications) to such a revised code as they apply to the first issue of a code.

(10) A failure on the part of any person to observe any provision of a code of practice shall not of itself render him liable to any proceedings; but in any proceedings under this Act before an [employment] tribunal [, a county court or, in Scotland, a sheriff court] any code of practice issued under this section shall be admissible in evidence, and if any provision of such a code appears to the tribunal [or the court] to be relevant to any question arising in the proceedings it shall be taken into account in determining that question.

(11) Without prejudice to subsection (1), a code of practice issued under this section may include such practical guidance as the Commission think fit as to what steps it is reasonably practicable for employers to take for the purpose of preventing their employees from doing in the course of their employment acts made unlawful by this Act.

Investigations

48. Power to conduct formal investigations

(1) Without prejudice to their general power to do anything requisite for the performance of their duties under section 43(1), the Commission may if they think fit, and shall if required by the Secretary of State, conduct a formal investigation for any purpose connected with the carrying out of those duties.

(2) The Commission may, with the approval of the Secretary of State, appoint, on a full-time or part-time basis, one or more individuals as additional Commissioners for the purposes of a formal investigation.

(3) The Commission may nominate one or more Commissioners, with or without one or more additional Commissioners, to conduct a formal investigation on their behalf, and may delegate any of their functions in relation to the investigation to the persons so nominated.

49. Terms of reference

(1) The Commission shall not embark on a formal investigation unless the requirements of this section have been complied with.

(2) Terms of reference for the investigation shall be drawn up by the Commission or, if the Commission were required by the Secretary of State to conduct the investigation, by the Secretary of State after consulting the Commission.

(3) It shall be the duty of the Commission to give general notice of the holding of the investigation unless the terms of reference confine it to activities of persons named in them, but in such a case the Commission shall in the prescribed manner give those persons notice of the holding of the investigation.

(4) Where the terms of reference of the investigation confine it to activities of persons named in them and the Commission in the course of it propose to investigate any act made unlawful by this Act which they believe that a person so named may have done, the Commission shall—

(a) inform that person of their belief and of their proposal to investigate the act in question; and

(b) offer him an opportunity of making oral or written representations with regard to it (or both oral and written representations if he thinks fit);

and a person so named who avails himself of an opportunity under this subsection of making oral representations may be represented—

(i) by counsel or a solicitor; or

(ii) by some other person of his choice, not being a person to whom the Commission object on the ground that he is unsuitable.

(5) The Commission or, if the Commission were required by the Secretary of State to conduct the investigation, the Secretary of State after consulting the Commission may from time to time revise the terms of reference; and subsections (1), (3) and (4) shall apply to the revised investigation and terms of reference as they applied to the original.

50. Power to obtain information

(1) For the purposes of a formal investigation the Commission, by a notice in the prescribed form served on him in the prescribed manner—

(a) may require any person to furnish such written information as may be described in the notice, and may specify the time at which, and the manner and form in which, the information is to be furnished;

(b) may require any person to attend at such time and place as is specified in the notice and give oral information about, and produce all documents in his possession or control relating to, any matter specified in the notice.

(2) Except as provided by section 60, a notice shall be served under subsection (1) only where—

(a) service of the notice was authorised by an order made by the Secretary of State: or

(b) the terms of reference of the investigation state that the Commission believe that a person named in them may have done or may be doing acts of all or any of the following descriptions—

(i) unlawful discriminatory acts;

(ii) contraventions of section 28; and

(iii) contraventions of sections 29, 30 or 31,

and confine the investigation to those acts.

(3) A notice under subsection (1) shall not require a person—

(a) to give information, or produce any documents, which he could not be compelled to give in evidence, or produce. in civil proceedings before the High Court or the Court of Session; or

(b) to attend at any place unless the necessary expenses of his journey to and from that place are paid or tendered to him.

(4) If a person fails to comply with a notice served on him under subsection (1) or the Commission have reasonable cause to believe that he intends not to comply with it, the Commission may apply to a county court or, in Scotland, a sheriff court for an order requiring him to comply with it or with such directions for the like purpose as may be contained in the order.

(5) [Section 55 of the County Courts Act 1984] (penalty for neglecting witness summons) shall apply to failure without reasonable excuse to comply with an order of a county court under subsection (4) as it applies in the cases provided in the [said section 55] . . .

(6) A person commits an offence if he—

(a) wilfully alters, suppresses, conceals or destroys a document which he has been required by a notice or order under this section to produce; or

(b) in complying with such a notice or order, knowingly or recklessly makes any statement which is false in a material particular,

and shall be liable on summary conviction to a fine not exceeding [level 5 on the standard scale].

(7) Proceedings for an offence under subsection (6) may (without prejudice to any jurisdiction exercisable apart from this subsection) be instituted—

(a) against any person at any place at which he has an office or other place of business;

(b) against an individual at any place where he resides, or at which he is for the time being.

51. Recommendations and reports on formal investigations

(1) If in the light of any of their findings in a formal investigation it appears to the Commission necessary or expedient, whether during the course of the investigation or after its conclusion—

(a) to make to any person, with a view to promoting equality of opportunity between persons of different racial groups who are affected by any of his activities, recommendations for changes in his policies or procedures, or as to any other matters; or

(b) to make to the Secretary of State any recommendations, whether for changes in the law or otherwise,

the Commission shall make those recommendations accordingly.

(2) The Commission shall prepare a report of their findings in any formal investigation conducted by them.

(3) If the formal investigation is one required by the Secretary of State—

(a) the Commission shall deliver the report to the Secretary of State; and

(b) the Secretary of State shall cause the report to be published,

and, unless required by the Secretary of State, the Commission shall not publish the report.

(4) If the formal investigation is not one required by the Secretary of State, the Commission shall either publish the report, or make it available for inspection in accordance with subsection (5).

(5) Where under subsection (4) a report is to be made available for inspection, any person shall be entitled, on payment of such fee (if any) as may be determined by the Commission—

(a) to inspect the report during ordinary office hours and take copies of all or any part of the report; or

(b) to obtain from the Commission a copy, certified by the Commission to be correct, of the report.

(6) The Commission may, if they think fit, determine that the right conferred by subsection (5)(a) shall be exercisable in relation to a copy of the report instead of, or in addition to, the original.

(7) The Commission shall give general notice of the place or places where, and the times when, reports may be inspected under subsection (5).

52. Restriction on disclosure of information

(1) No information given to the Commission by any person ('the informant') in connection with a formal investigation shall be disclosed by the Commission, or by any person who is or has been a Commissioner, additional Commissioner or employee of the Commission, except—

(a) on the order of any court; or

(b) with the informant's consent; or

(c) in the form of a summary or other general statement published by the Commission which does not identify the informant or any other person to whom the information relates; or

(d) in a report of the investigation published by the Commission or made available for inspection under section 51(5); or

(e) to the Commissioners, additional Commissioners or employees of the Commission, or, so far as may be necessary for the proper performance of the functions of the Commission, to other persons; or

(f) for the purpose of any civil proceedings under this Act to which the Commission are a party, or any criminal proceedings.

(2) Any person who discloses information in contravention of subsection (1) commits an offence and shall be liable on summary conviction to a fine not exceeding £400.

(3) In preparing any report for publication or for inspection the Commission shall exclude, so far as is consistent with their duties and the object of the report, any matter which relates to the private affairs of any individual or the business interests of any person where the publication of that matter might, in the opinion of the Commission, prejudicially affect that individual or person.

PART VIII
ENFORCEMENT

General

53. Restriction of proceedings for breach of Act

(1) Except as provided by this Act [or the Special Immigration Appeals Commission Act 1997 or Part IV of the Immigration and Asylum Act 1999] no proceedings, whether civil or criminal, shall lie against any person in respect of an act by reason that the act is unlawful by virtue of a provision of this Act.

(2) Subsection (1) does not preclude the making of an order of certiorari, mandamus or prohibition.

(3) In Scotland, subsection (1) does not preclude the exercise of the jurisdiction of the Court of Session to entertain an application for reduction or suspension of any order or determination or otherwise to consider the validity of any order or determination, or to require reasons for any order or determination to be stated.

[(4) Subsections (2) and (3) do not, except so far as provided by section 76, apply to any act which is unlawful by virtue of section 76(5) or (9) or by virtue of section 76 (10)(b) and (11).]

Enforcement in employment field

54. Jurisdiction of [employment] tribunals

(1) A complaint by any person ('the complainant') that another person ('the respondent')—

(a) has committed an act of discrimination against the complainant which is unlawful by virtue of Part II; or

(b) is by virtue of section 32 or 33 to be treated as having committed such an act of discrimination against the complainant,

may be presented to an [employment] tribunal.

(2) Subsection (1) does not apply to a complaint under section 12(1) of an act in respect of which an appeal, or proceedings in the nature of an appeal, may be brought under any enactment, . . .

55. . . .

56. Remedies on complaint under s. 54

(1) Where an [employment] tribunal finds that a complaint presented to it under section 54 is well-founded, the tribunal shall make such of the following as it considers just and equitable—

(a) an order declaring the rights of the complainant and the respondent in relation to the act to which the complaint relates;

(b) an order requiring the respondent to pay to the complainant compensation of an amount corresponding to any damages he could have been ordered by a county court or by a sheriff court to pay to the complainant if the complaint had fallen to be dealt with under section 57;

(c) a recommendation that the respondent take within a specified period action appearing to the tribunal to be practicable for the purpose of obviating or reducing the adverse effect on the complainant of any act of discrimination to which the complaint relates.

(2) . . .

(3) . . .

(4) If without reasonable justification the respondent to a complaint fails to comply with a recommendation made by an [employment] tribunal under subsection (1)(c), then, if it thinks it just and equitable to do so—

(a) the tribunal may . . . increase the amount of compensation required to be paid to the complainant in respect of the complaint by an order made under subsection (1)(b); or

(b) if an order under subsection (1)(b) could have been made but was not, the tribunal may make such an order.

[(5) The Secretary of State may by regulations make provision—

(a) for enabling a tribunal, where an amount of compensation falls to be awarded under subsection (1)(b), to include in the award interest on that amount; and

(b) specifying, for cases where a tribunal decides that an award is to include an amount in respect of interest, the manner in which and the periods and rate by reference to which the interest is to be determined;

and the regulations may contain such incidental and supplementary provisions as the Secretary of State considers appropriate.

(6) The Secretary of State may by regulations modify the operation of any order made under [section 14 of [the Employment Tribunals Act 1996]] (power to make provision as to interest on sums payable in pursuance of [employment tribunal] decisions) to the extent that it relates to any award of compensation under subsection (1)(b).]

Enforcement of Part III

57. Claims under Part III

(1) A claim by any person ('the claimant') that another person ('the respondent')—

(a) has committed an act of discrimination against the claimant which is unlawful by virtue of Part III; or

(b) is by virtue of section 32 or 33 to be treated as having committed such an act of discrimination against the claimant,

may be made the subject of civil proceedings in like manner as any other claim in tort or (in Scotland) in reparation for breach of statutory duty.

(2) Proceedings under subsection (1)—

(a) shall, in England and Wales, be brought only in a designated county court; and

(b) shall, in Scotland, be brought only in a sheriff court;

but all such remedies shall be obtainable in such proceedings as, apart from this subsection and section 53(1), would be obtainable in the High Court or the Court of Session, as the case may be.

(3) As respects an unlawful act of discrimination falling within section 1(1)(b), no award of damages shall be made if the respondent proves that the requirement or condition in question was not applied with the intention of treating the claimant unfavourably on racial grounds.

(4) For the avoidance of doubt it is hereby declared that damages in respect of an unlawful act of discrimination may include compensation for injury to feelings whether or not they include compensation under any other head.

[(4A) As respects an act which is done, or by virtue of section 32 or 33 is treated as done, by a person in carrying out public investigator functions or functions as a public prosecutor and which is unlawful by virtue of section 1 9B, no remedy other than—

(a) damages; or

(b) a declaration or, in Scotland, a declarator;

shall be obtainable unless the court is satisfied that the remedy concerned would not prejudice a criminal investigation, a decision to institute criminal proceedings or any criminal proceedings.

(4B) In this section—

'criminal investigation' means—

(a) any investigation which a person in carrying out functions to which section 19B applies has a duty to conduct with a view to it being ascertained whether a person should be charged with, or in Scotland prosecuted for, an offence, or whether a person charged with or prosecuted for an offence is guilty of it;

(b) any investigation which is conducted by a person in carrying out functions to which section 19B applies and which in the circumstances may lead to a decision by that person to institute criminal proceedings which the person has power to conduct; or

(c) any investigation which is conducted by a person in carrying out functions to which section 19B applies and which in the circumstances may lead to a decision by that person to make a report to the procurator fiscal for the purpose of enabling him to determine whether criminal proceedings should be instituted; and

'public investigator functions' means functions of conducting criminal investigations or charging offenders;

and in this subsection 'offence' includes any offence under the Army Act 1955, the Air Force Act 1955 or the Naval Discipline Act 1957 (and 'offender' shall be construed accordingly).

(4C) Subsection (4D) applies where a party to proceedings under subsection (1) which have arisen by virtue of section 19B has applied for a stay or sist of those proceedings on the grounds of prejudice to—

(a) particular criminal proceedings;

(b) a criminal investigation; or

(c) a decision to institute criminal proceedings.

(4D) The court shall grant the stay or sist unless it is satisfied that the continuance of the proceedings under subsection (1) would not result in the prejudice alleged.]

(5) Civil proceedings in respect of a claim by any person that he has been discriminated against in contravention of section 17 or 18 by a body to which [subsection (5A)] applies shall not be instituted unless the claimant has given notice of the claim to the Secretary of State . . .

[(5A) This subsection applies to—

(a) local education authorities in England and Wales;

(b) education authorities in Scotland; and

(c) any body which is a responsible body in relation to an establishment falling within paragraph 3, 3B or 7B of the table in section 17.]

(6) In Scotland, when any proceedings are brought under this section, in addition to the service on the defender of a copy of the summons or initial writ initiating the action a copy thereof shall be sent as soon as practicable to the Commission in a manner to be prescribed by Act of Sederunt.

[(7) This section has effect subject to section 57A.]

57A. Claims under section 19B in immigration cases

(1) No proceedings may be brought by a claimant under section 57(1) in respect of an immigration claim if—

(a) the act to which the claim relates was done in the taking by an immigration authority of a relevant decision and the question whether that act was unlawful by virtue of section 19B has been or could be raised in proceedings on an appeal which is pending, or could be brought, under the 1997 Act or Part IV of the 1999 Act; or

(b) it has been decided in relevant immigration proceedings that that act was not unlawful by virtue of that section.

(2) For the purposes of this section an immigration claim is a claim that a person—

(a) has committed a relevant act of discrimination against the claimant which is unlawful by virtue of section 19B; or

(b) is by virtue of section 32 or 33 to be treated as having committed such an act of discrimination against the claimant.

(3) Where it has been decided in relevant immigration proceedings that an act to which an immigration claim relates was unlawful by virtue of section 19B, any court hearing that claim under section 57 shall treat that act as an act which is unlawful by virtue of section 19B for the purposes of the proceedings before it.

(4) No relevant decision of an immigration authority involving an act to which an immigration claim relates and no relevant decision of an immigration appellate body in relation to such a decision shall be subject to challenge or otherwise affected by virtue of a decision of a court hearing the immigration claim under section 57.

(5) In this section—

'the Immigration Acts' has the same meaning as in the 1999 Act;

'immigration appellate body' means an adjudicator appointed for the purposes of the 1999 Act, the Immigration Appeal Tribunal, the Special Immigration Appeals Commission, the Court of Appeal, the Court of Session or the House of Lords;

'immigration authority' means an authority within the meaning of section 65 of the 1999 Act (human rights and racial discrimination cases);

'immigration claim' has the meaning given by subsection (2) above;

'pending' has the same meaning as in the 1997 Act or, as the case may be, Part IV of the 1999 Act;

'relevant act of discrimination' means an act of discrimination done by an immigration authority in taking any relevant decision;

'relevant decision' means—

(a) in relation to an immigration authority, any decision under the Immigration Acts relating to the entitlement of the claimant to enter or remain in the United Kingdom; and

(b) in relation to an immigration appellate body, any decision on an appeal under the 1997 Act or Part IV of the 1999 Act in relation to a decision falling within paragraph (a);

'relevant immigration proceedings' means proceedings on an appeal under the 1997 Act or Part IV of the 1999 Act;

'the 1997 Act' means the Special Immigration Appeals Commission Act 1997;

'the 1999 Act' means the Immigration and Asylum Act 1999;

and, for the purposes of subsection (1)(a), any power to grant leave to appeal out of time shall be disregarded.]

Non-discrimination notices

58. Issue of non-discrimination notice

(1) This section applies to—

(a) an unlawful discriminatory act; and

(b) an act contravening section 28; and

(c) an act contravening section 29, 30 or 31,

and so applies whether or not proceedings have been brought in respect of the act.

(2) If in the course of a formal investigation the Commission become satisfied that a person is committing, or has committed, any such acts, the Commission may in the prescribed manner serve on him a notice in the prescribed form ('a non-discrimination notice') requiring him—

(a) not to commit any such acts; and

(b) where compliance with paragraph (a) involves changes in any of his practices or other arrangements—

(i) to inform the Commission that he has effected those changes and what those changes are; and

(ii) to take such steps as may be reasonably required by the notice for the purpose of affording that information to other persons concerned.

(3) A non-discrimination notice may also require the person on whom it is served to furnish the Commission with such other information as may be reasonably required by the notice in order to verify that the notice has been complied with.

(4) The notice may specify the time at which, and the manner and form in which, any information is to be furnished to the Commission, but the time at which any information is to be furnished in compliance with the notice shall not be later than five years after the notice has become final.

(5) The Commission shall not serve a non-discrimination notice in respect of any person unless they have first—

(a) given him notice that they are minded to issue a non-discrimination notice in his case, specifying the grounds on which they contemplate doing so; and

(b) offered him an opportunity of making oral or written representations in the matter (or both oral and written representations if he thinks fit) within a period of not less than 28 days specified in the notice; and

(c) taken account of any representations so made by him.

(6) . . .

(7) Section 50(4) shall apply to requirements under subsection (2)(b), (3) and (4) contained in a non-discrimination notice which has become final as it applies to requirements in a notice served under section 50(1).

59. Appeal against non-discrimination notice

(1) Not later than six weeks after a non-discrimination notice is served on any person he may appeal against any requirement of the notice—

(a) to an [employment] tribunal, so far as the requirement relates to acts which are within the jurisdiction of the tribunal;

(b) to a designated county court or a sheriff court, so far as the requirement relates to acts which are within the jurisdiction of the court [(ignoring section 57A)] and are not within the jurisdiction of an [employment] tribunal.

(2) Where the tribunal or court considers a requirement in respect of which an appeal is brought under subsection (1) to be unreasonable because it is based on an incorrect finding of fact or for any other reason, the tribunal or court shall quash the requirement.

(3) On quashing a requirement under subsection (2) the tribunal or court may direct that the non-discrimination notice shall be treated as if, in place of the requirement quashed, it had contained a requirement in terms specified in the direction.

(4) Subsection (1) does not apply to a requirement treated as included in a non-discrimination notice by virtue of a direction under subsection (3).

60. Investigation as to compliance with non-discrimination notice

(1) If—

(a) the terms of reference of a formal investigation state that its purpose is to determine whether any requirements of a non-discrimination notice are being or have been carried out, but section 50(2)(b) does not apply; and

(b) section 49(3) is complied with in relation to the investigation on a date ('the commencement date') not later than the expiration of the period of five years beginning when the non-discrimination notice became final,

the Commission may within the period referred to in subsection (2) serve notices under section 50(1) for the purposes of the investigation without needing to obtain the consent of the Secretary of State.

(2) The said period begins on the commencement date and ends on the later of the following dates—

(a) the date on which the period of five years mentioned in subsection (1)(b) expires;
(b) the date two years after the commencement date.

61. Register of non-discrimination notices

(1) The Commission shall establish and maintain a register ('the register') of non-discrimination notices which have become final.

(2) Any person shall be entitled, on payment of such fee (if any) as may be determined by the Commission—

(a) to inspect the register during ordinary office hours and take copies of any entry; or
(b) to obtain from the Commission a copy, certified by the Commission to be correct, of any entry in the register.

(3) The Commission may, if they think fit, determine that the right conferred by subsection (2)(a) shall be exercisable in relation to a copy of the register instead of, or in addition to, the original.

(4) The Commission shall give general notice of the place or places where, and the times when, the register or a copy of it may be inspected.

Other enforcement by Commission

62. Persistent discrimination

(1) If, during the period of five years beginning on the date on which any of the following became final in the case of any person, namely—

(a) a non-discrimination notice served on him; or

(b) a finding by a tribunal or court under section 54 or 57; that he has done an unlawful discriminatory act; or

[(ba) a finding under the Special Immigration Appeals Commission Act 1997 or Part IV of the Immigration and Asylum Act 1999 that he has done an act which was unlawful by virtue of section 19B; or]

(c) a finding by a court in proceedings under section 19 or 20 of the Race Relations Act 1968 that he has done an act which was unlawful by virtue of any provision of Part I of that Act,

it appears to the Commission that unless restrained he is likely to do one or more acts falling within paragraph (b), or contravening section 28, the Commission may apply to a designated county court for an injunction, or to a sheriff court for an order, restraining him from doing so; and the court, if satisfied that the application is well-founded, may grant the injunction or order in the terms applied for or in more limited terms.

(2) In proceedings under this section the Commission shall not allege that the person to whom the proceedings relate has done an act falling within subsection (1)(b) or contravening section 28 which is within the jurisdiction of an [employment] tribunal unless a finding by an [employment] tribunal that he did that act has become final.

63. Enforcement of ss. 29 to 31

(1) Proceedings in respect of a contravention of section 29, 30 or 31 shall be brought only by the Commission in accordance with the following provisions of this section.

(2) The proceedings shall be—

(a) an application for a decision whether the alleged contravention occurred; or
(b) an application under subsection (4),

or both.

(3) An application under subsection (2)(a) shall be made—

(a) in a case based on any provision of Part II, to an [employment] tribunal; and
(b) in any other case, to a designated county court or a sheriff court.

(4) If it appears to the Commission—

(a) that a person has done an act which by virtue of section 29, 30 or 31 was unlawful; and

(b) that unless restrained he is likely to do further acts which by virtue of that section are unlawful,

the Commission may apply to a designated county court for an injunction, or to a sheriff court for an order, restraining him from doing such acts; and the court, if satisfied that the application is well-founded, may grant the injunction or order in the terms applied for or more limited terms.

(5) In proceedings under subsection (4) the Commission shall not allege that the person to whom the proceedings relate has done an act which is unlawful under this Act and within the jurisdiction of an [employment] tribunal unless a finding by an [employment] tribunal that he did that act has become final.

64. Preliminary action in employment cases

(1) With a view to making an application under section 62(1) or 63(4) in relation to a person the Commission may present to an [employment] tribunal a complaint that he has done an act within the jurisdiction of an [employment] tribunal, and if the tribunal considers that the complaint is well-founded it shall make a finding to that effect and, if it thinks it just and equitable to do so in the case of an act contravening any provision of Part II may also (as if the complaint had been presented by the person discriminated against) make an order such as is referred to in section 56(1)(a), or a recommendation such as is referred to in section 56(1)(c), or both.

(2) Subsection (1) is without prejudice to the jurisdiction conferred by section 63(2).

(3) In sections 62 and 63 and this section, the acts 'within the jurisdiction of an [employment] tribunal' are those in respect of which such jurisdiction is conferred by sections 54 and 63.

Help for persons suffering discrimination

65. Help for aggrieved persons in obtaining information etc.

(1) With a view to helping a person ('the person aggrieved') who considers he may have been discriminated against in contravention of this Act to decide whether to institute proceedings and, if he does so, to formulate and present his case in the most effective manner, the Secretary of State shall by order prescribe—

(a) forms by which the person aggrieved may question the respondent on his reasons for doing any relevant act, or on any other matter which is or may be relevant; and

(b) forms by which the respondent may if he so wishes reply to any questions.

(2) Where the person aggrieved questions the respondent (whether in accordance with an order under subsection (1) or not)—

(a) the question, and any reply by the respondent (whether in accordance with such an order or not) shall, subject to the following provisions of this section, be admissible as evidence in the proceedings;

(b) if it appears to the court or tribunal that the respondent deliberately, and without reasonable excuse, omitted to reply within a reasonable period or that his reply is evasive or equivocal, the court or tribunal may draw any inference from that fact that it considers it just and equitable to draw, including an inference that he committed an unlawful act.

(3) The Secretary of State may by order—

(a) prescribe the period within which questions must be duly served in order to be admissible under subsection (2)(a); and

(b) prescribe the manner in which a question, and any reply by the respondent, may be duly served.

(4) Rules may enable the court entertaining a claim under section 57 to determine, before the date fixed for the hearing of the claim, whether a question or reply is admissible under this section or not.

[(4A) In section 19B proceedings, subsection (2)(b) does not apply in relation to a failure to reply, or a particular reply, if the conditions specified in subsection (4B) are satisfied.

(4B) Those conditions are that—

(a) at the time of doing any relevant act, the respondent was carrying out public investigator functions or was a public prosecutor; and

(b) he reasonably believes that a reply or (as the case may be) a different reply would be likely to prejudice any criminal investigation, any decision to institute criminal proceedings or any criminal proceedings or would reveal the reasons behind a decision not to institute, or a decision not to continue, criminal proceedings.

(4C) For the purposes of subsections (4A) and (4B)—

'public investigator functions' has the same meaning as in section 57;

'section 19B proceedings' means proceedings in respect of a claim under section 57 which has arisen by virtue of section 19B.]

(5) This section is without prejudice to any other enactment or rule of law regulating interlocutory and preliminary matters in proceedings before a county court, sheriff court or [employment] tribunal, and has effect subject to any enactment or rule of law regulating the admissibility of evidence in such proceedings.

(6) In this section 'respondent' includes a prospective respondent and 'rules'—

(a) in relation to county court proceedings, means county court rules;

(b) in relation to sheriff court proceedings, means sheriff court rules.

[(7) This section does not apply in relation to any proceedings under—

(a) the Special Immigration Appeals Commission Act 1997; or

(b) Part IV of the Immigration and Asylum Act 1999.]

66. Assistance by Commission

(1) Where, in relation to proceedings or prospective proceedings under this Act, an individual who is an actual or prospective complainant or claimant applies to the Commission for assistance under this section, the Commission shall consider the application and may grant it if they think fit to do so—

(a) on the ground that the case raises a question of principle; or

(b) on the ground that it is unreasonable, having regard to the complexity of the case, or to the applicant's position in relation to the respondent or another person involved, or to any other matter, to expect the applicant to deal with the case unaided; or

(c) by reason of any other special consideration.

(2) Assistance by the Commission under this section may include—

(a) giving advice;

(b) procuring or attempting to procure the settlement of any matter in dispute;

(c) arranging for the giving of advice or assistance by a solicitor or counsel;

(d) arranging for representation by any person, including all such assistance as is usually given by a solicitor or counsel in the steps preliminary or incidental to any proceedings, or in arriving at or giving effect to a compromise to avoid or bring to an end any proceedings;

(e) any other form of assistance which the Commission may consider appropriate,

but paragraph (d) shall not affect the law and practice regulating the descriptions of persons who may appear in, conduct, defend, and address the court in, any proceedings.

(3) Where under subsection (1) an application for assistance under this section is made in writing, the Commission shall, within the period of two months beginning when the application is received—

(a) consider the application after making such enquiries as they think fit; and

(b) decide whether or not to grant it; and

(c) inform the applicant of their decision, stating whether or not assistance under this section is to be provided by the Commission and, if so, what form it will take.

(4) If, in a case where subsection (3) applies, the Commission within the period of two months there mentioned give notice to the applicant that, in relation to his application—

(a) the period of two months allowed them by that subsection is by virtue of the notice extended to three months; and

(b) the reference to two months in section 68(3) is by virtue of the notice to be read as a reference to three months,

subsection (3) and section 68(3) shall have effect accordingly.

(5) In so far as expenses are incurred by the Commission in providing the applicant with assistance under this section, the recovery of those expenses (as taxed or assessed in such manner as may be prescribed by rules or regulations) shall constitute a first charge for the benefit of the Commission—

(a) on any costs or expenses which (whether by virtue of a judgment or order of a court or tribunal or an agreement or otherwise) are payable to the applicant by any other person in respect of the matter in connection with which the assistance is given; and

(b) so far as relates to any costs or expenses, on his rights under any compromise or settlement arrived at in connection with that matter to avoid or bring to an end any proceedings.

(6) The charge conferred by subsection (5) is subject to any charge [imposed by section 10(7) of the Access to Justice Act 1999], or any charge or obligation for payment in priority to other debts under the Legal Aid and Advice (Scotland) Acts 1967 and 1972, and is subject to any provision in [or made under] any of those Acts for payment of any sum [to the Legal Services Commission] or into the Scottish Legal Aid Fund.

(7) In this section 'respondent' includes a prospective respondent and 'rules or regulations'—

(a) in relation to county court proceedings, means county court rules;

(b) in relation to sheriff court proceedings, means sheriff court rules;

(c) in relation to [employment] tribunal proceedings, means [employment tribunal procedure] regulations made under [Part I of the Employment Tribunals Act 1996].

[(8) This section (except for subsection (4)) applies to proceedings or prospective proceedings under the Special Immigration Appeals Commission Act 1997 or Part IV of the Immigration and Asylum Act 1999 so far as they relate to acts which may be unlawful by virtue of section 19B as it applies to proceedings or prospective proceedings under this Act.

(9) In this section as it applies by virtue of subsection (8) 'rules and regulations' means—

(a) in relation to proceedings under the Act of 1997, rules under section 5 or 8 of that Act;

(b) in relation to proceedings under Part IV of the Act of 1999, rules under paragraph 3 or 4 of Schedule 4 to that Act.]

Sheriff courts and designated county courts

67. Sheriff courts and designated county courts

(1) For the purposes of this Act a 'designated' county court is one designated for the time being for those purposes by an order made by the Lord Chancellor.

(2) An order under subsection (1) designating any county court for the purposes of this Act shall assign to that court as its district for those purposes any county court district or two or more county court districts.

(3) A designated county court or a sheriff court shall have jurisdiction to entertain proceedings under this Act with respect to an act done on a ship, aircraft or hovercraft outside its district, including such an act done outside Great Britain.

[(3A) A designated county court or a sheriff court shall have jurisdiction to entertain proceedings under this Act with respect to an act done outside the United Kingdom where section 19B applies in relation to such an act by virtue of section 27(1A).]

(4) In any proceedings under this Act in a designated county court or a sheriff court the judge or sheriff shall, unless with the consent of the parties he sits without assessors, be assisted by two assessors appointed from a list of persons prepared and maintained by the Secretary of State, being persons appearing to the Secretary of State to have special

knowledge and experience of problems connected with relations between persons of different racial groups.

(5) The remuneration of assessors appointed under subsection (4) shall be at such rate as may, with the approval of the Minister for the Civil Service, be determined by the Lord Chancellor (for proceedings in England and Wales) or the Lord President of the Court of Session (for proceedings in Scotland).

(6) Without prejudice to section 74(3), an order for the discontinuance of the jurisdiction of any county court under this Act, whether wholly or within a part of the district assigned to it for the purposes of this Act, may include provision with respect to any proceedings under this Act commenced in that court before the order comes into operation.

[67A. National security: procedure

(1) Rules may make provision for enabling a court in which relevant proceedings have been brought, where it considers it expedient in the interests of national security—

(a) to exclude from all or part of the proceedings—

(i) the claimant;

(ii) the claimant's representatives; or

(iii) the assessors (if any) appointed by virtue of section 67(4);

(b) to permit a claimant or representative who has been excluded to make a statement to the court before the commencement of the proceedings, or the part of the proceedings, from which he is excluded;

(c) to take steps to keep secret all or part of the reasons for its decision in the proceedings.

(2) The Attorney General or, in Scotland, the Advocate General for Scotland, may appoint a person to represent the interests of a claimant in, or in any part of, any proceedings from which the claimant and his representatives are excluded by virtue of subsection (1).

(3) A person appointed under subsection (2)—

(a) if appointed for the purposes of proceedings in England and Wales, must have a general qualification (within the meaning of section 71 of the Courts and Legal Services Act 1990); and

(b) if appointed for the purposes of proceedings in Scotland, must be—

(i) an advocate; or

(ii) a solicitor who has by virtue of section 25A of the Solicitors (Scotland) Act 1980 rights of audience in the Court of Session or the High Court of Justiciary.

(4) A person appointed under subsection (2) shall not be responsible to the person whose interests he is appointed to represent.

(5) In this section—

'relevant proceedings' means proceedings brought under this Act—

(a) in England and Wales, in a designated county court; or

(b) in Scotland, in a sheriff court; and

'rules' has the same meaning as in section 65.]

Period within which proceedings to be brought

68. Period within which proceedings to be brought

(1) An [employment] tribunal shall not consider a complaint under section 54 unless it is presented to the tribunal before the end of—

[(a) the period of three months beginning when the act complained of was done; or

(b) in a case to which section 75(8) applies, the period of six months so beginning.]

(2) [Subject to subsection (2A)] a county court or a sheriff court shall not consider a claim under section 57 unless proceedings in respect of the claim are instituted before the end of—

(a) the period of six months beginning when the act complained of was done;

(b) . . .

[(2A) In relation to an immigration claim within the meaning of section 57A, the period of six months mentioned in subsection (2)(a) begins on the expiry of the period during which, by virtue of section 57A(1)(a), no proceedings may be brought under section 57(1) in respect of the claim.]

(3) Where, in relation to proceedings or prospective proceedings by way of a claim under section 57, an application for assistance under section 66 is made to the Commission before the end of the period of six . . . months mentioned in paragraph (a) . . . of subsection (2), the period allowed by that paragraph for instituting proceedings in respect of the claim shall be extended by two months.

(4) An [employment] tribunal, county court or sheriff court shall not consider an application under section 63(2)(a) unless it is made before the end of the period of six months beginning when the act to which it relates was done; and a county court or sheriff court shall not consider an application under section 63(4) unless it is made before the end of the period of five years so beginning.

(5) An [employment] tribunal shall not consider a complaint under section 64(1) unless it is presented to the tribunal before the end of the period of six months beginning when the act complained of was done.

(6) A court or tribunal may nevertheless consider any such complaint, claim or application which is out of time if, in all the circumstances of the case, it considers that it is just and equitable to do so.

(7) For the purposes of this section—

(a) when the inclusion of any term in a contract renders the making of the contract an unlawful act, that act shall be treated as extending throughout the duration of the contract; and

(b) any act extending over a period shall be treated as done at the end of that period; and

(c) a deliberate omission shall be treated as done when the person in question decided upon it;

and in the absence of evidence establishing the contrary a person shall be taken for the purposes of this section to decide upon an omission when he does an act inconsistent with doing the omitted act or, if he has done no such inconsistent act, when the period expires within which he might reasonably have been expected to do the omitted act if it was to be done.

Evidence

69. Evidence

(1) Any finding by a court under section 19 or 20 of the Race Relations Act 1968, or by a court or [employment] tribunal under this Act, in respect of any act shall, if it has become final, be treated as conclusive in any proceedings under this Act.

(2) In any proceedings under this Act [or any enactment mentioned in section 19D(5)] a certificate signed by or on behalf of a Minister of the Crown and certifying—

(a) that any arrangements or conditions specified in the certificate were made, approved or imposed by a Minister of the Crown and were in operation at a time or throughout a period so specified;

(b) . . .

shall be conclusive evidence of the matters certified.

[(2A) . . .]

(3) A document purporting to be a certificate such as is mentioned in subsection (2) shall be received in evidence and, unless the contrary is proved, shall be deemed to be such a certificate.

. . .

70. . . .

PART X
SUPPLEMENTAL

[71. Specified authorities: general statutory duty

(1) Every body or other person specified in Schedule 1A or of a description falling within that Schedule shall, in carrying out its functions, have due regard to the need—

(a) to eliminate unlawful racial discrimination; and

(b) to promote equality of opportunity and good relations between persons of different racial groups.

(2) The Secretary of State may by order impose, on such persons falling within Schedule 1A as he considers appropriate, such duties as he considers appropriate for the purpose of ensuring the better performance by those persons of their duties under subsection (1).

(3) An order under subsection (2)—

(a) may be made in relation to a particular person falling within Schedule 1A, any description of persons falling within that Schedule or every person falling within that Schedule;

(b) may make different provision for different purposes.

(4) Before making an order under subsection (2), the Secretary of State shall consult the Commission.

(5) The Secretary of State may by order amend Schedule 1A; but no such order may extend the application of this section unless the Secretary of State considers that the extension relates to a person who exercises functions of a public nature.

(6) An order under subsection (2) or (5) may contain such incidental, supplementary or consequential provision as the Secretary of State considers appropriate (including provision amending or repealing provision made by or under this Act or any other enactment).

(7) This section is subject to section 71A and 71B and is without prejudice to the obligation of any person to comply with any other provision of this Act.

71A. General statutory duty: special cases

(1) In relation to the carrying out of immigration and nationality functions (within the meaning of section 19D(1)), section 71(1)(b) has effect with the omission of the words 'equality of opportunity and'.

(2) Where an entry in Schedule 1A is limited to a person in a particular capacity, section 71(1) does not apply to that person in any other capacity.

(3) Where an entry in Schedule 1A is limited to particular functions of a person, section 71(1) does not apply to that person in relation to any other functions.

71B. General statutory duty: Scotland and Wales

(1) For the purposes of the Scotland Act 1998, subsections (2) to (4) of section 71 (and sections 71(6) and 74 so far as they apply to the power conferred by subsection (2) of section 71) shall be taken to be pre-commencement enactments within the meaning of that Act.

(2) Before making an order under section 71(2) in relation to functions exercisable in relation to Wales by a person who is not a Welsh public authority, the Secretary of State shall consult the National Assembly for Wales.

(3) The Secretary of State shall not make an order under section 71(2) in relation to functions of a Welsh public authority except with the consent of the National Assembly for Wales.

(4) In this section 'Welsh public authority' means any person whose functions are exercisable only in relation to Wales and includes the National Assembly for Wales.

71C. General statutory duty: codes of practice

(1) The Commission may issue codes of practice containing such practical guidance as the Commission think fit in relation to the performance by persons of duties imposed on them by virtue of subsections (1) and (2) of section 71.

(2) When the Commission propose to issue a code of practice under this section, they—

(a) shall prepare and publish a draft of the code;

(b) shall consider any representations made to them about the draft; and

(c) may modify the draft accordingly.

(3) In the course of preparing any draft code of practice under this section the Commission shall consult such organisations or bodies as appear to the Commission to be appropriate having regard to the content of the draft code.

(4) If the Commission determine to proceed with a draft code of practice, they shall transmit the draft to the Secretary of State who shall consult the Scottish Ministers and the National Assembly for Wales.

(5) After consulting the Scottish Ministers and the National Assembly for Wales, the Secretary of State shall—

(a) if he approves of the draft code, lay it before both Houses of Parliament; and

(b) if he does not approve of it, publish details of his reasons for withholding approval.

(6) If, within the period of forty days beginning with the day on which a copy of a draft code of practice is laid before each House of Parliament, or, if such copies are laid on different days, with the later of the two days, either House so resolves, no further proceedings shall be taken on the draft code of practice, but without prejudice to the laying before Parliament of a new draft.

(7) In reckoning the period of forty days referred to in subsection (6), no account shall be taken of any period during which Parliament is dissolved or prorogued or during which both Houses are adjourned for more than four days.

(8) If no such resolution is passed as is referred to in subsection (6), the Commission shall issue the code in the form of the draft and the code shall come into effect on such day as the Secretary of State may, after consulting the Scottish Ministers and the National Assembly for Wales, by order appoint.

(9) Without prejudice to section 74(3), an order under subsection (8) may contain such transitional provisions or savings as appear to the Secretary of State to be necessary or expedient in connection with the code of practice thereby brought into operation.

(10) The Commission may revoke, or from time to time revise, the whole or any part of a code of practice issued under this section; and, where they revise the whole or any part of such a code, they shall issue the revised code, and subsections (2) to (9) shall apply (with appropriate modifications) to such a revised code as they apply to the first issue of a code.

(11) A failure on the part of any person to observe any provision of a code of practice shall not of itself render that person liable to any proceedings; but any code of practice issued under this section shall be admissible in evidence in any legal proceedings, and if any provision of such a code appears to the court or tribunal concerned to be relevant to any question arising in the proceedings it shall be taken into account in determining that question.

(12) Without prejudice to subsection (1), a code of practice issued under this section may include such practical guidance as the Commission think fit as to what steps it is reasonably practicable for persons to take for the purpose of preventing their staff from doing in the course of their duties acts made unlawful by this Act.

71D. General statutory duty: compliance notices

(1) If the Commission are satisfied that a person has failed to comply with, or is failing to comply with, any duty imposed by an order under section 71(2), the Commission may serve on that person a notice ('a compliance notice').

(2) A compliance notice shall require the person concerned—

(a) to comply with the duty concerned; and

(b) to inform the Commission, within 28 days of the date on which the notice is served, of the steps that the person has taken, or is taking, to comply with the duty.

(3) A compliance notice may also require the person concerned to furnish the Commission with such other written information as may be reasonably required by the notice in order to verify that the duty has been complied with.

(4) The notice may specify—

(a) the time (no later than three months from the date on which the notice is served) at which any information is to be furnished to the Commission;

(b) the manner and form in which any such information is to be so furnished.

(5) A compliance notice shall not require a person to furnish information which the person could not be compelled to furnish in evidence in civil proceedings before the High Court or the Court of Session.

71E. Enforcement of compliance notices

(1) The Commission may apply to a designated county court or, in Scotland, a sheriff court for an order requiring a person falling within Schedule 1A to furnish any information required by a compliance notice if—

(a) the person fails to furnish the information to the Commission in accordance with the notice; or

(b) the Commission have reasonable cause to believe that the person does not intend to furnish the information.

(2) If the Commission consider that a person has not, within three months of the date on which a compliance notice was served on that person, complied with any requirement of the notice for that person to comply with a duty imposed by an order under section 71(2), the Commission may apply to a designated county court or, in Scotland, a sheriff court for an order requiring the person to comply with the requirement of the notice.

(3) If the court is satisfied that the application is well-founded, it may grant the order in the terms applied for or in more limited terms.

(4) The sanctions in section 71D and this section shall be the only sanctions for breach of any duty imposed by an order under section 71(2), but without prejudice to the enforcement under section 57 or otherwise of any other provision of this Act (where the breach is also a contravention of that provision).]

72. Validity and revision of contracts

(1) A term of a contract is void where—

(a) its inclusion renders the making of the contract unlawful by virtue of this Act; or

(b) it is included in furtherance of an act rendered unlawful by this Act; or

(c) it provides for the doing of an act which would be rendered unlawful by this Act.

(2) Subsection (1) does not apply to a term the inclusion of which constitutes, or is in furtherance of, or provides for, unlawful discrimination against a party to the contract, but the term shall be unenforceable against that party.

(3) A term in a contract which purports to exclude or limit any provision of this Act is unenforceable by any person in whose favour the term would operate apart from this subsection.

(4) Subsection (3) does not apply—

(a) to a contract settling a complaint to which section 54(1) applies where the contract is made with the assistance of a conciliation officer;

[(aa) to a contract settling a complaint to which section 54(1) applies if the conditions regulating compromise contracts under this Act are satisfied in relation to the contract;] or

(b) to a contract settling a claim to which section 57 applies.

[(4A) The conditions regulating compromise contracts under this Act are that—

(a) the contract must be in writing;

(b) the contract must relate to the particular complaint;

(c) the complainant must have received [advice from a relevant independent adviser] as to the terms and effect of the proposed contract and in particular its effect on his ability to pursue his complaint before an [employment tribunal];

(d) there must be in force, when the adviser gives the advice, a [contract of insurance, or an indemnity provided for members of a profession or professional body,] covering the risk of a claim by the complainant in respect of loss arising in consequence of the advice; and

(e) the contract must identify the adviser; and

(f) the contract must state that the conditions regulating compromise contracts under this Act are satisfied.

[(4B) A person is a relevant independent adviser for the purposes of subsection (4A)(c)—

(a) if he is a qualified lawyer,

(b) if he is an officer, official, employee or member of an independent trade union who has been certified in writing by the trade union as competent to give advice and as authorised to do so on behalf of the trade union.

(c) if he works at an advice centre (whether as an employee or a volunteer) and has been certified in writing by the centre as competent to give advice and as authorised to do so on behalf of the centre, or

(d) if he is a person of a description specified in an order made by the Secretary of State.

(4BA) But a person is not a relevant independent adviser for the purposes of subsection (4A)(c) in relation to the complainant—

(a) if he is, is employed by or is acting in the matter for the other party or a person who is connected with the other party,

(b) in the case of a person within subsection (4B)(b) or (c), if the trade union or advice centre is the other party or a person who is connected with the other party,

(c) in the case of a person within subsection (4B)(c), if the complainant makes a payment for the advice received from him, or

(d) in the case of a person of a description specified in an order under subsection (4B)(d), if any condition specified in the order in relation to the giving of advice by persons of that description is not satisfied.

(4BB) In subsection (4B)(a) 'qualified lawyer' means—

(a) as respects England and Wales, a barrister (whether in practice as such or employed to give legal advice), a solicitor who holds a practising certificate, or a person other than a barrister or solicitor who is an authorised advocate or authorised litigator (within the meaning of the Courts and Legal Services Act 1990), and

(b) as respects Scotland, an advocate (whether in practice as such or employed to give legal advice), or a solicitor who holds a practising certificate.

(4BC) In subsection (4B)(b) 'independent trade union' has the same meaning as in the Trade Union and Labour Relations (Consolidation) Act 1992.

(4C) For the purposes of subsection (4BA) any two persons are to be treated as connected—

(a) if one is a company of which the other (directly or indirectly) has control, or

(b) if both are companies of which a third person (directly or indirectly) has control.]]

[(4D) An agreement under which the parties agree to submit a dispute to arbitration—

(a) shall be regarded for the purposes of subsection (4)(a) and (aa) as being a contract settling a complaint if—

(i) the dispute is covered by a scheme having effect by virtue of an order under section 212A of the Trade Union and Labour Relations (Consolidation) Act 1992, and

(ii) the agreement is to submit it to arbitration in accordance with the scheme, but

(b) shall be regarded for those purposes as neither being nor including such a contract in any other case.]

(5) On the application of any person interested in a contract to which subsection (2) applies, a designated county court or a sheriff court may make such order as it thinks just for removing or modifying any term made unenforceable by that subsection; but such an

order shall not be made unless all persons affected have been given notice of the application (except where under rules of court notice may be dispensed with) and have been afforded an opportunity to make representations to the court.

(6) An order under subsection (5) may include provision as respects any period before the making of the order.

73. Power to amend certain provisions of Act

(1) The Secretary of State may by an order the draft of which has been approved by each House of Parliament—

(a) amend or repeal section 9 (including that section as amended by a previous order under this subsection);

(b) amend Part II, III or IV so as to render lawful an act which, apart from the amendment, would be unlawful by reason of section 4(1) or (2), [19B,] 20(1), 21, 24 or 25;

(c) amend section 10(1) or 25(1)(a) so as to alter the number of partners or members specified in that provision.

(2) The Secretary of State shall not lay before Parliament the draft of an order under subsection (1) unless he has consulted the Commission about the contents of the draft.

74. Orders and regulations

(1) Any power of a Minister of the Crown to make orders or regulations under the provisions of this Act (except section . . . 50(2)(a)) shall be exercisable by statutory instrument.

(2) An order made by a Minister of the Crown under the preceding provisions of this Act (except sections . . . 50(2)(a) and 73(1)), and any regulations made under section [56(5), (6), or] 75(5)(a), [or (9A)] shall be subject to annulment in pursuance of a resolution of either House of Parliament.

(3) An order under this Act may make different provision in relation to different cases or classes of case, may exclude certain cases or classes of case, and may contain transitional provisions and savings.

(4) Any power conferred by this Act to make orders includes power (exercisable in the like manner and subject to the like conditions) to vary or revoke any order so made.

(5) Any document purporting to be an order made by the Secretary of State under section . . . 50(2)(a) and to be signed by him or on his behalf shall be received in evidence, and shall, unless the contrary is proved, be deemed to be made by him.

75. Application to Crown etc.

(1) This Act applies—

(a) to an act done by or for purposes of a Minister of the Crown or government department; or

(b) to an act done on behalf of the Crown by a statutory body, or a person holding a statutory office,

as it applies to an act done by a private person.

(2) Parts II and IV apply to—

(a) service for purposes of a Minister of the Crown or government department, other than service of a person holding a statutory office; or

(b) service on behalf of the Crown for purposes of a person holding a statutory office or purposes of a statutory body; or

(c) service in the armed forces,

as they apply to employment by a private person, and shall so apply as if references to a contract of employment included references to the terms of service.

[(2A) Subsections (1) and (2) do not apply in relation to the provisions mentioned in subsection (2B).

(2B) Sections 19B to 19F, sections 71 to 71E (including Schedule 1A) and section 76 bind the Crown; and the other provisions of this Act so far as they relate to those provisions shall be construed accordingly (including, in particular, references to employment in Part IV).]

(3) Subsections (1) [to (2B)] have effect subject to [sections 76A and 76B].

(4) Subsection (2) of section 8 and subsection (4) of section 27 shall have effect in relation to any ship, aircraft or hovercraft belonging to or possessed by Her Majesty in right of the Government of the United Kingdom as it has effect in relation to a ship, aircraft or hovercraft such as is mentioned in paragraph (a) or (b) of the subsection in question; and section 8(3) shall apply accordingly.

(5) Nothing in this Act shall—

(a) invalidate any rules (whether made before or after the passing of this Act) restricting employment in the service of the Crown or by any public body prescribed for the purposes of this subsection by regulations made by the Minister for the Civil Service to persons of particular birth, nationality, descent or residence; or

(b) render unlawful the publication, display or implementation of any such rules, or the publication of advertisements stating the gist of any such rules.

In this subsection 'employment' includes service of any kind, and 'public body' means a body of persons, whether corporate or unincorporate, carrying on a service or undertaking of a public nature.

(6) The provisions of Parts II to IV of the Crown Proceedings Act 1947 shall apply to proceedings against the Crown under this Act as they apply to proceedings in England and Wales which by virtue of section 23 of that Act are treated for the purposes of Part II of that Act as civil proceedings by or against the Crown, except that in their application to proceedings under this Act section 20 of that Act (removal of proceedings from county court to High Court) shall not apply.

(7) The provisions of Part V of the Crown Proceedings Act 1947 shall apply to proceedings against the Crown under this Act as they apply to proceedings in Scotland which by virtue of the said Part are treated as civil proceedings by or against the Crown, except that in their application to proceedings under this Act the proviso to section 44 of that Act (removal of proceedings from the sheriff court to the Court of Session) shall not apply.

(8) This subsection applies to any complaint by a person ('the complainant') that another person—

(a) has committed an act of discrimination against the complainant which is unlawful by virtue of section 4 or

(b) is by virtue of section 32 or 33 to be treated as having committed such an act of discrimination against the complainant,

if at the time when the act complained of was done the complainant was serving in the armed forces and the discrimination in question relates to his service in those forces.

[(9) No complaint to which subsection (8) applies shall he presented to an [employment tribunal] under section 54 unless—

(a) the complainant has made a complaint to an officer under the service redress procedures applicable to him and has submitted that complaint to the Defence Council under those procedures; and

(b) the Defence Council have made a determination with respect to the complaint.

(9A) Regulations may make provision enabling a complaint to which subsection (8) applies to be presented to an [employment tribunal] under section 54 in such circumstances as may be specified by the regulations, notwithstanding that subsection (9) would otherwise preclude the presentation of the complaint to an [employment tribunal].

(9B) Where a complaint is presented to an [employment tribunal] under section 54 by virtue of regulations under subsection (9A), the service redress procedures may continue after the complaint is so presented.]

(10) In this section—

(a) 'the armed forces' means any of the naval, military or air forces of the Crown . . .;

[(aa) 'regulations' means regulations made by the Secretary of State;

(ab) 'the service redress procedures' means the procedures, excluding those which relate to the making of a report on a complaint to Her Majesty, referred to in section 180 of the Army Act 1955, section 180 of the Air Force Act 1955 and section 130 of the Naval Discipline Act 1957;]

(b) 'statutory body' means a body set up by or in pursuance of an enactment, and 'statutory office' means an office so set up; and

(c) service 'for purposes of' a Minister of the Crown or government department does not include service in any office in Schedule 2 (Ministerial offices) to the House of Commons Disqualification Act 1975 as for the time being in force.

[75A. Application to House of Commons Staff

(1) Parts II and IV apply to an act done by an employer of a relevant member of the House of Commons staff, and to service as such a member, as they apply to an act done by and to service for the purposes of a Minister of the Crown or government department. and accordingly apply as if references to a contract of employment included references to the terms of service of such a member.

(2) in this section 'relevant member of the House of Commons staff' has the same meaning as in [section 195 of the Employment Rights Act 1996]; and [subsections (6) to (12)] of that section (person to be treated as employer of House of Commons staff) apply, with any necessary modifications, for the purposes of Parts II and IV as they apply by virtue of this section.]

[75B. Application to House of Lords staff

(1) Parts II and IV apply in relation to employment as a relevant member of the House of Lords staff as they apply in relation to other employment.

(2) In this section 'relevant member of the House of Lords staff' has the same meaning as in [section 194 of the Employment Rights Act 1996]; and [subsection (7)] of that section applies for the purposes of this section.]

76. Government appointments outside section 4

(1) [Subsection (2)] applies to any appointment by a Minister of the Crown or government department to an office or post where section 4 does not apply in relation to the appointment.

(2) In making the appointment, and in making the arrangements for determining who should be offered the office or post, the Minister of the Crown or government department shall not do an act which would be unlawful under section 4 if the Crown were the employer for the purposes of this Act.

[(3) Subsection (5) applies to—

(a) any recommendation made by a Minister of the Crown or government department in relation to an appointment to an office or post where section 4 does not apply in relation to the appointment; and

(b) any approval given by such a Minister or department in relation to any such appointment.

(4) Subsection (5) also applies to—

(a) any recommendation made by a Minister of the Crown or government department in relation to a conferment by the Crown of a dignity or honour; and

(b) any approval given by such a Minister or department in relation to any such conferment.

(5) In making the recommendation, or giving the approval, and in making the arrangements for determining who should be recommended or approved, the Minister of the Crown or government department shall not do an act which would be unlawful under section 4 if the recommendation or approval were an offer of employment and the Crown were the employer for the purposes of this Act.

(6) Subsections (3) to (5) do not apply in relation to the making of negative recommendations.

(7) Subsection (9) applies to—

(a) any negative recommendation made by a Minister of the Crown or government department, or any refusal to make a recommendation by such a Minister or department, in relation to an appointment to an office or post where section 4 does not apply in relation to the appointment; and

(b) any approval refused by such a Minister or department in relation to any such appointment.

(8) Subsection (9) also applies to—

(a) any negative recommendation made by a Minister of the Crown or government department, or any refusal to make a recommendation by such a Minister or department, in relation to a conferment by the Crown of a dignity or honour; and

(b) any approval refused by such a Minister or department in relation to any such conferment.

(9) In making a negative recommendation or in refusing to make a recommendation or give an approval, and in making the arrangements for determining whether to make such a recommendation or refusal, the Minister of the Crown or government department shall not do an act which would be unlawful under section 4 if the recommendation or refusal were a refusal to offer the person concerned employment and the Crown were the employer for the purposes of this Act.

(10) Subsection (11) applies in relation to any appointment to an office or post where section 4 does not apply and—

(a) the appointment is made by a Minister of the Crown or government department; or

(b) the office or post is an office or post in relation to which a Minister of the Crown or government department has made a recommendation (other than a negative recommendation) or given an approval.

(11) A Minister of the Crown or government department shall not do an act in connection with—

(a) the terms of the appointment;

(b) access for the person appointed to opportunities for promotion, transfer or training, or to any other benefits, facilities or services; or

(c) the termination of the appointment, or subjecting the person appointed to any other detriment;

which would be unlawful under section 4 if the Crown were the employer for the purposes of this Act.

(12) The High Court may, on an application for judicial review, make a declaration to the effect that a Minister of the Crown or government department has contravened subsection (5), subsection (9) or, in relation to an appointment falling within subsection (10)(b), subsection (11), and may award damages in respect of the contravention.

(13) In Scotland, the Court of Session may, in a petition for judicial review, grant declarator to the like effect and may award damages in respect of the contravention.

(14) The sanctions provided by virtue of the operation of section 53(2) to (4) in relation to this section shall be the only sanctions under this Act in relation to appointments, conferments and other acts to which this section applies.

(15) In this section—

(a) references to refusal include references to deliberate omission;

(b) references to Ministers of the Crown and government departments include references to the National Assembly for Wales and any part of the Scottish Administration; and

(c) references to Ministers of the Crown and government departments so far as they relate to the making of a recommendation or a refusal to make a recommendation, or the giving or refusal of an approval, in relation to a conferment of a peerage for life under section 1 of the Life Peerages Act 1958 include references to any body established by a Minister of the Crown to make such a recommendation to the Prime Minister or to determine whether to give such an approval.]

[*Police*

76A. Police forces

(1) In this section, 'relevant police office' means—

(a) the office of constable held—

(i) as a member of a police force; or

(ii) on appointment as a special constable for a police area; or

(b) an appointment as police cadet to undergo training with a view to becoming a member of a police force.

(2) For the purposes of Part II, the holding of a relevant police office shall be treated as employment—

(a) by the chief officer of police as respects any act done by him in relation to that office or a holder of it;

(b) by the police authority as respects any act done by it in relation to that office or a holder of it.

(3) For the purposes of section 32—

(a) the holding of a relevant police office shall be treated as employment by the chief officer of police (and as not being employment by any other person); and

(b) anything done by a person holding such an office in the performance, or purported performance, of his functions shall be treated as done in the course of that employment.

(4) There shall be paid out of the police fund—

(a) any compensation, costs or expenses awarded against a chief officer of police in any proceedings brought against him under this Act, and any costs or expenses incurred by him in any such proceedings so far as not recovered by him in the proceedings; and

(b) any sum required by a chief officer of police for the settlement of any claim made against him under this Act if the settlement is approved by the police authority.

(5) Any proceedings under this Act which, by virtue of this section, would lie against a chief officer of police shall be brought against—

(a) the chief officer of police for the time being; or

(b) in the case of a vacancy in that office, against the person for the time being performing the functions of that office;

and references in subsection (4) to the chief officer of police shall be construed accordingly.

(6) A police authority may, in such cases and to such extent as appear to it to be appropriate, pay out of the police fund—

(a) any damages or costs awarded in proceedings under this Act against a person under the direction and control of the chief officer of police;

(b) any costs incurred and not recovered by such a person in such proceedings; and

(c) any sum required in connection with the settlement of a claim that has or might have given rise to such proceedings.

76B. Other police bodies etc.

(1) Section 76A applies in relation to the National Criminal Intelligence Service ('NCIS') and the National Crime Squad ('the NCS') as it applies in relation to a police force but as if any reference—

(a) to the chief officer of police were to the Director General of NCIS or of the NCS, as the case may be;

(b) to the police authority were to the Service Authority for the National Criminal Intelligence Service or the Service Authority for the National Crime Squad, as the case may be;

(c) to the police fund were to the service fund established under section 16 of the Police Act 1997 (NCIS service fund) or section 61 of that Act (the NCS service fund), as the case may be.

(2) Section 76A also applies in relation to any other body of constables or cadets as it applies in relation to a police force, but as if any reference—

(a) to the chief officer of police were to the officer or other person who has the direction and control of the body in question;

(b) to the police authority were to the authority by whom the members of the body are paid;

(c) to the police fund were to money provided by that authority.

(3) In relation to a member of a police force or a special constable who is not under the direction and control of the chief officer of police for that police force or, as the case may be, for the police area to which he is appointed, references in section 76A to the chief officer of police are references to the chief officer under whose direction and control he is.]

77. Financial provisions

There shall be defrayed out of money provided by Parliament—

(a) sums required by the Secretary of State for making payments under paragraph 5 or 16 of Schedule 1 or paragraph 12 of Schedule 2, and for defraying any other expenditure falling to be made by him under or by virtue of this Act;

(b) any expenses incurred by the Secretary of State with the consent of the Treasury in undertaking, or financially assisting the undertaking by other persons of, research into any matter connected with relations between persons of different racial groups;

(c) payments falling to be made under section 67(5) in respect of the remuneration of assessors; and

(d) any increase attributable to the provisions of this Act in the sums payable out of money provided by Parliament under any other Act.

78. General interpretation provisions

(1) In this Act, unless the context otherwise requires—

'access' shall be construed in accordance with section 40;

'act' includes a deliberate omission;

'advertisement' includes every form of advertisement or notice, whether to the public or not, and whether in a newspaper or other publication, by television or radio, by display of notices, signs, labels, showcards or goods, by distribution of samples, circulars, catalogues, price lists or other material, by exhibition of pictures, models or films, or in any other way, and references to the publishing of advertisements shall be construed accordingly;

['board of management' in relation to a college of further education within the meaning of Part I of the Further and Higher Education (Scotland) Act 1992, has the same meaning as in that Part;]

['body' includes an unincorporated association;]

. . .

'the Commission' means the Commission for Racial Equality;

'Commissioner' means a member of the Commission;

['criminal investigation' has the meaning given by section 57(4B);]

['criminal proceedings' includes—

(a) proceedings on dealing summarily with a charge under the Army Act 1955 or the Air Force Act 1955 or on summary trial under the Naval Discipline Act 1957;

(b) proceedings before a summary appeal court constituted under any of those Acts;

(c) proceedings before a court-martial constituted under any of those Acts or a disciplinary court constituted under section 52G of the Act of 1957;

(d) proceedings before the Courts-Martial Appeal Court; and
(e) proceedings before a Standing Civilian Court;]

'designated county court' has the meaning given by section 67(1);
'discrimination' and related terms shall be construed in accordance with section 3(3);
'dispose', in relation to premises, includes granting a right to occupy the premises, and any reference to acquiring premises shall be construed accordingly;
'education' include any form of training or instruction;
['the Education Acts' has the meaning given by section 578 of the Education Act 1996;]

. . .

'employment' means employment under a contract of service or of apprenticeship or a contract personally to execute any work or labour, and related expressions shall be construed accordingly;
'employment agency' means a person who, for profit or not, provides services for the purpose of finding employment for workers or supplying employers with workers;
['enactment' includes an enactment comprised in, or in an instrument made under, an Act of the Scottish Parliament.]
'estate agent' means a person who, by way of profession or trade, provides services for the purpose of finding premises for persons seeking to acquire them or assisting in the disposal of premises;
'final' shall be construed in accordance with subsection (4);
'firm' has the meaning given by section 4 of the Partnership Act 1890;
'formal investigation' means an investigation under section 48;

. . .

'general notice', in relation to any person, mean a notice published by him at a time and in a manner appearing to him suitable for securing that the notice is seen within a reasonable time by persons likely to be affected by it;
'genuine occupational qualification' shall be construed in accordance with section 5;
'Great Britain' includes such of the territorial waters of the United Kingdom as are adjacent to Great Britain;
'independent school' has for England and Wales the meaning given by section [463] of the Education Act [1996], and for Scotland the meaning given by section 145(23) of the Education (Scotland) Act 1962;

. . .

'Minister of the Crown' includes the Treasury and the Defence Council;
'nationality' includes citizenship;
'near relative' shall be construed in accordance with subsection (5);
'non-discrimination notice' means a notice under section 58;
'notice' means a notice in writing;
'prescribed' means prescribed by regulations made by the Secretary of State;
'profession' includes any vocation or occupation;
'proprietor', in relation to a school, has for England and Wales the meaning given by section [579] of the Education Act [1996], and for Scotland the meaning given by section 145(37) of the Education (Scotland) Act 1962;

. . .

'racial grounds' and 'racial group' have the meaning given by section 3(1);
'school' has for England and Wales the meaning given by section [4] of the Education Act [1996], and for Scotland the meaning given by section 145(42) of the Education (Scotland) Act 1962;

. . .

'trade' includes any business;
'training' includes any form of education or instruction;

'university' includes a university college and the college, school or hall of a university;

. . .

(2) It is hereby declared that in this Act 'premises', unless the context otherwise requires, includes land of any description.

(3) Any power conferred by this Act to designate establishments or persons may be exercised either by naming them or by identifying them by reference to a class or other description.

(4) For the purposes of this Act a non-discrimination notice or a finding by a court or tribunal becomes final when an appeal against the notice or finding is dismissed, withdrawn or abandoned or when the time for appealing expires without an appeal having been brought; and for this purpose an appeal against a non-discrimination notice shall be taken to be dismissed if, notwithstanding that a requirement of the notice is quashed on appeal, a direction is given in respect of it under section 59(3).

(5) For the purposes of this Act a person is a near relative of another if that person is the wife or husband, a parent or child, a grandparent or grandchild, or a brother or sister of the other (whether of full blood or half-blood or by affinity), and 'child' includes an illegitimate child and the wife or husband of an illegitimate child.

(6) Except so far as the context otherwise requires, any reference in this Act to an enactment shall be construed as a reference to that enactment as amended by or under any other enactment, including this Act.

(7) In this Act, except where otherwise indicated—

(a) a reference to a numbered Part, section or Schedule is a reference to the Part or section of, or the Schedule to, this Act so numbered; and

(b) a reference in a section to a numbered subsection is a reference to the subsection of that section so numbered; and

(c) a reference in a section, subsection or Schedule to a numbered paragraph is a reference to the paragraph of that section, subsection or Schedule so numbered; and

(d) a reference to any provision of an Act (including this Act) includes a Schedule incorporated in the Act by that provision.

79. Transitional and commencement provisions, amendments and repeals

(1) The provisions of Schedule 2 shall have effect for making transitional provision for the purposes of this Act.

(2) This Act shall come into operation on such day as the Secretary of State may by order appoint, and different days may be so appointed for different provisions and for different purposes.

(3) The enactments specified in Schedule 3 shall have effect subject to the amendments specified in that Schedule (being minor amendments or amendments consequential on the preceding provisions of this Act).

(4) The Sex Discrimination Act 1975 shall have effect subject to the amendments specified in Schedule 4, being amendments for bringing provisions in that Act relating to its administration and enforcement into conformity with the corresponding provisions in this Act.

(5) Subject to the provisions of Schedule 2, the enactments specified in Schedule 5 are hereby repealed to the extent shown in column 3 of that Schedule.

(6) . . .

(7) An order under this section may make such transitional provision as appears to the Secretary of State to be necessary or expedient in connection with the provisions thereby brought into operation, including such adaptations of those provisions, or of any provisions of this Act then in operation, as appear to the Secretary of State necessary or expedient in consequence of the partial operation of this Act.

80. Short title and extent

(1) This Act may be cited as the Race Relations Act 1976.

(2) This Act, except so far as it amends or repeals any provision of the House of Commons Disqualification Act 1975 or the Northern Ireland Assembly Disqualification Act 1975, does not extend to Northern Ireland.

SCHEDULES

Section 43

SCHEDULE 1
THE COMMISSION FOR RACIAL EQUALITY

Incorporation and status

1. On the appointment by the Secretary of State of the first Commissioners, the Commission shall come into existence as a body corporate.

2.—(1) The Commission is not an emanation of the Crown, and shall not act or be treated as the servant or agent of the Crown.

(2) Accordingly—

(a) neither the Commission nor a Commissioner or member of its staff as such is entitled to any status, immunity, privilege or exemption enjoyed by the Crown;

(b) the Commissioners and members of the staff of the Commission as such are not civil servants; and

(c) the Commission's property is not property of, or held on behalf of, the Crown.

Tenure of office of Commissioners

3.—(1) A Commissioner shall hold and vacate his office in accordance with the terms of his appointment.

(2) A person shall not be appointed a Commissioner for more than five years.

(3) With the consent of the Commissioner concerned, the Secretary of State may alter the terms of an appointment so as to make a full-time Commissioner into a part-time Commissioner or vice versa, or for any other purpose.

(4) a Commissioner may resign by notice to the Secretary of State.

(5) The Secretary of State may terminate the appointment of a Commissioner if satisfied that—

(a) without the consent of the Commission, he failed to attend the meetings of the Commission during a continuous period of six months beginning not earlier than nine months before the termination; or

(b) he is an undischarged bankrupt, or has made an arrangement with his creditors, or is insolvent within the meaning of paragraph 9(2) of Schedule 3 to the Conveyancing and Feudal Reform (Scotland) Act 1970; or

(c) he is by reason of physical or mental illness, or for any other reason, incapable of carrying out his duties.

(6) Past service as a Commissioner is no bar to re-appointment.

Tenure of office of chairman and deputy chairmen

4.—(1) The chairman and each deputy chairman shall hold and vacate his office in accordance with the terms of his appointment, and may resign by notice to the Secretary of State.

(2) The office of the chairman or a deputy chairman is vacated if he ceases to be a Commissioner.

(3) Past service as chairman or a deputy chairman is no bar to re-appointment.

Remuneration of Commissioners

5. The Secretary of State may pay, or make such payments towards the provision of, such remuneration, pensions, allowances or gratuities to or in respect of the Commissioners or any of them as, with the consent of the Minister for the Civil Service, he may determine.

6. Where a person ceases to be a Commissioner otherwise than on the expiry of his term of office, and it appears to the Secretary of State that there are special circumstances which make it right for that person to receive compensation, the Secretary of State may, with the consent of the Minister for the Civil Service, direct the Commission to make to that person a payment of such amount as, with the consent of that Minister, the Secretary of State may determine.

Additional Commissioners

7.—(1) Paragraphs 2(2), 3(1) and (6), and 6 shall apply to additional Commissioners appointed under section 48(2) as they apply to Commissioners.

(2) The Commission may pay, or make such payments towards the provision of, such remuneration, pensions, allowances or gratuities to or in respect of an additional Commissioner as the Secretary of State, with the consent of the Minister for the Civil Service, may determine.

(3) With the approval of the Secretary of State and the consent of the additional Commissioner concerned, the Commission may alter the terms of an appointment of an additional Commissioner so as to make a full-time additional Commissioner into a part-time additional Commissioner or vice versa, or for any other purpose.

(4) An additional Commissioner may resign by notice to the Commission.

(5) The Secretary of State, or the Commission acting with the approval of the Secretary of State, may terminate the appointment of an additional Commissioner if satisfied that—

(a) without reasonable excuse he failed to carry out the duties for which he was appointed during a continuous period of three months beginning not earlier than six months before the termination; or

(b) he is a person such as is mentioned in paragraph 3(5)(b); or

(c) he is by reason of physical or mental illness, or for any other reason, incapable of carrying out his duties.

(6) The appointment of an additional Commissioner shall terminate at the conclusion of the investigation for which he was appointed, if not sooner.

Staff

8. The Commission may, after consultation with the Secretary of State, appoint such officers and servants as they think fit, subject to the approval of the Minister for the Civil Service as to numbers and as to remuneration and other terms and conditions of service.

9.—(1) Employment with the Commission shall be included among the kinds of employment to which a superannuation scheme under section 1 of the Superannuation Act 1972 can apply, and accordingly in Schedule 1 to that Act (in which those kinds of employment are listed) the words 'Commission for Racial Equality' shall be inserted after the words 'Commission on Industrial Relations.'

(2) Where a person who is employed by the Commission and is by reference to that employment a participant in a scheme under section 1 of the Superannuation Act 1972 becomes a Commissioner or an additional Commissioner, the Minister for the Civil Service may determine that his service as a Commissioner or additional Commissioner shall be treated for the purposes of the scheme as service as an employee of the Commission.

10.—(1) In this paragraph—

'the new Commission' means the Commission for Racial Equality;

'present Commission employee' means a person who immediately before the repeal date is employed by the Community Relations Commission;

'private pension scheme' means a scheme for the payment of pensions, allowances or gratuities other than one made under section 1 of the Superannuation Act 1972;

'the repeal date' means the date on which the repeal of the Race Relations Act 1968 by this Act takes effect.

(2) If a present Commission employee enters the employment of the new Commission on the repeal date and on so doing elects to be covered for his service in that employment by a private pension scheme in which he was a participant in respect of his service in the employment of the Community Relations Commission, the new Commission may make such payments towards the provision of benefits to or in respect of him under that scheme (or any other private pension scheme replacing it) as may be determined by the new Commission with the consent of the Secretary of State given with the approval of the Minister for the Civil Service; and it shall be the duty of the new Commission and those Ministers in the exercise of their functions under this sub-paragraph to ensure that his rights under the scheme do not become less advantageous than they were when he entered the employment of the new Commission.

(3) Where a person who is employed by the new Commission and is in respect of that employment a participant in a private pension scheme becomes a Commissioner or an additional Commissioner, his service as a Commissioner or additional Commissioner may be treated for the purposes of the scheme as service as an employee of the new Commission.

11. The Employers' Liability (Compulsory Insurance) Act 1969 shall not require insurance to be effected by the Commission.

Advisory committees

12. The Commission may, with the approval of the Secretary of State, appoint advisory committees for the purpose of such of their functions as they think fit.

Proceedings and business

13.—(1) Subject to the provisions of this Act—

(a) the Commission shall discharge their functions in accordance with arrangements made by the Commission and approved by the Secretary of State; and

(b) arrangements so made and approved may provide for the discharge under the general direction of the Commission of any of the Commission's functions by a committee of the Commission, or by two or more Commissioners.

(2) Anything done by or in relation to a committee of the Commission or Commissioners in the discharge of the Commission's functions shall have the same effect as if done by or in relation to the Commission.

14. The validity of any proceedings of the Commission shall not be affected by any vacancy among the members of the Commission or by any defect in the appointment of any Commissioner or additional Commissioner.

15. The quorum for meetings of the Commission shall in the first instance be determined by a meeting of the Commission attended by not less than five Commissioners.

Finance

16. The Secretary of State shall pay to the Commission expenses incurred or to be incurred by them under paragraph 6, 7, 8 or 10 of this Schedule or paragraph 7 of Schedule 2, and, with the consent of the Minister for the Civil Service and the Treasury, shall pay to the Commission such sums as the Secretary of State thinks fit for enabling the Commission to meet other expenses.

17.—(1) The accounting year of the Commission shall be the twelve months ending on 31st March.

(2) It shall be the duty of the Commission—

(a) to keep proper accounts and proper records in relation to the accounts;

(b) to prepare in respect of each accounting year a statement of accounts in such form as the Secretary of State may direct with the approval of the Treasury; and

(c) to send copies of the statement to the Secretary of State and the Comptroller and Auditor General before the end of the month of November next following the accounting year to which the statement relates.

(3) The Comptroller and Auditor General shall examine, certify and report on each statement received by him in pursuance of this Schedule and shall lay copies of each statement and of his report before each House of Parliament.

Disqualification Acts

18.—(1) In Part II of Schedule 1 to the House of Commons Disqualification Act 1975 and Part II of Schedule 1 to the Northern Ireland Assembly Disqualification Act 1975 (bodies of which all members are disqualified under those Acts), there shall (at the appropriate place in alphabetical order) be inserted the following entry:—

'The Commission for Racial Equality'.

(2) In Part III of Schedule 1 to each of those Acts of 1975 (other disqualifying offices) there shall (at the appropriate place in alphabetical order) be inserted the following entry:—

'Additional Commissioner of the Commission for Racial Equality'.

[SCHEDULE 1A

BODIES AND OTHER PERSONS SUBJECT TO GENERAL STATUTORY DUTY

Ministers of the Crown and government departments

1.—(1) A Minister of the Crown or government department.

(2) Sub-paragraph (1) does not include the Security Service, the Intelligence Service or the Government Communications Headquarters.

Scottish Administration

2.—(1) An office-holder in the Scottish Administration within the meaning given by section 126(7)(a) of the Scotland Act 1998.

(2) Members of the staff of the Scottish Administration within the meaning given by section 126(7)(b) of that Act.

National Assembly for Wales

3.—(1) The National Assembly for Wales.

(2) An Assembly subsidiary as defined by section 99(4) of the Government of Wales Act 1998.

Armed forces

4. Any of the naval, military or air forces of the Crown.

National Health Service: England and Wales

5. A Health Authority established under section 8 of the National Health Service Act 1977.

6. A special health authority established under section 11 of that Act.

7. A primary care trust established under section 16A of that Act.

8. A National Health Service trust established under section 5 of the National Health Service and Community Care Act 1990.

National Health Service: Scotland

9. A Health Board constituted under section 2 of the National Health Service (Scotland) Act 1978.

10. A Special Health Board constituted under section 2 of that Act.

11. A National Health Service Trust established under section 12A of that Act.

Local government

12. A local authority within the meaning of the Local Government Act 1972, namely—
   (a) in England, a county council, a London borough council, a district council or a parish council;
   (b) in Wales, a county council, a county borough council or a community council.

13. A council constituted under section 2 of the Local Government etc. (Scotland) Act 1994.

14. A community council established under section 51 of the Local Government (Scotland) Act 1973.

15. The Greater London Authority.

16. The Common Council of the City of London in its capacity as a local authority or port health authority.

17. The Sub-Treasurer of the Inner Temple or the Under-Treasurer of the Middle Temple, in his capacity as a local authority.

18. The Council of the Isles of Scilly.

19. A parish meeting constituted under section 13 of the Local Government Act 1972.

20. Any charter trustees constituted under section 246 of that Act.

21. A fire authority constituted by a combination scheme under section 5 or 6 of the Fire Services Act 1947.

22. A waste disposal authority established by virtue of an order under section 10(1) of the Local Government Act 1985.

23. A water or sewerage authority constituted under section 62 of the Local Government etc. (Scotland) Act 1994.

24. A port health authority constituted by an order under section 2 of the Public Health (Control of Disease) Act 1984.

25. A licensing planning committee constituted under section 119 of the Licensing Act 1964.

26. A licensing board constituted under section 1 of the Licensing (Scotland) Act 1976.

27. An internal drainage board which is continued in being by virtue of section 1 of the Land Drainage Act 1991.

28. A probation committee constituted under section 3 of the Probation Service Act 1993.

29. A joint authority established under Part IV of the Local Government Act 1985 (fire services, civil defence and transport).

30. A joint board within the meaning of section 235(1) of the Local Government (Scotland) Act 1973.

31. The London Fire and Emergency Planning Authority.

32. A body corporate established pursuant to an order under section 67 of the Local Government Act 1985 (transfer of functions to successors of residuary bodies, etc.).

33. A body corporate established pursuant to an order under section 22 of the Local Government Act 1992 (residuary bodies).

34. The Broads Authority established by section 1 of the Norfolk and Suffolk Broads Act 1988.

35. A joint committee constituted in accordance with section 102(1)(b) of the Local Government Act 1972.

36. A joint board which is continued in being by virtue of section 263(1) of that Act.

37. A joint authority established under section 21 of the Local Government Act 1992.

38. A Passenger Transport Executive for a passenger transport area within the meaning of Part II of the Transport Act 1968.

39. Transport for London.

40. The London Development Agency.

41. A regional development agency established under the Regional Development Agencies Act 1998 (other than the London Development Agency).

42. Scottish Enterprise and Highland and Islands Enterprise, established under the Enterprise and New Towns (Scotland) Act 1990.

43. A National Park authority established by an order under section 63 of the Environment Act 1995.

44. A joint planning board constituted for an area in Wales outside a National Park by an order under section 2(1B) of the Town and Country Planning Act 1990.

45. A magistrates' courts committee established under section 27 of the Justices of the Peace Act 1997.

Other educational bodies

46. Governing bodies of—

(a) educational establishments maintained by local education authorities;

(b) institutions within the further education sector (within the meaning of section 91(3) of the Further and Higher Education Act 1992); or

(c) institutions within the higher education sector (within the meaning of section 91(5) of the Act of 1992).

47. The managers of a grant-aided school (within the meaning of section 135 of the Education (Scotland) Act 1980).

48. The managers of a central institution (within the meaning of section 135 of the Act of 1980).

49. The board of management of a self-governing school (within the meaning of the Self-Governing Schools etc. (Scotland) Act 1989).

50. The board of management of a college of further education (within the meaning of section 36(1) of the Further and Higher Education (Scotland) Act 1992).

51. The governing body of an institution within the higher education sector (within the meaning of Part II of the Further and Higher Education (Scotland) Act 1992).

Other housing bodies

52. The Housing Corporation.

53. Scottish Homes.

54. A housing action trust established under Part III of the Housing Act 1988.

Police

55. A police authority established under section 3 of the Police Act 1996.

56. A police authority established under section 2 of the Police (Scotland) Act 1967.

57. The Metropolitan Police Authority established under section 5B of the Police Act 1996.

58. The Common Council of the City of London in its capacity as a police authority.

59. The Service Authority for the National Criminal Intelligence Service.

60. The Service Authority for the National Crime Squad.]

Section 79

SCHEDULE 2
TRANSITIONAL PROVISIONS

Interpretation

1. In this Schedule—
'the 1968 Act' means the Race Relations Act 1968;
'the repeal date' means the date on which the repeal of the 1968 Act by this Act takes effect;
'the Board' means the Race Relations Board.

Enforcement

2. The repeal of the 1968 Act shall not—
(a) invalidate any injunction or order granted or made under section 21 or 23 of that Act which is in force immediately before the repeal date; or
(b) remove from any court any jurisdiction which, but for that repeal, it would have in relation to any such injunction or order.

3. Any proceedings under section 19 or 20 of the 1968 Act which are pending immediately before the repeal date may be continued on and after that date by the Commission as if that Act had not been repealed and the Commission were the Board.

4.—(1) Where a complaint such as is mentioned in section 15(1) or 16(1) of the 1968 Act was made but not disposed of before the repeal date, the relevant provisions of the 1968 Act shall, notwithstanding their repeal, continue to apply in relation to the complaint and the act complained of, but as if anything falling to be done in that connection by or in relation to the Board or a conciliation committee fell to be done by or in relation to the Commission or, in so far as the Commission may so direct, a committee appointed for that purpose by the Commission.
(2) For the purposes of this paragraph the relevant provisions of the 1968 Act are—
(a) for a complaint such as is mentioned in section 15(1) of that Act, sections 15, 18 to 24 and 27 to 29 of that Act; or
(b) for a complaint such as is mentioned in section 16(1) of that Act, section 16(1) of, Schedule 2 to, and sections 18 to 24 and 27 to 29 of, that Act.

5. Where a complaint such as is mentioned in section 15(1) or 16(1) of the 1968 Act could have been, but was not, made before the repeal date in respect of an act done before that date, the relevant provisions of the 1968 Act (within the meaning of paragraph 4) shall, notwithstanding their repeal, continue to apply in relation to that act and any such complaint made in respect of it, but as if anything falling to be done in that connection by or in relation to the Board or a conciliation committee fell to be done as mentioned in paragraph 4(1).

6.—(1) Where—
(a) an investigation under subsection (1) of section 17 of the 1968 Act was begun but not completed before the repeal date; or
(b) a matter was before that date referred for investigation under that subsection but was at that date still awaiting investigation; or

(c) an investigation under that subsection having been completed before that date, some action arising out of the investigation would have fallen to be taken or continued under the 1968 Act on or after that date if that Act had not been repealed,
the relevant provisions of the 1968 Act shall, notwithstanding their repeal, continue to apply in relation to the investigation and its subject-matter, but as if anything falling to be done in that connection by or in relation to the Board or a conciliation committee fell to be done as mentioned in paragraph 4(1).

(2) For the purposes of this paragraph the relevant provisions of the 1968 Act are section 17(1) of, Schedule 3 to, and sections 18 to 24 and 27 to 29 of, that Act.

7. The Commission—

(a) may pay to members of any committee appointed by the Commission for the purposes of paragraph 4, 5 or 6 travelling or other allowances in accordance with such scales as may be approved by the Secretary of State with the consent of the Treasury, and may defray any other expenses of such a committee to such amount as may be so approved; and

(b) shall pay to any assessors appointed by the Commission under section 18 of the 1968 Act such remuneration and allowances as the Commission may, with the consent of the Treasury and after consultation with the Secretary of State, determine.

8.—(1) An order under section 19 of the 1968 Act appointing a county court to have jurisdiction under, and assigning to it a district for the purposes of, that section, or providing for the discontinuance of any jurisdiction of a county court for those purposes, shall, so far as it is in force immediately before the repeal date, have effect with the necessary modifications as if made under section 67(1) for the purposes of this Act.

In its application on or after the repeal date by virtue of paragraph 3, 4, 5 or 6, section 19 of the 1968 Act shall have effect as if—

(a) subsections (3) to (5) were omitted; and

(b) any reference to, or to the district assigned to, a county court appointed to have jurisdiction thereunder were a reference to, or to the district of, a designated county court;
and section 67(6) shall apply in relation to proceedings under that section in its application as aforesaid as if they were proceedings under this Act.

Regulations under s. 27(9) of 1968 Act

9. Any regulations under section 27(9) of the 1968 Act shall, so far as they are in force immediately before the repeal date, have effect as if made under section 75(5).

Property, rights and liabilities of Race Relations Board and Community Relations Commission

10.—(1) On the repeal date all property, rights and liabilities which immediately before that date were property, rights and liabilities of the Board or of the Community Relations Commission shall vest in the Commission for Racial Equality by virtue of this paragraph and without further assurance.

(2) Section 12 of the Finance Act 1895 (which requires Acts to be stamped as conveyances on sale in certain cases) shall not apply to any transfer of property effected by this paragraph.

(3) Any damages recovered by the Commission for Racial Equality on or after the repeal date by virtue of an award made under section 22 of the 1968 Act shall be accounted for by the Commission to the person in respect of whom they were awarded.

Staff

11.—(1) In this . . . paragraph 'present employee' means a person who immediately before the repeal date is employed by the Board or the Community Relations Commission.

(2) . . .

(3) . . .

(4) For the purposes of—

[(a) the Employment Rights Act 1996 except Part XI;

(b) the Trade Union and Labour Relations (Consolidation) Act 1992; and];

(d) any scheme under section 1 of the Superannuation Act 1972,

there shall be deemed to have been no break at the repeal date in the employment of a present employee who as from that date is employed by the Commission.

(5) . . .

12. . . .

13. . . .

Section 79 SCHEDULE 4

AMENDMENTS OF SEX DISCRIMINATION ACT 1975

1. After section 56 insert the cross-heading '*Codes of Practice*' and, below it, insert as section 56A a section in terms identical with those of section 47 of this Act except for the following adaptations, namely—

(a) in subsection (1), for 'persons of different racial groups' substitute 'men and women';

(b) in subsection (8), for 'section 74(3)' substitute 'section 81(4)'.

2.—(1) After section 58(3) (terms of reference of an investigation) insert as subsection (3A) a subsection in terms identical with those of section 49(4) of this Act.

(2) In section 58(4) for 'and (3) substitute '(3) and (3A)'.

3. For section 62 (no further sanctions for breach of Act) substitute—

'62. Restriction of proceedings for breach of Act

(1) Except as provided by this Act no proceedings, whether civil or criminal, shall lie against any person in respect of an act by reason that the act is unlawful by virtue of a provision of this Act.

(2) Subsection (1) does not preclude the making of an order of certiorari, mandamus or prohibition.

(3) In Scotland, subsection (1) does not preclude the exercise of the jurisdiction of the Court of Session to entertain an application for reduction or suspension of any order or determination, or otherwise to consider the validity of any order or determination, or to require reasons for any order or determination to be stated.'.

4. In section 65(3)(a), after 'may' insert '(subject to the limit in subsection (2))'.

5.—(1) In section 66(2) (claims under Part III) after 'this subsection' insert 'and section 62(1)'.

(2) After section 66(5) insert—

'(5A) In Scotland, when any proceedings are brought under this section, in addition to the service on the defender of a copy of the summons or initial writ initiating the action a copy thereof shall be sent as soon as practicable to the Commission in a manner to be prescribed by Act of Sederunt.'

6. In section 72(4) (enforcement of sections 38 to 40) omit 'an' in the last place where it occurs.

7. In section 75(2), after paragraph (d) insert—

'(e) any other form of assistance which the Commission may consider appropriate,'.

8. In section 76 (period within which proceedings to be brought)—

(a) in subsection (2), for the words from 'the period' onwards substitute—

'(a) the period of six months beginning when the act complained of was done; or

(b) in a case to which section 66(5) applies, the period of eight months so beginning.';

(b) for subsection (3) substitute—

'(3) An industrial tribunal, county court or sheriff court shall not consider an application under section 72(2)(a) unless it is made before the end of the period of six months beginning when the act to which it relates was done; and a county court or sheriff court shall not consider an application under section 72(4) unless it is made before the end of the period of five years so beginning.'

9. For paragraph 15 of Schedule 3 (accounts) substitute—

'15.—(1) The accounting year of the Commission shall be the twelve months ending on 31st March.

(2) It shall be the duty of the Commission—

(a) to keep proper accounts and proper records in relation to the accounts;

(b) to prepare in respect of each accounting year a statement of accounts in such form as the Secretary of State may direct with the approval of the Treasury; and

(c) to send copies of the statement to the Secretary of State and the Comptroller and Auditor General before the end of the month of November next following the accounting year to which the statement relates.

(3) The Comptroller and Auditor General shall examine, certify and report on each statement received by him in pursuance of this Schedule and shall lay copies of each statement and of his report before each House of Parliament.'.

Section 79

SCHEDULE 5
REPEALS

Session and Chapter	Short title	Extent of repeal
1965 c. 73.	Race Relations Act 1965.	The whole Act, so far as unrepealed.
1968 c. 71.	Race Relations Act 1968.	The whole Act.
1972 c. 11.	Superannuation Act 1972.	In Schedule 1, the words 'Race Relations Board'.
1973 c. 50.	Employment and Training Act 1973.	In Schedule 3, paragraph 10.
1974 c. 52.	Trade Union and Labour Relations Act 1974.	In Schedule 1, paragraph 28.
1975 c. 24.	House of Commons Disqualification Act 1975.	In Part II of Schedule 1, the words 'The Community Relations Commission' and the entry beginning 'The Race Relations Board'.
1975 c. 25.	Northern Ireland Assembly Disqualification Act 1975.	In Part II of Schedule 1, the entry beginning 'The Race Relations Board'.
1975 c. 65.	Sex Discrimination Act 1975.	In section 72(4) the word 'an', in the last place where it occurs.
1975 c. 71.	Employment Protection Act 1975.	In Part III of Schedule 16, paragraph 28.

B. The Race Relations (Amendment) Act 2000

An Act to extend further the application of the Race Relations Act 1976 to the police and other public authorities; to amend the exemption under that Act for acts done for the purpose of safeguarding national security; and for connected purposes. [30th November 2000]

BE IT ENACTED by the Queen's most Excellent Majesty, by and with the advice and consent of the Lords Spiritual and Temporal, and Commons, in this present Parliament assembled, and by the authority of the same, as follows:—

Further extension of 1976 Act to police and other public authorities

1. Discrimination by police and other public authorities
After section 19A of the Race Relations Act 1976 (in this Act referred to as 'the 1976 Act') there is inserted—

'*Public authorities*

19B. Discrimination by public authorities

(1) It is unlawful for a public authority in carrying out any functions of the authority to do any act which constitutes discrimination.

(2) In this section "public authority"—

(a) includes any person certain of whose functions are functions of a public nature; but

(b) does not include any person mentioned in subsection (3).

(3) The persons mentioned in this subsection are—

(a) either House of Parliament;

(b) a person exercising functions in connection with proceedings in Parliament;

(c) the Security Service;

(d) the Secret Intelligence Service;

(e) the Government Communications Headquarters; and

(f) any unit or part of a unit of any of the naval, military or air forces of the Crown which is for the time being required by the Secretary of State to assist the Government Communications Headquarters in carrying out its functions.

(4) In relation to a particular act, a person is not a public authority by virtue only of subsection (2)(a) if the nature of the act is private.

(5) This section is subject to sections 19C to 19F.

(6) Nothing in this section makes unlawful any act of discrimination which—

(a) is made unlawful by virtue of any other provision of this Act; or

(b) would be so made but for any provision made by or under this Act.

19C. Exceptions or further exceptions from section 19B for judicial and legislative acts etc.

(1) Section 19B does not apply to—

(a) any judicial act (whether done by a court, tribunal or other person); or

(b) any act done on the instructions, or on behalf, of a person acting in a judicial capacity.

(2) Section 19B does not apply to any act of, or relating to, making, confirming or approving any enactment or Order in Council or any instrument made by a Minister of the Crown under an enactment.

(3) Section 19B does not apply to any act of, or relating to, making or approving arrangements, or imposing requirements or conditions, of a kind falling within section 41.

(4) Section 19B does not apply to any act of, or relating to, imposing a requirement, or giving an express authorisation, of a kind mentioned in section 19D(3) in relation to the carrying out of immigration and nationality functions.

(5) In this section—

"immigration and nationality functions" has the meaning given in section 19D; and

"Minister of the Crown" includes the National Assembly for Wales and a member of the Scottish Executive.

19D. Exception from section 19B for certain acts in immigration and nationality cases

(1) Section 19B does not make it unlawful for a relevant person to discriminate against another person on grounds of nationality or ethnic or national origins in carrying out immigration and nationality functions.

(2) For the purposes of subsection (1), "relevant person" means—

(a) a Minister of the Crown acting personally; or

(b) any other person acting in accordance with a relevant authorisation.

(3) In subsection (2), "relevant authorisation" means a requirement imposed or express authorisation given—

(a) with respect to a particular case or class of case, by a Minister of the Crown acting personally;

(b) with respect to a particular class of case—

(i) by any of the enactments mentioned in subsection (5); or

(ii) by any instrument made under or by virtue of any of those enactments.

(4) For the purposes of subsection (1),

"immigration and nationality functions" means functions exercisable by virtue of any of the enactments mentioned in subsection (5).

(5) Those enactments are—

(a) the Immigration Acts (within the meaning of the Immigration and Asylum Act 1999 but excluding sections 28A to 28K of the Immigration Act 1971 so far as they relate to offences under Part III of that Act);

(b) the British Nationality Act 1981;

(c) the British Nationality (Falkland Islands) Act 1983;

(d) the British Nationality (Hong Kong) Act 1990;

(e) the Hong Kong (War Wives and Widows) Act 1996;

(f) the British Nationality (Hong Kong) Act 1997; and

(g) the Special Immigration Appeals Commission Act 1997;

and include any provision made under section 2(2) of the European Communities Act 1972, or any provision of Community law, which relates to the subject-matter of any of the enactments mentioned above.

19E. Monitoring of exception in relation to immigration and nationality cases

(1) The Secretary of State shall appoint a person who is not a member of his staff to act as a monitor.

(2) Before appointing any such person, the Secretary of State shall consult the Commission.

(3) The person so appointed shall monitor, in such manner as the Secretary of State may determine—

(a) the likely effect on the operation of the exception in section 19D of any relevant authorisation relating to the carrying out of immigration and nationality functions which has been given by a Minister of the Crown acting personally; and

(b) the operation of that exception in relation to acts which have been done by a person acting in accordance with such an authorisation.

(4) The monitor shall make an annual report on the discharge of his functions to the Secretary of State.

(5) The Secretary of State shall lay a copy of any report made to him under subsection (4) before each House of Parliament.

(6) The Secretary of State shall pay to the monitor such fees and allowances (if any) as he may determine.

(7) In this section "immigration and nationality functions" and "relevant authorisation" have the meanings given to them in section 19D.

19F. Exceptions from section 19B for decisions not to prosecute etc

Section 19B does not apply to—

(a) a decision not to institute criminal proceedings and, where such a decision has been made, any act done for the purpose of enabling the decision whether to institute criminal proceedings to be made;

(b) where criminal proceedings are not continued as a result of a decision not to continue them, the decision and, where such a decision has been made—

(i) any act done for the purpose of enabling the decision whether to continue the proceedings to be made; and

(ii) any act done for the purpose of securing that the proceedings are not continued.'

2. Specified authorities: general statutory duty

(1) For section 71 of the 1976 Act (local authorities: general statutory duty) there is substituted—

'71. Specified authorities: general statutory duty

(1) Every body or other person specified in Schedule 1A or of a description falling within that Schedule shall, in carrying out its functions, have due regard to the need—

(a) to eliminate unlawful racial discrimination; and

(b) to promote equality of opportunity and good relations between persons of different racial groups.

(2) The Secretary of State may by order impose, on such persons falling within Schedule 1A as he considers appropriate, such duties as he considers appropriate for the purpose of ensuring the better performance by those persons of their duties under subsection (1).

(3) An order under subsection (2)—

(a) may be made in relation to a particular person falling within Schedule 1A, any description of persons falling within that Schedule or every person falling within that Schedule;

(b) may make different provision for different purposes.

(4) Before making an order under subsection (2), the Secretary of State shall consult the Commission.

(5) The Secretary of State may by order amend Schedule 1A; but no such order may extend the application of this section unless the Secretary of State considers that the extension relates to a person who exercises functions of a public nature.

(6) An order under subsection (2) or (5) may contain such incidental, supplementary or consequential provision as the Secretary of State considers appropriate

(including provision amending or repealing provision made by or under this Act or any other enactment).

(7) This section is subject to section 71A and 71B and is without prejudice to the obligation of any person to comply with any other provision of this Act.

71A. General statutory duty: special cases

(1) In relation to the carrying out of immigration and nationality functions (within the meaning of section 19D(1)), section 71(1)(b) has effect with the omission of the words "equality of opportunity and".

(2) Where an entry in Schedule 1A is limited to a person in a particular capacity, section 71(1) does not apply to that person in any other capacity.

(3) Where an entry in Schedule 1A is limited to particular functions of a person, section 71(1) does not apply to that person in relation to any other functions.

71B. General statutory duty: Scotland and Wales

(1) For the purposes of the Scotland Act 1998, subsections (2) to (4) of section 71 (and sections 71(6) and 74 so far as they apply to the power conferred by subsection (2) of section 71) shall be taken to be pre-commencement enactments within the meaning of that Act.

(2) Before making an order under section 71(2) in relation to functions exercisable in relation to Wales by a person who is not a Welsh public authority, the Secretary of State shall consult the National Assembly for Wales.

(3) The Secretary of State shall not make an order under section 71(2) in relation to functions of a Welsh public authority except with the consent of the National Assembly for Wales.

(4) In this section "Welsh public authority" means any person whose functions are exercisable only in relation to Wales and includes the National Assembly for Wales.

71C. General statutory duty: codes of practice

(1) The Commission may issue codes of practice containing such practical guidance as the Commission think fit in relation to the performance by persons of duties imposed on them by virtue of subsections (1) and (2) of section 71.

(2) When the Commission propose to issue a code of practice under this section, they—

(a) shall prepare and publish a draft of the code;
(b) shall consider any representations made to them about the draft; and
(c) may modify the draft accordingly.

(3) In the course of preparing any draft code of practice under this section the Commission shall consult such organisations or bodies as appear to the Commission to be appropriate having regard to the content of the draft code.

(4) If the Commission determine to proceed with a draft code of practice, they shall transmit the draft to the Secretary of State who shall consult the Scottish Ministers and the National Assembly for Wales.

(5) After consulting the Scottish Ministers and the National Assembly for Wales, the Secretary of State shall—

(a) if he approves of the draft code, lay it before both Houses of Parliament; and
(b) if he does not approve of it, publish details of his reasons for withholding approval.

(6) If, within the period of forty days beginning with the day on which a copy of a draft code of practice is laid before each House of Parliament, or, if such copies are laid on different days, with the later of the two days, either House so resolves, no further proceedings shall be taken on the draft code of practice, but without prejudice to the laying before Parliament of a new draft.

(7) In reckoning the period of forty days referred to in subsection (6), no account shall be taken of any period during which Parliament is dissolved or prorogued or during which both Houses are adjourned for more than four days.

(8) If no such resolution is passed as is referred to in subsection (6), the Commission shall issue the code in the form of the draft and the code shall come into effect on such day as the Secretary of State may, after consulting the Scottish Ministers and the National Assembly for Wales, by order appoint.

(9) Without prejudice to section 74(3), an order under subsection (8) may contain such transitional provisions or savings as appear to the Secretary of State to be necessary or expedient in connection with the code of practice thereby brought into operation.

(10) The Commission may revoke, or from time to time revise, the whole or any part of a code of practice issued under this section; and, where they revise the whole or any part of such a code, they shall issue the revised code, and subsections (2) to (9) shall apply (with appropriate modifications) to such a revised code as they apply to the first issue of a code.

(11) A failure on the part of any person to observe any provision of a code of practice shall not of itself render that person liable to any proceedings; but any code of practice issued under this section shall be admissible in evidence in any legal proceedings, and if any provision of such a code appears to the court or tribunal concerned to be relevant to any question arising in the proceedings it shall be taken into account in determining that question.

(12) Without prejudice to subsection (1), a code of practice issued under this section may include such practical guidance as the Commission think fit as to what steps it is reasonably practicable for persons to take for the purpose of preventing their staff from doing in the course of their duties acts made unlawful by this Act.

71D. General statutory duty: compliance notices

(1) If the Commission are satisfied that a person has failed to comply with, or is failing to comply with, any duty imposed by an order under section 71(2), the Commission may serve on that person a notice ("a compliance notice").

(2) A compliance notice shall require the person concerned—

(a) to comply with the duty concerned; and

(b) to inform the Commission, within 28 days of the date on which the notice is served, of the steps that the person has taken, or is taking, to comply with the duty.

(3) A compliance notice may also require the person concerned to furnish the Commission with such other written information as may be reasonably required by the notice in order to verify that the duty has been complied with.

(4) The notice may specify—

(a) the time (no later than three months from the date on which the notice is served) at which any information is to be furnished to the Commission;

(b) the manner and form in which any such information is to be so furnished.

(5) A compliance notice shall not require a person to furnish information which the person could not be compelled to furnish in evidence in civil proceedings before the High Court or the Court of Session.

71E. Enforcement of compliance notices

(1) The Commission may apply to a designated county court or, in Scotland, a sheriff court for an order requiring a person falling within Schedule 1A to furnish any information required by a compliance notice if—

(a) the person fails to furnish the information to the Commission in accordance with the notice; or

(b) the Commission have reasonable cause to believe that the person does not intend to furnish the information.

(2) If the Commission consider that a person has not, within three months of the date on which a compliance notice was served on that person, complied with any requirement of the notice for that person to comply with a duty imposed by an order under section 71(2), the Commission may apply to a designated county court or, in Scotland, a sheriff court for an order requiring the person to comply with the requirement of the notice.

(3) If the court is satisfied that the application is well-founded, it may grant the order in the terms applied for or in more limited terms.

(4) The sanctions in section 71D and this section shall be the only sanctions for breach of any duty imposed by an order under section 71(2), but without prejudice to the enforcement under section 57 or otherwise of any other provision of this Act (where the breach is also a contravention of that provision).'

(2) Schedule 1 (which inserts Schedule 1A into the 1976 Act) is to have effect.

3. Certain appointment functions outside the employment field

(1) Section 76 of the 1976 Act (government appointments outside the employment field) is amended as follows.

(2) In subsection (1) for 'This section' there is substituted 'Subsection (2)'.

(3) After subsection (2) there is added—

'(3) Subsection (5) applies to—

(a) any recommendation made by a Minister of the Crown or government department in relation to an appointment to an office or post where section 4 does not apply in relation to the appointment; and

(b) any approval given by such a Minister or department in relation to any such appointment.

(4) Subsection (5) also applies to—

(a) any recommendation made by a Minister of the Crown or government department in relation to a conferment by the Crown of a dignity or honour; and

(b) any approval given by such a Minister or department in relation to any such conferment.

(5) In making the recommendation, or giving the approval, and in making the arrangements for determining who should be recommended or approved, the Minister of the Crown or government department shall not do an act which would be unlawful under section 4 if the recommendation or approval were an offer of employment and the Crown were the employer for the purposes of this Act.

(6) Subsections (3) to (5) do not apply in relation to the making of negative recommendations.

(7) Subsection (9) applies to—

(a) any negative recommendation made by a Minister of the Crown or government department, or any refusal to make a recommendation by such a Minister or department, in relation to an appointment to an office or post where section 4 does not apply in relation to the appointment; and

(b) any approval refused by such a Minister or department in relation to any such appointment.

(8) Subsection (9) also applies to—

(a) any negative recommendation made by a Minister of the Crown or government department, or any refusal to make a recommendation by such a Minister or department, in relation to a conferment by the Crown of a dignity or honour; and

(b) any approval refused by such a Minister or department in relation to any such conferment.

(9) In making a negative recommendation or in refusing to make a recommendation or give an approval, and in making the arrangements for determining whether to make such a recommendation or refusal, the Minister of the Crown or government

department shall not do an act which would be unlawful under section 4 if the recommendation or refusal were a refusal to offer the person concerned employment and the Crown were the employer for the purposes of this Act.

(10) Subsection (11) applies in relation to any appointment to an office or post where section 4 does not apply and—

(a) the appointment is made by a Minister of the Crown or government department; or

(b) the office or post is an office or post in relation to which a Minister of the Crown or government department has made a recommendation (other than a negative recommendation) or given an approval.

(11) A Minister of the Crown or government department shall not do an act in connection with—

(a) the terms of the appointment;

(b) access for the person appointed to opportunities for promotion, transfer or training, or to any other benefits, facilities or services; or

(c) the termination of the appointment, or subjecting the person appointed to any other detriment;

which would be unlawful under section 4 if the Crown were the employer for the purposes of this Act.

(12) The High Court may, on an application for judicial review, make a declaration to the effect that a Minister of the Crown or government department has contravened subsection (5), subsection (9) or, in relation to an appointment falling within subsection (10)(b), subsection (11), and may award damages in respect of the contravention.

(13) In Scotland, the Court of Session may, in a petition for judicial review, grant declarator to the like effect and may award damages in respect of the contravention.

(14) The sanctions provided by virtue of the operation of section 53(2) to (4) in relation to this section shall be the only sanctions under this Act in relation to appointments, conferments and other acts to which this section applies.

(15) In this section—

(a) references to refusal include references to deliberate omission;

(b) references to Ministers of the Crown and government departments include references to the National Assembly for Wales and any part of the Scottish Administration; and

(c) references to Ministers of the Crown and government departments so far as they relate to the making of a recommendation or a refusal to make a recommendation, or the giving or refusal of an approval, in relation to a conferment of a peerage for life under section 1 of the Life Peerages Act 1958 include references to any body established by a Minister of the Crown to make such a recommendation to the Prime Minister or to determine whether to give such an approval.'

4. Police: extension of liability of chief officers etc.

After section 76 of the 1976 Act there is inserted—

'*Police*

76A. Police forces

(1) In this section, "relevant police office" means—

(a) the office of constable held—

(i) as a member of a police force; or

(ii) on appointment as a special constable for a police area; or

(b) an appointment as police cadet to undergo training with a view to becoming a member of a police force.

(2) For the purposes of Part II, the holding of a relevant police office shall be treated as employment—

(a) by the chief officer of police as respects any act done by him in relation to that office or a holder of it;

(b) by the police authority as respects any act done by it in relation to that office or a holder of it.

(3) For the purposes of section 32—

(a) the holding of a relevant police office shall be treated as employment by the chief officer of police (and as not being employment by any other person); and

(b) anything done by a person holding such an office in the performance, or purported performance, of his functions shall be treated as done in the course of that employment.

(4) There shall be paid out of the police fund—

(a) any compensation, costs or expenses awarded against a chief officer of police in any proceedings brought against him under this Act, and any costs or expenses incurred by him in any such proceedings so far as not recovered by him in the proceedings; and

(b) any sum required by a chief officer of police for the settlement of any claim made against him under this Act if the settlement is approved by the police authority.

(5) Any proceedings under this Act which, by virtue of this section, would lie against a chief officer of police shall be brought against—

(a) the chief officer of police for the time being; or

(b) in the case of a vacancy in that office, against the person for the time being performing the functions of that office;

and references in subsection (4) to the chief officer of police shall be construed accordingly.

(6) A police authority may, in such cases and to such extent as appear to it to be appropriate, pay out of the police fund—

(a) any damages or costs awarded in proceedings under this Act against a person under the direction and control of the chief officer of police;

(b) any costs incurred and not recovered by such a person in such proceedings; and

(c) any sum required in connection with the settlement of a claim that has or might have given rise to such proceedings.

76B. Other police bodies etc.

(1) Section 76A applies in relation to the National Criminal Intelligence Service ("NCJS") and the National Crime Squad ("the NCS") as it applies in relation to a police force but as if any reference—

(a) to the chief officer of police were to the Director General of NCIS or of the NCS, as the case may be;

(b) to the police authority were to the Service Authority for the National Criminal Intelligence Service or the Service Authority for the National Crime Squad, as the case may be;

(c) to the police fund were to the service fund established under section 16 of the Police Act 1997 (NCIS service fund) or section 61 of that Act (the NCS service fund), as the case may be.

(2) Section 76A also applies in relation to any other body of constables or cadets as it applies in relation to a police force, but as if any reference—

(a) to the chief officer of police were to the officer or other person who has the direction and control of the body in question;

(b) to the police authority were to the authority by whom the members of the body are paid;

(c) to the police fund were to money provided by that authority.

(3) In relation to a member of a police force or a special constable who is not under the direction and control of the chief officer of police for that police force or, as the case may be, for the police area to which he is appointed, references in section 76A to the

chief officer of police are references to the chief officer under whose direction and control he is.'

Special cases: procedural and other consequences

5. Criminal investigations and proceedings

(1) After section 57(4) of the 1976 Act (enforcement of Part III of that Act) there is inserted—

'(4A) As respects an act which is done, or by virtue of section 32 or 33 is treated as done, by a person in carrying out public investigator functions or functions as a public prosecutor and which is unlawful by virtue of section 19B, no remedy other than—

(a) damages; or

(b) a declaration or, in Scotland, a declarator;

shall be obtainable unless the court is satisfied that the remedy concerned would not prejudice a criminal investigation, a decision to institute criminal proceedings or any criminal proceedings.

(4B) In this section—

"criminal investigation" means—

(a) any investigation which a person in carrying out functions to which section 19B applies has a duty to conduct with a view to it being ascertained whether a person should be charged with, or in Scotland prosecuted for, an offence, or whether a person charged with or prosecuted for an offence is guilty of it;

(b) any investigation which is conducted by a person in carrying out functions to which section 19B applies and which in the circumstances may lead to a decision by that person to institute criminal proceedings which the person has power to conduct; or

(c) any investigation which is conducted by a person in carrying out functions to which section 19B applies and which in the circumstances may lead to a decision by that person to make a report to the procurator fiscal for the purpose of enabling him to determine whether criminal proceedings should be instituted; and

"public investigator functions" means functions of conducting criminal investigations or charging offenders;

and in this subsection "offence" includes any offence under the Army Act 1955, the Air Force Act 1955 or the Naval Discipline Act 1957 (and "offender" shall be construed accordingly).

(4C) Subsection (4D) applies where a party to proceedings under subsection (1) which have arisen by virtue of section 19B has applied for a stay or sist of those proceedings on the grounds of prejudice to—

(a) particular criminal proceedings;

(b) a criminal investigation; or

(c) a decision to institute criminal proceedings.

(4D) The court shall grant the stay or sist unless it is satisfied that the continuance of the proceedings under subsection (1) would not result in the prejudice alleged.'

(2) After section 65(4) of the 1976 Act (help for aggrieved persons in obtaining information etc.) there is inserted—

'(4A) In section 19B proceedings, subsection (2)(b) does not apply in relation to a failure to reply, or a particular reply, if the conditions specified in subsection (4B) are satisfied.

(4B) Those conditions are that—

(a) at the time of doing any relevant act, the respondent was carrying out public investigator functions or was a public prosecutor; and

(b) he reasonably believes that a reply or (as the case may be) a different reply would be likely to prejudice any criminal investigation, any decision to institute criminal proceedings or any criminal proceedings or would reveal the reasons behind a decision not to institute, or a decision not to continue, criminal proceedings.

(4C) For the purposes of subsections (4A) and (4B)—

"public investigator functions" has the same meaning as in section 57;

"section 19B proceedings" means proceedings in respect of a claim under section 57 which has arisen by virtue of section 19B.'

6. Immigration and asylum appeals

(1) After section 57(6) of the 1976 Act (enforcement of Part III of that Act) there is added—

'(7) This section has effect subject to section 57A.'

(2) After section 57 of that Act there is inserted—

'57A. Claims under section 19B in immigration cases

(1) No proceedings may be brought by a claimant under section 57(1) in respect of an immigration claim if—

(a) the act to which the claim relates was done in the taking by an immigration authority of a relevant decision and the question whether that act was unlawful by virtue of section 19B has been or could be raised in proceedings on an appeal which is pending, or could be brought, under the 1997 Act or Part IV of the 1999 Act; or

(b) it has been decided in relevant immigration proceedings that that act was not unlawful by virtue of that section.

(2) For the purposes of this section an immigration claim is a claim that a person—

(a) has committed a relevant act of discrimination against the claimant which is unlawful by virtue of section 19B; or

(b) is by virtue of section 32 or 33 to be treated as having committed such an act of discrimination against the claimant.

(3) Where it has been decided in relevant immigration proceedings that an act to which an immigration claim relates was unlawful by virtue of section 19B, any court hearing that claim under section 57 shall treat that act as an act which is unlawful by virtue of section 19B for the purposes of the proceedings before it.

(4) No relevant decision of an immigration authority involving an act to which an immigration claim relates and no relevant decision of an immigration appellate body in relation to such a decision shall be subject to challenge or otherwise affected by virtue of a decision of a court hearing the immigration claim under section 57.

(5) In this section—

"the Immigration Acts" has the same meaning as in the 1999 Act;

"immigration appellate body" means an adjudicator appointed for the purposes of the 1999 Act, the Immigration Appeal Tribunal, the Special Immigration Appeals Commission, the Court of Appeal, the Court of Session or the House of Lords;

"immigration authority" means an authority within the meaning of section 65 of the 1999 Act (human rights and racial discrimination cases);

"immigration claim" has the meaning given by subsection (2) above;

"pending" has the same meaning as in the 1997 Act or, as the case may be, Part IV of the 1999 Act;

"relevant act of discrimination" means an act of discrimination done by an immigration authority in taking any relevant decision;

"relevant decision" means—

(a) in relation to an immigration authority, any decision under the Immigration Acts relating to the entitlement of the claimant to enter or remain in the United Kingdom; and

(b) in relation to an immigration appellate body, any decision on an appeal under the 1997 Act or Part IV of the 1999 Act in relation to a decision falling within paragraph (a);

"relevant immigration proceedings" means proceedings on an appeal under the 1997 Act or Part IV of the 1999 Act;

"the 1997 Act' means the Special Immigration Appeals Commission Act 1997;

"the 1999 Act" means the Immigration and Asylum Act 1999;

and, for the purposes of subsection (1)(a), any power to grant leave to appeal out of time shall be disregarded.'

(3) In section 65(1) of the Immigration and Asylum Act 1999 (acts made unlawful by section 6(1) of the Human Rights Act 1998) after 'United Kingdom,' there is inserted 'racially discriminated against him or'.

(4) In section 65(2) of that Act, after 'Part' there is inserted'—

(a) an authority racially discriminates against a person if he acts, or fails to act, in relation to that other person in a way which is unlawful by virtue of section 19B of the Race Relations Act 1976; and

(b) '.

National security

7. National security

(1) In section 42 of the 1976 Act (exclusion for acts safeguarding national security), at the end there is added 'if the doing of the act was justified by that purpose'.

(2) Section 69(2)(b) of that Act (provision for national security certificates) is omitted.

8. National security: procedure

After section 67 of the 1976 Act there is inserted—

'67A. National security: procedure

(1) Rules may make provision for enabling a court in which relevant proceedings have been brought, where it considers it expedient in the interests of national security—

(a) to exclude from all or part of the proceedings—

(i) the claimant;

(ii) the claimant's representatives; or

(iii) the assessors (if any) appointed by virtue of section 67(4);

(b) to permit a claimant or representative who has been excluded to make a statement to the court before the commencement of the proceedings, or the part of the proceedings, from which he is excluded;

(c) to take steps to keep secret all or part of the reasons for its decision in the proceedings.

(2) The Attorney General or, in Scotland, the Advocate General for Scotland, may appoint a person to represent the interests of a claimant in, or in any part of, any proceedings from which the claimant and his representatives are excluded by virtue of subsection (1).

(3) A person appointed under subsection (2)—

(a) if appointed for the purposes of proceedings in England and Wales, must have a general qualification (within the meaning of section 71 of the Courts and Legal Services Act 1990); and

(b) if appointed for the purposes of proceedings in Scotland, must be—

(i) an advocate; or

(ii) a solicitor who has by virtue of section 25A of the Solicitors (Scotland) Act 1980 rights of audience in the Court of Session or the High Court of Justiciary.

(4) A person appointed under subsection (2) shall not be responsible to the person whose interests he is appointed to represent.

(5) In this section—

"relevant proceedings" means proceedings brought under this Act—
(a) in England and Wales, in a designated county court; or
(b) in Scotland, in a sheriff court; and
"rules" has the same meaning as in section 65.'

Supplementary and final provisions

9. Consequential amendments and repeals

(1) Schedule 2 (which makes further consequential amendments of enactments) is to have effect.

(2) The enactments mentioned in Schedule 3 are repealed to the extent specified there.

10. Short title, commencement and extent

(1) This Act may be cited as the Race Relations (Amendment) Act 2000.

(2) Sections 1 to 9 (including Schedules 1 to 3) shall come into force on such day as the Secretary of State may by order appoint; and different days may be appointed for different purposes.

(3) An order under this section—
(a) shall be made by statutory instrument; and
(b) may make such transitory, transitional or saving provision as the Secretary of State considers appropriate.

(4) Transitory provision made in exercise of the power conferred by subsection (3)(b) may, in particular, include provision made in consequence of any provision of any other Act passed before, or in the same session as, this Act not having come into force.

(5) No amendment by this Act of an enactment shall be taken, for the purposes of the Scotland Act 1998, to be a pre-commencement enactment within the meaning of that Act unless the amendment so provides.

(6) Any amendment or repeal by this Act of an enactment has the same extent as the enactment amended or repealed.

SCHEDULES

SCHEDULE 1
BODIES AND OTHER PERSONS SUBJECT TO GENERAL STATUTORY DUTY

The following Schedule is inserted into the 1976 Act after Schedule 1—

'SCHEDULE 1A
BODIES AND OTHER PERSONS SUBJECT TO GENERAL STATUTORY DUTY

Ministers of the Crown and government departments

1.—(1) A Minister of the Crown or government department.

(2) Sub-paragraph (1) does not include the Security Service, the Intelligence Service or the Government Communications Headquarters.

Scottish Administration

2.—(1) An office-holder in the Scottish Administration within the meaning given by section 126(7)(a) of the Scotland Act 1998.

(2) Members of the staff of the Scottish Administration within the meaning given by section 126(7)(b) of that Act.

National Assembly for Wales

3.—(1) The National Assembly for Wales.

(2) An Assembly subsidiary as defined by section 99(4) of the Government of Wales Act 1998.

Armed forces

4. Any of the naval, military or air forces of the Crown.

National Health Service: England and Wales

5. A Health Authority established under section 8 of the National Health Service Act 1977.

6. A special health authority established under section 11 of that Act.

7. A primary care trust established under section 16A of that Act.

8. A National Health Service trust established under section 5 of the National Health Service and Community Care Act 1990.

National Health Service: Scotland

9. A Health Board constituted under section 2 of the National Health Service (Scotland) Act 1978.

10. A Special Health Board constituted under section 2 of that Act.

11. A National Health Service Trust established under section 12A of that Act.

Local government

12. A local authority within the meaning of the Local Government Act 1972, namely—
(a) in England, a county council, a London borough council, a district council or a parish council;
(b) in Wales, a county council, a county borough council or a community council.

13. A council constituted under section 2 of the Local Government etc. (Scotland) Act 1994.

14. A community council established under section 51 of the Local Government (Scotland) Act 1973.

15. The Greater London Authority.

16. The Common Council of the City of London in its capacity as a local authority or port health authority.

17. The Sub-Treasurer of the Inner Temple or the Under-Treasurer of the Middle Temple, in his capacity as a local authority.

18. The Council of the Isles of Scilly.

19. A parish meeting constituted under section 13 of the Local Government Act 1972.

20. Any charter trustees constituted under section 246 of that Act.

21. A fire authority constituted by a combination scheme under section 5 or 6 of the Fire Services Act 1947.

22. A waste disposal authority established by virtue of an order under section 10(1) of the Local Government Act 1985.

23. A water or sewerage authority constituted under section 62 of the Local Government etc. (Scotland) Act 1994.

24. A port health authority constituted by an order under section 2 of the Public Health (Control of Disease) Act 1984.

25. A licensing planning committee constituted under section 119 of the Licensing Act 1964.

26. A licensing board constituted under section 1 of the Licensing (Scotland) Act 1976.

27. An internal drainage board which is continued in being by virtue of section 1 of the Land Drainage Act 1991.

28. A probation committee constituted under section 3 of the Probation Service Act 1993.

29. A joint authority established under Part IV of the Local Government Act 1985 (fire services, civil defence and transport).

30. A joint board within the meaning of section 235(1) of the Local Government (Scotland) Act 1973.

31. The London Fire and Emergency Planning Authority.

32. A body corporate established pursuant to an order under section 67 of the Local Government Act 1985 (transfer of functions to successors of residuary bodies, etc.).

33. A body corporate established pursuant to an order under section 22 of the Local Government Act 1992 (residuary bodies).

34. The Broads Authority established by section 1 of the Norfolk and Suffolk Broads Act 1988.

35. A joint committee constituted in accordance with section 102(1)(b) of the Local Government Act 1972.

36. A joint board which is continued in being by virtue of section 263(1) of that Act.

37. A joint authority established under section 21 of the Local Government Act 1992.

38. A Passenger Transport Executive for a passenger transport area within the meaning of Part II of the Transport Act 1968.

39. Transport for London.

40. The London Development Agency.

41. A regional development agency established under the Regional Development Agencies Act 1998 (other than the London Development Agency).

42. Scottish Enterprise and Highland and Islands Enterprise, established under the Enterprise and New Towns (Scotland) Act 1990.

43. A National Park authority established by an order under section 63 of the Environment Act 1995.

44. A joint planning board constituted for an area in Wales outside a National Park by an order under section 2(1B) of the Town and Country Planning Act 1990.

45. A magistrates' courts committee established under section 27 of the Justices of the Peace Act 1997.

Other educational bodies

46. Governing bodies of—

(a) educational establishments maintained by local education authorities;

(b) institutions within the further education sector (within the meaning of section 91(3) of the Further and Higher Education Act 1992); or

(c) institutions within the higher education sector (within the meaning of section 91(5) of the Act of 1992).

47. The managers of a grant-aided school (within the meaning of section 135 of the Education (Scotland) Act 1980).

48. The managers of a central institution (within the meaning of section 135 of the Act of 1980).

49. The board of management of a self-governing school (within the meaning of the Self-Governing Schools etc. (Scotland) Act 1989).

50. The board of management of a college of further education (within the meaning of section 36(1) of the Further and Higher Education (Scotland) Act 1992).

51. The governing body of an institution within the higher education sector (within the meaning of Part II of the Further and Higher Education (Scotland) Act 1992).

Other housing bodies

52. The Housing Corporation.

53. Scottish Homes.

54. A housing action trust established under Part III of the Housing Act 1988.

Police

55. A police authority established under section 3 of the Police Act 1996.

56. A police authority established under section 2 of the Police (Scotland) Act 1967.

57. The Metropolitan Police Authority established under section 5B of the Police Act 1996.

58. The Common Council of the City of London in its capacity as a police authority.

59. The Service Authority for the National Criminal Intelligence Service.

60. The Service Authority for the National Crime Squad.'

SCHEDULE 2
CONSEQUENTIAL AMENDMENTS

Race Relations Act 1976 (c. 74)

1. In section 17 of the 1976 Act (prohibition on discrimination by certain education bodies), in the Table—

(a) in paragraph 7 for '73(c) or (d)' there is substituted '73(d)'; and

(b) after paragraph 7 there is inserted—

'7AA. A grant-aided school, within the meaning of section 135 of the Education (Scotland) Act 1980.'	The managers of the school

2. In section 27(1) of the 1976 Act (extent of Part III), for '19' there is substituted '18D'.

3. After section 27(1) of that Act, there is inserted—

'(1A) In its application in relation to granting entry clearance (within the meaning of the Immigration Act 1971) section 19B applies in relation to acts done outside the United Kingdom, as well as those done within Great Britain.'

4. In section 53(1) of that Act (restriction of proceedings for breach of Act), after first 'Act' there is inserted 'or the Special Immigration Appeals Commission Act 1997 or Part IV of the Immigration and Asylum Act 1999'.

5. After section 53(3) of that Act (judicial review to be available for government appointments outside the employment field), there is added—

'(4) Subsections (2) and (3) do not, except so far as provided by section 76, apply to any act which is unlawful by virtue of section 76(5) or (9) or by virtue of section 76(10)(b) and (11).'

6. In section 57(5) of that Act (claims under Part III in relation to certain educational bodies)—

(a) for the words 'section 19(1)' there is substituted 'subsection (5A)'; and

(b) the words from 'and' to the end of the subsection are omitted.

7. After section 57(5) of that Act, there is inserted—

'(5A) This subsection applies to—

(a) local education authorities in England and Wales;

(b) education authorities in Scotland; and

(c) any body which is a responsible body in relation to an establishment falling within paragraph 3, 3B or 7B of the table in section 17.'

8. In section 59(1)(b) of that Act (appeal against non-discrimination notice), after 'the court' there is inserted '(ignoring section 57A)'.

9. In section 62(1) of that Act (persistent discrimination), after 'or' at the end of paragraph (b) there is inserted—

'(ba) a finding under the Special Immigration Appeals Commission Act 1997 or Part IV of the Immigration and Asylum Act 1999 that he has done an act which was unlawful by virtue of section 19B; or'.

10. After section 65(6) of that Act (help for aggrieved persons in obtaining information etc.), there is added—

'(7) This section does not apply in relation to any proceedings under—

(a) the Special Immigration Appeals Commission Act 1997; or

(b) Part IV of the Immigration and Asylum Act 1999.'

11. After section 66(7) of that Act (assistance by Commission), there is added—

'(8) This section (except for subsection (4)) applies to proceedings or prospective proceedings under the Special Immigration Appeals Commission Act 1997 or Part IV of the Immigration and Asylum Act 1999 so far as they relate to acts which may be unlawful by virtue of section 19B as it applies to proceedings or prospective proceedings under this Act.

(9) In this section as it applies by virtue of subsection (8) "rules and regulations" means—

(a) in relation to proceedings under the Act of 1997, rules under section 5 or 8 of that Act;

(b) in relation to proceedings under Part IV of the Act of 1999, rules under paragraph 3 or 4 of Schedule 4 to that Act.'

12. After section 67(3) of that Act (extension of jurisdiction of county courts and sheriff courts), there is inserted—

'(3A) A designated county court or a sheriff court shall have jurisdiction to entertain proceedings under this Act with respect to an act done outside the United Kingdom where section 19B applies in relation to such an act by virtue of section 27(1A).'

13. In section 68(2) of that Act (period within which proceedings to be brought), at the beginning there is inserted 'Subject to subsection (2A)'.

14. After section 68(2) of that Act, there is inserted—

'(2A) In relation to an immigration claim within the meaning of section 57A, the period of six months mentioned in subsection (2)(a) begins on the expiry of the period during which, by virtue of section 57A(1)(a), no proceedings may be brought under section 57(1) in respect of the claim.'

15. In section 69(2) of that Act (evidence), after 'Act' there is inserted 'or any enactment mentioned in section 19D(5)'.

16. In section 73(1)(b) of that Act (power to amend certain provisions of Act), after 'or (2),' there is inserted '19B,'.

17. After section 75(2) of that Act (application to Crown etc.), there is inserted—

'(2A) Subsections (1) and (2) do not apply in relation to the provisions mentioned in subsection (2B).

(2B) Sections 19B to 19F, sections 71 to 71E (including Schedule 1A) and section 76 bind the Crown; and the other provisions of this Act so far as they relate to those provisions shall be construed accordingly (including, in particular, references to employment in Part IV).'

18. In section 75(3) of that Act—

(a) for 'and (2)' there is substituted 'to (2B)'; and

(b) for 'section 16' there is substituted 'sections 76A and 76B'.

19. In section 78(1) of that Act (general interpretation provisions), at the appropriate places, there are inserted—

'"body" includes an unincorporated association;'

'"criminal investigation" has the meaning given by section 57(4B);' and

'"criminal proceedings" includes—

(a) proceedings on dealing summarily with a charge under the Army Act 1955 or the Air Force Act 1955 or on summary trial under the Naval Discipline Act 1957;

(b) proceedings before a summary appeal court constituted under any of those Acts;

(c) proceedings before a court-martial constituted under any of those Acts or a disciplinary court constituted under section 52G of the Act of 1957;

(d) proceedings before the Courts-Martial Appeal Court; and

(e) proceedings before a Standing Civilian Court;'.

Local Government Act 1988 (c. 9)

20. In section 18(1) of the Local Government Act 1988 (race relations matters)—

(a) for the words from '71' to 'regard to' there is substituted '71(1) of the Race Relations Act 1976 and any duty imposed by an order under section 71(2) of that Act (duties relating to the'; and

(b) for 'local authority' there is substituted 'public authority to which section 17 above applies'.

21. In section 18(2) of that Act—

(a) for 'local authority' there is substituted 'public authority to which that section applies'; and

(b) for '71' there is substituted '71(1) or any duty imposed by an order under the said section 71(2)'.

22. Section 18(7A) of that Act is omitted.

Special Immigration Appeals Commission Act 1997 (c. 68)

23. In section 2A(1) of the Special Immigration Appeals Commission Act 1997 (jurisdiction: human rights), after 'appealable decision,' there is inserted 'racially discriminated against him or'.

24. In section 2A(2) of that Act, after 'this section,' there is inserted'—

(a) an authority racially discriminates against a person if he acts, or fails to act, in relation to that other person in a way which is unlawful by virtue of section 19B of the Race Relations Act 1976; and

(b) '.

25. In section 2A(3) of that Act, after 'the proceedings,' there is inserted 'racially discriminated against the appellant or'.

26. In section 2A(5) of that Act—

(a) after 'concerned' there is inserted'—

(a) racially discriminated against the appellant; or

(b) '; and

(b) for 'that ground' there is substituted 'the ground in question'.

27. In the side note to section 2A of that Act, after 'Jurisdiction:' there is inserted 'racial discrimination and'.

28. In section 5 of that Act (procedure in relation to jurisdiction under section 2 of that Act etc.)—

(a) in subsection (1)(a) after '2' there is inserted 'or 2A';

(b) in subsection (1)(b) for 'that section' there is substituted 'section 2 or 2A above'; and

(c) in subsection (2) after '2' there is inserted 'or 2A'.

29. In Schedule 2 to that Act (appeals: supplementary)—

(a) in paragraph 4 after '2' there is inserted 'or 2A'; and

(b) in paragraphs 6 and 7 after '2' there is inserted 'and 2A'.

School Standards and Framework Act 1998 (c. 31)

30. In paragraph 8(b) of Schedule 4 to the School Standards and Framework Act 1998 (school organisation committees to have regard to certain obligations owed by local education authorities and governing bodies under the Race Relations Act 1976), after 'Part III' there shall be inserted 'or section 71'.

31. In paragraph 6(b) of Schedule 5 to the Act of 1998 (adjudicators to have regard to certain obligations owed by local education authorities and governing bodies under the Race Relations Act 1976), after 'Part III' there shall be inserted 'or section 71'.

Immigration and Asylum Act 1999 (c.33)

32. In section 65(3) of the Immigration and Asylum Act 1999 (acts made unlawful by section 6(1) of the Human Rights Act 1998), after 'Kingdom,' there is inserted 'racially discriminated against the appellant or'.

33. In section 65(5) of the Act of 1999—

(a) after 'concerned' there is inserted'—

(a) racially discriminated against the appellant; or

(b) '; and

(b) for 'that ground' there is substituted 'the ground in question'.

34. For the side-note to section 65 of that Act, there is substituted 'Racial discrimination and breach of human rights.'

35. In section 72(2)(a) of that Act (miscellaneous limitations on rights of appeal), after 'rights' there is inserted 'or racially discriminated against him'.

36. In section 73(2) of that Act (limitation on further appeals), after 'a claim that' there is inserted 'in taking a decision, a decision-maker racially discriminated against the appellant or that'.

37. In section 74(7) of that Act (duty to disclose grounds for appeal etc.), after paragraph (a) there is inserted—

'(aa) if he claims that he was racially discriminated against, include notice of that claim;'.

38. In section 76(3)(a) of that Act (result of failure to give statement of additional grounds for appeal), for 'breached the applicant's' there is substituted 'racially discriminated against the applicant or breached his'.

39. In Schedule 4 to that Act (appeals), in paragraph 9(2) for the words 'that the claim is one to which this paragraph applies' there is substituted 'with the opinion expressed in the Secretary of State's certificate'.

40. In that Schedule to that Act, after paragraph 9 there is inserted—

'Racial discrimination

9A.—(1) This paragraph applies to an appeal under Part IV of this Act by a person who claims that he has been racially discriminated against, if the Secretary of State has certified that, in his opinion, the claim is manifestly unfounded.

(2) If, on an appeal to which this paragraph applies, the adjudicator agrees with the opinion expressed in the Secretary of State's certificate, paragraph 22 does not confer on the appellant any right to appeal to the Immigration Appeal Tribunal.'

SCHEDULE 3
REPEALS

Chapter	Short title	Extent of repeal
1976 c. 74.	Race Relations Act 1976.	Section 16. Section 19. Section 19ZA. In section 57(5), the words from 'and' to the end of the subsection. Section 58(6). In section 68, subsection (2)(b) and the word 'or' immediately preceding it and, in subsection (3), the words 'or, as the case may be, eight' and 'or (b)'. In section 69, subsection (2)(b) and the word 'or' immediately preceding it and subsection (2A).
1980 c. 44.	Education (Scotland) Act 1980.	In Schedule 4, paragraph 14.
1985 c. 51.	Local Government Act 1985.	In Schedule 13, paragraph 13(h). In Schedule 14, paragraph 54.
1985 c. 69.	Housing Associations Act 1985.	Section 75(5).
1988 c. 4.	Norfolk and Suffolk Broads Act 1988.	In Schedule 6, paragraph 16.
1988 c. 9.	Local Government Act 1988.	Section 18(7A).

Chapter	Short title	Extent of repeal
1988 c. 40.	Education Reform Act 1988.	In Schedule 12, paragraphs 19 and 79.
1988 c. 43.	Housing (Scotland) Act 1988.	Section 2(11).
1988 c. 50.	Housing Act 1988.	Sections 56 and 63(5).
1989 c. 39.	Self-Governing Schools etc. (Scotland) Act 1989.	In Schedule 10, paragraph 6(3).
1992 c. 13.	Further and Higher Education Act 1992.	In Schedule 8, paragraph 88.
1992 c. 37.	Further and Higher Education (Scotland) Act 1992.	In Schedule 9, paragraph 5(4).
1994 c. 19.	Local Government (Wales) Act 1994.	In Schedule 13, paragraph 20(g).
1994 c. 29.	Police and Magistrates' Courts Act 1994.	In Schedule 4, paragraph 51.
1994 c. 30.	Education Act 1994.	In Schedule 2, paragraph 6(4).
1994 c. 39.	Local Government etc. (Scotland) Act 1994.	In Schedule 13, paragraph 108.
1995 c. 25.	Environment Act 1995.	In Schedule 8, paragraph 8(4). In Schedule 10, paragraph 15(2).
1996 c. 16.	Police Act 1996.	In Schedule 7, paragraphs 1(2)(l) and 31.
1996 c. 56.	Education Act 1996.	In Schedule 37, paragraph 42 and, in paragraph 117(4), paragraph (b) and the word 'and' immediately preceding it.
1997 c. 50.	Police Act 1997.	In Schedule 9, paragraphs 35 and 36.
1998 c. 38.	Government of Wales Act 1998.	In Schedule 16, paragraph 30.
1999 c. 26.	Employment Relations Act 1999.	In Schedule 8, paragraph 6.
1999 c. 29.	Greater London Authority Act 1999.	Section 391.
2000 c. 21.	Learning and Skills Act 2000.	In Schedule 9, paragraph 10.

Appendix 2
Key Hansard debates

This is a selection of some of the statements made by introducing ministers and some of the more lively debates during the passage of the Race Relations (Amendment) Act 2000. The extracts are given section by section in the following format:

Place, [Stage]
Hansard reference
Speaker: text

INTRODUCTION

Aims of the Act

House of Lords, Second Reading Debate
Hansard HL, 14 December 1999, col. 128
Lord Bassam of Brighton

The Bill significantly updates the Race Relations Act 1976 for the first time in almost 25 years. . . . it is a significant part, but only one aspect, of our wider equality agenda. We want to transform Britain into a society that is inclusive and prosperous, eliminating unjustified discrimination wherever it exists. Making equality of opportunity a reality for all is very much at the heart of our agenda. It is not only inherently right but also essential for Britain's economic and social success. Our aim is to provide the right legislative and administrative framework to achieve just this. . . .

The Bill has three main purposes: to extend the Race Relations Act in relation to public authorities; to make chief officers of police vicariously liable for acts of racial discrimination by police officers; and to amend an exemption under the Act for acts done for the purposes of safeguarding national security, thus remedying a provision that we think is incompatible with the European Convention on Human Rights. The first two proposals implement a government commitment made in response to one of the key recommendations of the report of the inquiry into the death of Stephen Lawrence. The report recommended, among other things, that the Race Relations Act should be extended to the police and that chief officers of police should be made vicariously liable for acts of racial discrimination by police officers. When the report was published, the Government said that they would go further and are now doing so. We are extending provisions of the Act not only to the police but also to the functions of other public authorities. . . . that are not currently covered. The Bill therefore tackles gaps in coverage which were left when the 1976 Act was introduced, or which have been found through the case law. The Commission for Racial Equality, in its third review of the Race Relations Act, also recommended that the Act should be extended in respect of public services, as, indeed, did the Better Regulation Task Force. So I am pleased to say that the Bill also meets a commitment made by the Government in response to both the CRE and the Better Regulation Task Force.

Context of the Act

House of Lords, Second Reading Debate
Hansard HL, 14 December 1999, col. 155
Lord Desai

Over the past 23 years, and especially over the past three or four years, people's awareness of still persistent racism has deepened. We must remember that the re-igniting of the Stephen Lawrence case was carried out by the Daily Mail, a newspaper normally thought to be right wing. Tabloids in this country no longer condone any form of racism; they are clearly anti-racist. As has been said by many noble Lords, we have all been shocked by the Stephen Lawrence case. However, my shock stems from the fact that no one seems to have been punished as a consequence of what we found out about the Stephen Lawrence case. . . . It is also shocking that murders of black or Asian teenagers must be dragged over many years into newspapers, petitions and so on in order to attain redress for grievances. Perhaps I may refer to the Ricky Reel case and the Satpal Ram case — his was not a murder case but he is in gaol. I believe that we shall not rid ourselves of racism in this country until parents of black and Asian teenagers and black and Asian teenagers themselves feel that they can achieve justice without the need to undergo the long haul of petitions, meetings, newspaper articles and so on. Far too many people who die in police custody are black or Asian, and I believe that that has not been properly investigated. I do not own a car but I am told that if you own a fancy car and if you are black, there is a high probability that you will be stopped by the police. Why should that be? If you are travelling late at night, look out of your car window. If a car has been stopped by the kerb, there is a 98 per cent chance that the driver will be black. At the end of this process, I should like to see established not simply a legal structure but a climate of equality so that the first, second and third generations of black and Asian people feel at home in this country. That is the challenge which we all face.

'Institutional Racism' and the Macpherson Inquiry

House of Lords, Second Reading Debate
Hansard HL, 14 December 1999, col. 148
Baroness Howells of St Davids

The history of racism is something of which we should be ashamed but from which we must learn. I distinguish racism from prejudice. I have always maintained that prejudice in an individual can be dealt with fairly easily, either through experience or education; or it can be ignored. But prejudice in an institution cannot be ignored. Racism in an institution is more pernicious than mere prejudice. Racism is the application of prejudice with power. Prejudice plus power is a dangerous combination. It was that combination of prejudice plus power that helped to capture, transport and sell my African ancestors into slavery in the new world. . . . The slave trade was institutionalised. We may have abolished slavery but we are still affected by the structures within our institutions which allowed such an abhorrence to flourish for so long. . . . [T]he black community rank Neville and Doreen Lawrence with the likes of Mahatma Gandhi and Nelson Mandela. They all share the ability to communicate their suffering to the world. Every mother and father, every brother and sister, black or white, all felt their pain and their anger. I would say that the murder of their son may become as significant historically as the murder of Martin Luther King.

The inquiry into Stephen's murder introduced institutional racism into the wider domain. The media have brought it to our attention. Some have argued that the concept of institutional racism was plucked out of the air by Sir William Macpherson earlier this year. But the concept of institutional racism is nothing new. As the Lawrence inquiry report pointed out, the noble and learned Lord, Lord Scarman, in his presentation to Parliament of his report into the Brixton disorders addressed that issue in 1981. In that important report, the noble and learned Lord responded to the suggestion that Britain is an institutionally racist society by saying:

> 'If by [institutionally racist] it is meant that [Britain] is a society which knowingly, as a matter of policy, discriminates against black people, I reject that allegation. If, however, the suggestion being made is that practices may be adopted by public bodies as well as private individuals which are unwittingly discriminatory against black people, then this is an allegation which deserves serious consideration, and where proved, swift remedy'.

The failure of the police and the CPS to assist the Lawrence family proved beyond all doubt that unwitting institutional racism has not been given serious consideration or swift remedy. Sadly, it has taken 18 years since the report of the noble and learned Lord, Lord Scarman, for this House to consider the issue seriously. The Bill is the Government's promised legislative response to the report of the Stephen Lawrence inquiry. Much credit is due to the Government for setting up the inquiry in the first place and to the Home Secretary for putting a comprehensive action plan in place to take forward its recommendations. There has been real progress in the 25 years since the Race Relations Act was passed, but the murder of Stephen Lawrence has given us the impetus to update the Act and give it more teeth.

House of Lords, Second Reading Debate
Hansard HL, 14 December 1999, col. 151
The Lord Bishop of Oxford

The murder of Stephen Lawrence and what the Macpherson inquiry revealed about the failure to bring his killers to justice was a turning point — and will be seen as such by future historians — in the history of policing in this country. The Macpherson inquiry revealed something terribly wrong not just with the police but with society as a whole, including the Church. The right reverend Prelate the Bishop of Birmingham, speaking in your Lordships' House on 15th April, said:

> 'It is about far more than the terrible death of Stephen Lawrence and all that ensued; about far more than the Metropolitan Police, or policing in general in this country. It is about an issue that affects all of us, because it affects the whole of British society: the cancer of racism. The basic moral question before us is this: are we ready to own up to that cancer, not as someone else's responsibility, but as ours?' — [Official Report, 15/4/99; col. 868.]

INDIRECT DISCRIMINATION

The Government's initial rationale for not including indirect discrimination in the Bill

House of Lords, Second Reading Debate
Hansard HL, 14 December 1999, col. 130
Lord Bassam of Brighton

My Lords, I anticipate that your Lordships will be interested to know why the Government are proposing that the new section should cover direct discrimination and victimisation but not indirect discrimination. The Government did not take this decision lightly. We reached it for many of the reasons that we concluded that it would have been inappropriate to include indirect discrimination in the Northern Ireland Act 1998 when that legislation was before us in the second parliamentary Session . . . [D]irect discrimination is where a person treats a person less favourably than he treats or would treat other people. Indirect discrimination is treatment that may be described as equal in a formal sense but that is discriminatory in its effect on a particular group. It occurs when a requirement or condition is applied equally to all, but the proportion of one group that can comply is considerably smaller than the proportion of another group that can comply.

To outlaw indirect discrimination in all the functions to be newly covered by the Act would have uncertain and potentially far-reaching effects on the Government's ability to make policy. Any policy or practice that had a differential impact on different racial groups because of a requirement or condition could be challenged in the courts. That could potentially include any age-based policy because of the different demographic profiles of different racial groups, and also any regional policy because of the different regional spread of different racial groups. Not least, challenges could be mounted to those policies that are helping individuals from ethnic minority communities the most. The Government are working to ensure that discriminatory policy-making and practice must stop. But we believe that the most effective way of ensuring this is to retain the flexibility necessary to pursue policies which can benefit ethnic minorities and others without the risk of frequent and counter-productive challenges in the courts while obliging public authorities to tackle unjustifiable discriminatory practices through the promotion of race equality. That means, for example, consulting those affected by policy proposals and monitoring the differential impact of policy on different groups so that unexpected, unjustifiable outcomes can be remedied. As announced in the Government's equality Statement, we are pursuing this administratively and are committed to placing a statutory duty on public authorities to promote equality as soon as parliamentary time permits.

Parliamentary debate as to the refusal to include indirect discrimination in the Bill

Almost every speaker in the House of Lords Second Reading Debate expressed concern at the fact that the Bill did not extend to indirect discrimination — see, for example, Lord Cope, Hansard HL, 14 December 1999 col. 137; Lord Lester, Hansard HL, 14 December 1999 col. 141; Baroness Howells, Hansard HL, 14 December 1999 col. 150; Lord Avebury, Hansard HL, 14 December 1999 col. 159; Lord Ahmed, Hansard HL, 14 December 1999 col. 165; Lord Dholakia, Hansard HL, 14 December 1999 col. 169. The following extracts provide a flavour of the arguments advanced.

(i) General criticism

House of Lords, Second Reading Debate
Hansard HL, 14 December 1999, col. 134
Lord Cope of Berkeley

The first, and much the most significant, is the limitation of a large part of the Bill to direct discrimination and victimisation; in other words, the omission of indirect discrimination. The Macpherson report indicated that what went wrong was primarily connected to indirect discrimination rather than direct discrimination and victimisation. However, it is also arguable how far what went wrong was due to sheer incompetence. In any case, as a supposed reaction to the report, it seems to me that the Bill fails, or certainly it falls short.

In practice, these days, most racial discrimination is indirect. Employers do not say, 'I am not employing you because you are black'. They know better than that. It is all much more subtle and indirect. Similarly, no constable is going to say, 'I'm stopping and searching you because you are black'. It is the overall pattern of stop and search which matters in this respect. That is what we need to look at. Clearly, the pattern of stopping and searching should mirror the likelihood of offences and the chances of success in preventing them or of bringing offenders to justice. It is those considerations which should make a policeman stop and search a particular suspect, not a fear of later arguments based on other factors.

The Home Office very helpfully published last week some statistics on race and the criminal justice system, including the use of stop and search powers. The statistics covered up to the year 1998–99. Among other things the statistics allow us to see the effect in terms of arrests of the stopping and searching of white people by comparison with black people or those of Asian or other ethnic minority groups. That is not the whole picture, but the statistics help us to understand the reality. There is considerable variation across the country between the different forces, but in England and Wales as a whole, there were just over 1 million stops in 1998–99. Of those, roughly 865,000 were white people. Of those whites, 11 per cent were arrested and followed up. Of the 95,000 black people who were stopped, 13 per cent were arrested. Of the 51,000 Asians who were stopped, 12 per cent were arrested. Of the 10,000 other ethnic minority groups, 14 per cent were arrested. In the Metropolitan Police the number of arrests of white and black people who were stopped was the same for both categories, at 13 per cent. In the West Midlands a slightly higher percentage of whites who were stopped were arrested — 13 per cent, compared with 12 per cent for black people. I find those figures, as far as they go, somewhat reassuring by comparison with some of the points that are made on this subject. But my point today is that I cannot see the Bill improving the situation, or the appreciation of the situation by the people involved.

House of Lords, Second Reading Debate
Hansard HL, 14 December 1999, col. 140
Lord Lester of Herne Hill

The Stephen Lawrence inquiry recommended that the full force of the race relations legislation should apply to all police officers. In his action plan, the Home Secretary stated that the Government had accepted that recommendation, and went further, saying:

> 'All public services are to be brought within the scope of race discrimination legislation'.

What Mr Straw did not say was that public services were to be brought within the scope of only half of the concept of unlawful racial discrimination: only direct, and not indirect discrimination.

By creating an exception for indirect racial discrimination by public authorities, including the police service, the Bill discriminates between the public sector and the private sector. Indirect racial discrimination is, as the Minister has explained, unfair treatment resulting from a rule or practice applied equally to everyone, in a formal sense, but which has a disproportionate and unjustified adverse impact upon a particular racial group. Instead of having a greater responsibility because of the public nature of its vital functions, under the Bill much of the public service is to be less legally responsible. It is to be immunised from the statutory duty to justify indirectly discriminatory practices to individuals affected, the courts and the CRE. A building society, a bank, a professional organisation, a security firm, a local authority or, in some circumstances, a government agency has, under Section 20, read with Section (1)(1)(b) of the 1976 Act, to justify indirectly discriminatory practices where they are concerned with providing services or facilities to the public or a section of the public. But under the Bill it will not be unlawful for Ministers, their officials, the police and immigration services, Her Majesty's Customs and Excise, the Inland Revenue, the Benefits Agency and other public authorities to operate practices and procedures which have a disproportionate adverse impact on ethnic minorities and which cannot be justified. The victims of indirect discrimination by the public sector will remain unprotected. For example, British Muslims, who cannot obtain a remedy for religious discrimination, will not be protected against indirect racial discrimination by public authorities in providing services stemming from hostility to Islam. . . . .

By clothing themselves and their departments with the immunity from liability for indirect racial discrimination, Ministers are judges in their own cause. They seek to be immune, not for reasons of principle but for administrative convenience. The problems suggested by the Minister about policy-making are, with respect, fanciful and unreal. There is no reason whatever why regional policies and policies related to a person's age cannot be objectively justified. If, under the Bill, decisions about national security need to be justified, why on earth should other less serious policy decisions not also need to be justified? I submit that the police service, the Government and other public authorities should be brought fully under the Race Relations Act, as the Macpherson inquiry envisaged.

House of Lords, Second Reading Debate
Hansard HL, 14 December 1999, col. 153
The Lord Bishop of Oxford

The Minister, in presenting the Bill, said that the Government had seriously considered the possibility of including indirect racism, but had decided not to do so because of the uncertain and far-reaching effect on government policy. . . . I do not believe that that is a good enough reason for not including such a provision in the Bill. The reason why the issue is so crucial is that Richard Stone, who was a member of the Macpherson inquiry, said,

> 'We found no evidence of direct racism. What we did find was indirect racial discrimination'.

If that is so and the Bill does not include discrimination by public authorities within its scope, a serious question arises. Would the Bill, had it been enacted before the murder of Stephen Lawrence, have been able to bring to book those who were in fact responsible for the failure of the investigation of the murder of Stephen Lawrence?

House of Lords, Second Reading Debate
Hansard HL, 14 December 1999, col. 163
Baroness Whitaker

To use another of the Home Secretary's phrases, it is not direct discrimination that holds up the 'building of an anti-racist society', but part of our culture that is often unacknowledged — unconscious attitudes flowing, no doubt, from a series of historical events. Those attitudes are the main underlying reason why people from visible ethnic minorities are treated unfairly and have unequal opportunities. It shows in the employment figures where those with higher qualifications are still two or three times more likely to be unemployed if they are black. And the position is getting worse according to the latest TUC figures. It shows in school attainment figures, so closely linked to teacher expectations. It shows in different and more custodial mental health treatment for black patients. And it shows in the criminal justice system in different patterns of sentencing. Those are the symptoms of institutional racism — specific groups of people defined by their race getting a worse deal from public services, and the cause is indirect discrimination. The Bill can do something about it, taking on board the reservations of my noble friend the Minister. We can work on that in Committee and it would be a milestone to achieve full coverage.

House of Lords, Second Reading Debate
Hansard HL, 14 December 1999, col. 170
Lord Dholakia

The chairman of the commission, Sir Herman Ouseley, who is shortly to retire from his post, has this to say:

> 'By leaving out indirect discrimination, what the Lawrence enquiry termed unwitting racism, we fear that it will increasingly weaken the ability of the CRE to help in tackling the very issue that the report highlighted'.

By concentrating on direct discrimination, the commission would be unable to launch investigations into areas such as the disproportionate number of black people who are stopped and searched by the police . . . The policing and criminal justice issues are very important. They are at the heart of our democratic society . . . Police have wide powers which, if they are misused, affect the lives of ordinary people. By excluding indirect discrimination, we are giving a message that it is perfectly lawful for the police to convert ways of using their powers to the disadvantage of people — in particular ethnic minorities — as long as they do not make their racism explicit. I do not believe that the Government intended such a message to be conveyed for the simple reason that they have a fairly good track record on race relations. Unfortunately, it is not the intent that I question but the effects of the Bill, about which we are all concerned. Call it 'sham' or call it 'shame', either word clearly describes the inadequacy of the legislation before us. On the day of the Queen's Speech, Paul Wilson, chair of the National Black Police Officers Association, said at his conference that in his experience most police officers are now very careful not to discriminate directly. If that is correct, then black and Asian people will be left with no redress when they believe that police policies — formal or informal — have resulted in them receiving unfair treatment. It is important to recognise that this perception exists — and the present Bill will reinforce that feeling.

House of Lords, Second Reading Debate
Hansard HL, 14 December 1999, col. 172
Lord Dholakia

Consider a black prisoner who believes that prison officers are treating him and other prisoners, on a wing where there is a disproportionately high number of black prisoners, more harshly than they treat other prisoners. While on these simple facts it would seem right that the prisoner could bring proceedings under the Race Relations Act, that may not be the case as there are a number of variables that need to be considered. If this treatment occurs in the context of the Prison Service providing 'services' to prisoners — that is, meeting daily living requirements, seeing to medical needs, providing education or recreational opportunities — under the existing provisions in Section 20, the prisoner could challenge his treatment as either direct discrimination, because he is black, or as indirect discrimination, because he is on a wing that is predominantly black. If this treatment occurs as part of the Prison Service's functions to maintain prison discipline and to inflict punishment, then the prisoner would need to rely on the new Clause 19B in the Bill, but he would be able to bring proceedings only if his claim was one of direct discrimination. It is hard to envisage how the prisoner would be able to make these fairly sophisticated assessments of his circumstances, which he will continue to read as racism directed against him.

If the prisoner were a Muslim who considered that he or she was being unfairly treated because of his or her religion or a wish to comply with certain observances that are part of the Muslim faith, the Bill would exclude any prospect of challenge or redress since, under the law at present, it is only in reliance on the indirect discrimination provisions of the Race Relations Act that religious discrimination can be challenged. In other words, Muslims are excluded substantially from certain provisions of the Act.

Let us consider a scenario very like that presented to the Stephen Lawrence inquiry as it heard evidence from ethnic minority communities across the country. Mr and Mrs A are an Asian family living on a housing estate where there is a high proportion of black and Asian households. Mr A reports to the police that he and his wife have been victims of a racist incident involving verbal abuse and assault. He identifies the perpetrators as two white youths who live on a different estate on the other side of the main road. When taking down his address, the police officer makes a comment about Mr A's estate as one that is causing the police too much bother; people always complaining for no reason. After a few days the police come to Mr and Mrs A's house, push their way in, roughly grab Mr A and arrest him for assault on one of the youths he had named as his attacker. One of the police officers says, 'You on this estate may look innocent but you are always causing trouble. This estate always breeds troublemakers'. After the CPS decline to prosecute Mr A, he is determined to complain under the Race Relations Act about his treatment by the police. Under existing law, the *Farah* case could enable him to complain under the Race Relations Act about his treatment as a victim of crime. He would need an amendment to the Bill to complain about his arrest. Was his treatment on the grounds of being Asian or because he lived on that estate? If it was the latter, he could not challenge what he was convinced was racially discriminatory treatment. The Home Office this week published statistics under Section 95 of the Criminal Justice Act that again show disproportionate rates of stop and search. Many speakers have dealt with that issue . . . It would be tragic if we were to miss this opportunity for ensuring that our institutions — in this case public institutions — are protected because we have failed to deal with the crucial omission of indirect discrimination.

House of Lords, Second Reading Debate
Hansard HL, 14 December 1999, col. 179
Lord Lester of Herne Hill

If it is the case that a public authority is imposing a requirement or condition which hits disproportionately at members of a particular ethnic group, is to the detriment of an individual member of that group and is unjustifiable, what is the policy reason why government Ministers and public authorities should not be under exactly the same duty to justify as the Bar Council, my chambers, the City, local authorities, education bodies, housing authorities, or any other institution? I do not understand the policy reason for shielding the Minister and his colleagues from scrutiny by the independent authority of the courts and the CRE.

(ii) Inability of the Commission for Racial Equality to tackle indirect discrimination strategically if it was excluded from the Bill

House of Lords, Second Reading Debate
Hansard HL, 14 December 1999, col. 141
Lord Lester of Herne Hill

[If indirect discrimination is excluded from the Bill] [t]he CRE will be unable to use its strategic law enforcement powers to tackle indirectly discriminatory practices and procedures in key public sector functions, because, unless such discrimination is direct, it will be outside the scope of the Bill. That is a particularly serious defect. The CRE has conducted several important formal investigations into unlawful indirect discrimination covered by the 1976 Act. Its practical experience demonstrates the value of the CRE's power to issue non-discrimination notices; for example, in the allocation of local authority housing in Tower Hamlets and in my own borough of Southwark, or in threatening to issue a non-discrimination notice unless an unlawful discriminatory practice is eliminated. The CRE has no such power unless a practice is unlawful. Under the Bill, indirect discriminatory practices by public authorities are not made unlawful, so the CRE will continue to lack a crucial investigative power in that area. Because of the immunity to be given to indirect discrimination by public authorities, there will also be much legal uncertainty and unnecessary litigation about opaque distinctions between what is direct and what is indirect discrimination by public authorities, about what discrimination (direct or indirect) by public authorities is already forbidden by Section 20 of the 1976 Act; and about the effects of the Bill on the recently recognised common law principle that public authorities must provide equal treatment to the public without discrimination (*Matadeen* v *Pointu* [1998] 3 WLR 18 (PC)).

(iii) Fact that indirect discrimination had been litigated without difficulty under the 1976 Act and the Sex Discrimination Act; and overlap with section 20 of the 1976 Act

House of Lords, Second Reading Debate
Hansard HL, 14 December 1999, col. 142
Lord Lester of Herne Hill

Both the Race Relations Act and the Sex Discrimination Act already apply the concept of indirect as well as direct discrimination, not only to the employment field but also to public authorities and private bodies, in education and housing, and in the provision of goods, facilities and services to the public or a section of the public. We are not aware of any complaint that has ever been made that the operation of the concept of indirect discrimination in any of these areas is unworkable or unfair. I should be grateful if the Minister would tell the House whether he and his department have any evidence that it has operated in a harmful way. Section 20 outlaws direct or indirect discrimination in the provision of certain services by public authorities. If a service falls within Section 20, it must be provided without direct or indirect discrimination. If it falls outside Section 20 but within the proposed new Section 19B, it must be provided without direct discrimination but it will not be unlawful if it is indirectly and unfairly discriminatory in its impact on ethnic minorities. Unless the Bill is amended, much needless confusion and costly uncertainty will arise, both because of the inevitable overlap in many cases between direct and indirect discrimination and because, by not applying the law to indirect discrimination by public authorities, it will remain necessary to revisit complex case law based on obscure and elusive distinctions as to whether a public authority is or is not providing services to the public within the meaning of Section 20 of the 1976 Act. . . . It is entirely fortuitous whether a function of a public body falls within or outside Section 20. It is quite ridiculous — I understate my indignation — for the concept of unlawful discrimination to depend upon making such an artificial distinction based upon an uncertain legal test in circumstances where the factual issues about purpose and effect will often be tangled together. It is difficult to imagine how vulnerable people — the alleged victims of institutional racism by the police, prison, immigration or social services — could reasonably be expected to untangle the legal and factual knots. Disentangling those knots will simply add to the legal costs of employing counsel like myself.

(iv) Argument that to exclude indirect discrimination would constitute a violation of the Human Rights Act, European Community law and other human rights instruments

House of Lords, Second Reading Debate
Hansard HL, 14 December 1999, col. 179
Lord Lester of Herne Hill

The Minister has certified under Section 19 of the Human Rights Act 1998 his view, which is no doubt based on legal advice, that the Bill's provisions comply with the human rights convention. Will the Minister inform the House, either now or in writing, as to whether the concept of discrimination contained in the European Convention on Human Rights covers indirect as well as direct discrimination? If it does, as I believe is indicated in case law, how can the Minister possibly make a statement under Section 19 that the legislation complies with the convention if it will authorise breaches of Article 14 of the convention, read with Article 5 in relation to police powers and Article 6 in relation to access to justice? Will the Minister be kind enough to consider the second question and let me have a view in writing? So far as concerns the question of policy justification, I should be grateful if he would illustrate that now.

House of Lords, Committee Stage
Hansard HL, 11 January 2000, col. 538
Lord Lester of Herne Hill

Your Lordships will be aware that the case law of the European Convention on Human Rights and the European Court of Justice makes it clear that the concept of discrimination in convention and Community Law is not limited to direct discrimination. Both recognise that there may be situations in which disguised or indirect discrimination may arise and may need to be justified. Accordingly, any limitation in the extensions to be made by the Bill to the Act to 'direct' discrimination or victimisation are likely to rub up against either Community or convention law sooner or later. In those circumstances, Mr Allen says:

'unless the limitation is itself objectively justified, the provisions of the Act (so amended) will have to give way sooner or later to these superior sources of law'.

While I, too, recognise the concerns of the Government about the need to justify policies that have an adverse impact, surely this is no more than the obligation on any modern, democratic government based on human rights.

House of Lords, Committee Stage
Hansard HL, 11 January 2000, col. 547
Lord Lester of Herne Hill

The concept of indirect discrimination is well recognised in the European convention and in international human rights treaties, such as the UN Convention on the Elimination of All Forms of Racial Discrimination and the UN International Covenant on Civil and Political Rights, which are all binding on the United Kingdom. Unless the amendment is accepted, our statute book will continue to authorise breaches of the UK's obligations under international and European law because the victims of indirect racial discrimination and sex discrimination will still be unable to obtain effective remedies for indirectly discriminatory acts by Ministers, government departments and statutory bodies acting on behalf of the Crown. The Government accept that the application of the concept of indirect discrimination by the courts and the CRE has not resulted in over-intrusive or unworkable decisions. The concept has worked well in practice, except for the artificial limitations imposed by statutory definition and by the *Amin* case. There is no case at all in which the concept of indirect discrimination has been taken too far, unnecessarily hampering or fettering the exercise of discretion by providers of public services.

Announcement that indirect discrimination would be included in the Bill

House of Lords, Report Stage
Hansard HL, 27 January 2000, col. 1673
Lord Bassam of Brighton

First, after careful consideration we have decided to extend the indirect discrimination provisions of the Race Relations Act 1976 to the functions of public authorities to be caught by the Bill. We intend to table an amendment to provide precisely for that. We have always been in favour of this principle but have been concerned, we believe rightly, to ensure that any such provision is effective without leaving public bodies open to routine or vexatious legal challenge in circumstances where their policies are entirely proper. Since the Bill was published, however, we have listened carefully to the arguments put forward and concluded that, on balance, the risk of spurious challenge is outweighed by the importance of the principle of including in the Bill indirect discrimination in respect of public sector functions. Direct and indirect racial discrimination is already prohibited under the terms of the Race Relations Act 1976 in the fields of employment, training, education, housing and the provision of goods, facilities and services in respect of the public and private sectors. The Act is already being extended by the Bill to new fields in the public sector which have previously been determined by case law not to be a service and to which prohibitions on direct or indirect discrimination do not therefore apply. The Act will now extend to areas such as the implementation of central and local government regulatory, economic and social policies and law enforcement in respect of indirect discrimination.

THE EXEMPTION FROM THE PROHIBITION ON DISCRIMINATION FOR DECISIONS NOT TO PROSECUTE

There were several debates during the passage of the Bill on the exemption from the prohibition on discrimination for decisions not to prosecute, and several amendments to the exemption table. The final text of the Act was that 'any act done for the purpose' of enabling the decision whether to institute or discontinue criminal proceedings is exempt from the new section 19B (new section 19F(a)). The following extracts illustrate the nature of the debate on the exemption and the concerns expressed about it.

The Government's justification for the exemption

House of Lords, Second Reading Debate
Hansard HL, 14 December 1999, col. 132
Lord Bassam of Brighton

New Section 19D seeks to preserve the role of the criminal courts as the sole forum for determining guilt by exempting decisions not to prosecute from the new Provisions of the Bill. The importance of this principle was recognised both by the White Paper on freedom of information and also by the Phillips Royal Commission in 1981 which stated,

> 'publicly calling into question a decision not to prosecute could amount to a trial of the suspect without the safeguards which criminal proceedings are designed to provide'.

Concerns about the exemption

House of Lords, Second Reading Debate
Hansard HL, 14 December 1999, col. 171
Lord Dholakia

The position of the CPS is probably more complicated in terms of the whole of the prosecution process. Your Lordships will see in the exemptions in the Bill that it probably lobbied quite hard to make it particularly difficult to pursue complaints, even of direct discrimination, where these involved criminal investigations, prosecutions or criminal proceedings. A decision not to institute criminal proceedings, or any acts leading to such a decision, is excluded; Clause 1 replacing Section 19D. In other words, the Lawrence family would have no redress through this Bill against the acts leading to the decision not to prosecute, or against the decision not to prosecute itself. This is a blanket ban on direct and indirect discrimination. What recourse is there against the police or the CPS for a black or Asian victim, or the family of such a victim? The Government's answer will obviously be a judicial review or a private prosecution. But look what happened when the Lawrence family tried that. They discovered to their cost that neither proved sufficient or satisfactory.

House of Lords, Second Reading Debate
Hansard HL, 14 December 1999, col. 180
Lord Bassam of Brighton

The noble Lord, Lord Cope . . . raised some important questions as well as making generalised comments on our approach. He raised a question on the proposed new Section 19D, which exempts decisions not to prosecute, and claimed that it was possibly too widely drawn. We, too, are concerned about the point and will look closely at ways of ensuring that the exemption is no wider than it needs to be to preserve the role of the criminal courts as the sole forum for determining guilt.

House of Lords, Committee Stage
Hansard HL, 11 January 2000, col. 588
Lord Lester of Herne Hill

The purpose of the amendment is to remove the exemption from the race relations legislation of acts leading to a decision not to prosecute. The amendment provides that such racially discriminatory acts are not to be exempt from being found to be unlawful under Section 19B. The valid justification for exempting from Section 19B decisions not to institute criminal proceedings — namely, to avoid a criminal trial in civil proceedings under the Race Relations Act — does not apply to the series of acts leading up to a decision not to prosecute, which could, for example, include significant but remote acts by the police in gathering or rejecting evidence. In particular, the vagueness of the words, 'acts leading to such a decision', is remarkable. Almost any police or prosecution practice that involved the gathering or assessment of the evidence could possibly come into a category of that breadth. Again, that stems from the Lawrence affair and the Macpherson report. We greatly hope that the amendment will be acceptable to the Government. I beg to move.

House of Lords, Report Stage
Hansard HL, 27 January 2000, col. 1698
Lord Bassam of Brighton

My Lords, the Government's policy objective with Section 19B of Clause 1 will preserve the role of the criminal court as the sole forum for determining guilt, while keeping the exemption in Section 19B as narrow as possible. I think there is agreement on all sides that this is a proper and necessary objective. At Committee stage the noble Lord, Lord Lester, brought forward an important amendment to narrow this exemption. I said in Committee that the Government felt that the clause was broader than would be ideal and I indicated that we would wish to bring forward an amendment which would meet our concerns in relation to the decision-making process while narrowing the exemption as much as possible. I believe that the Government's amendment achieves that objective. It is intended to leave significant but remote acts such as the initial arrest itself and, where appropriate, the gathering and assessment of evidence subject to Section 19B. However, it would continue to provide the protection that we believe is necessary for acts done for the purpose of making a decision about instituting criminal proceedings which may result in any decision not to prosecute. The Government believe that if the role of the criminal court as the sole forum for determining guilt is to be preserved it is every bit as important to protect such acts from action under Section 19B as it is to protect the decision not to prosecute. As was acknowledged on all sides at Committee stage, there is a balance to be struck between two laudable aims and objectives. On the one hand, there is the need to ensure that individuals have a right to a remedy where discrimination has taken place and, on the other hand, there is the need to ensure that matters of criminal guilt are determined in the criminal court. I believe that this amendment strikes the right balance and on that basis I would commend it to your Lordships. I beg to move.

House of Commons, Standing Committee Stage
Hansard HC, Standing Committee D, 18 April 2000 (morning)
The Parliamentary Under-Secretary of State for the Home Department (Mr Mike O'Brien)

The effect of the amendment is that the collection of evidence by the police would not be covered by an exemption if it were improperly done. However, if the information was an 'act done for the purpose of' making a decision to prosecute, not collecting information, that would be the subject of the exemption. For example, a decision not to prosecute by the police will be covered and any act done in the making of it will be covered by the exemption; but if they have interviewed a suspect at any earlier stage and behaved wrongly, that will not be covered by an exemption. I take the hon. Gentleman's point that clarity is needed and I will make sure that we provide it to cover that situation, so that those who subsequently read the legislation will be clear about our aims.

(See, further, all of the Standing Committee D debate on 18 April 2000).

THE IMMIGRATION EXEMPTION

The Hansard debates illustrate that the immigration exemption was one of, if not the, most controversial provisions in the Bill. The debates on the exemption were lengthy, and only some of them are included here, to give a flavour of the arguments advanced.

The Government's justification for the exemption

House of Lords, Second Reading Debate
Hansard HL, 14 December 1999, col. 131
Lord Bassam of Brighton

The operation of an immigration policy necessarily and legitimately entails discrimination between individuals on the basis of their nationality. Differential treatment is unavoidable because, for example, arrangements for the operation of our immigration control at ports must distinguish between our own citizens, who are free from immigration control, and other nationalities who are subject to such control. Furthermore, there are different rules for those who enjoy free movement rights under our international obligations and those who do not. The immigration rules make distinct provisions for those nationals who require visas to come to the UK and those who do not. Some rules and policies apply only to Commonwealth countries or specified nationalities. There are other examples.

The operation of a rational asylum determination process also requires the ability to differentiate between people of different nationalities and ethnic and national origins who are at risk of persecution overseas and those who are not. A recent example of such differential treatment was the special exercise to evacuate and provide protection to Kosovo Albanians during the crisis in the Balkans. The existing safeguards in the Race Relations Act for covering acts of discrimination done in pursuance to other statutory provisions are insufficient to allow the immigration system to continue to operate as it should. If consequential provisions were not made, Ministers would, for example, be unable to authorise special compassionate exercises where necessary for particular ethnic or national groups and immigration staff would be unable to exercise the operational discretion necessary to carry out their duties in accordance with ministerial instructions. That is why the Bill provides in new Section 19C that acts of discrimination by immigration staff will not be unlawful if such acts are required or authorised by specified immigration and nationality laws, or expressly authorised by Ministers who of course are themselves accountable to Parliament.

Overall, therefore, it will be unlawful for immigration staff to discriminate on the grounds of race or colour, or, in the case of nationality and ethnic and national origins, where they go beyond what is specified in immigration and nationality laws or what is expressly authorised by Ministers. The personal decisions of Ministers in individual immigration and asylum cases will also be exempt, as such decisions may make legitimate distinctions on the grounds of nationality not covered by existing approved arrangements. The Bill seeks to strike a sensible balance between prohibiting discriminatory behaviour we would all regard as abhorrent on the one hand, and allowing justified and necessary acts of discrimination to maintain the Government's immigration and nationality policies on the other.

Criticism of the immigration exemption

House of Lords, Second Reading Debate
Hansard HL, 14 December 1999, col. 144
Lord Lester of Herne Hill

I turn to Section 19C, which creates a blanket exemption for any directly discriminatory act, in relation to any of the wide range of immigration or nationality functions, done against another person on grounds of nationality or ethnic or national origins by a Minister or by officials acting in accordance with a relevant authorisation. That section empowers Ministers to authorise officials to act because, in the words of the Explanatory Notes,

> 'the way officials actually carry out their duties is necessarily detailed in operational staff instructions approved by Ministers. It would be impracticable to set out in statutory or

> subordinate legislation every set of circumstances where discrimination would be required'.

In other words, again for reasons of administrative convenience, the Government seek to bypass the need for parliamentary approval of racially discriminatory practices and procedures operated by their officials. I have expressed my concern about this and other provisions to the Delegated Powers Scrutiny Committee, whose report will inform subsequent discussion of the Bill. If an exemption is needed for discriminatory treatment based on nationality or residence, a wide exemption is already provided in Section 41(2) of the Race Relations Act 1976 to cover such treatment. No further provision is needed for this. What is novel and objectionable is the blanket exemption for discrimination on grounds of ethnic or national origins.

Unlike discrimination on grounds of nationality or place of residence, discrimination based on ethnic or national origins is as much racial discrimination as is discrimination based on colour or race, as the definition of racial discrimination in Article 1 of the United Nations Convention on the Elimination of All Forms of Discrimination 1966 makes crystal clear. Such discrimination involves treating one individual less favourably than another for what is not chosen by them but for what is innate in them at birth — their genetic inheritance — whether as ethnic Jews, Roma gypsies or Hong Kong Indians. It is as invidious and unfair as is discrimination based on the colour of a person's skin. That is why the Race Relations Act 1976 forbids direct discrimination on any of those racial grounds, apart from a range of clearly defined exceptions.

The sweepingly broad exception in Section 19C is incompatible with the very principle of non-discrimination which the legislation is intended to secure. If the Home Office wishes to make special arrangements aimed at providing protection to particular groups seeking shelter in the United Kingdom, such as the Bosnians and Kosovars who were granted exceptional leave to remain during the recent crisis in the Balkans, it is difficult to understand how that would require an exception. The reason for affording favourable treatment to some of those groups is surely not their ethnic or national origins but their well-founded fear of persecution, the urgency of their humanitarian needs and the need to comply with the UK's obligations under the refugee convention. The policy is not based upon or caused by their ethnicity. It does not involve discriminating against anyone on the grounds of their ethnic or national origins. As the Government have correctly stated in the UK report to the CERD Committee, which is the UN committee (CERD/C/299/Add.9, 2nd December 1966, paragraph 58),

> 'There is nothing racist about designating countries which produce large numbers of unfounded asylum applications'.

The same is true of refugee situations, if humanitarian provision is made, not on the basis of nationality or ethnic or national origin, but on the basis of an objective assessment of the conditions in the country concerned. The Section 19C exception is therefore not only unsightly, but unnecessary.

I go further. Even if it were appropriate, for the avoidance of doubt, to include an exception to cover situations of that kind, the exception to the fundamental right to equal treatment without discrimination would need to be prescribed in legislation in a way carefully tailored to what is necessary to give effect to the Government's legitimate aims, with adequate judicial safeguards against the abuse of this extraordinary power, to ensure that the doing of a discriminatory act is justified by its purpose, as with national security. The functions covered by Section 19C include decisions to deport, exclusion directions, leave to enter or remain, the grant of asylum, exceptional leave to remain, and even naturalisation as a British citizen. Section 44 of the British Nationality Act 1981 provides that any discretion vested by that Act in the Secretary of State, a governor or lieutenant governor, must be exercised,

> 'without regard to the race, colour or religion of any person who may be affected by its exercise'.

Yet Section 19C would allow the discretion to be exercised on the basis of ethnic or national origins which are part of the international legal definition of what constitutes 'racial discrimination'. As it stands, Section 19C authorises breaches by a future populist illiberal Home Secretary, or by a prejudiced administration, of the various international human rights conventions by which the UK is bound: notably, Articles 2, 5 and 6 of the Convention on the Elimination of Racial Discrimination and Articles 2 and 26 of the International Covenant on Civil and Political Rights. Article 3 of the Convention Relating to the Status of Refugees 1951 obliges contracting states to apply the convention's provisions to refugees,

> 'without discrimination as to race, religion or country of origin'.

That covers discrimination on grounds of a refugee's ethnic or national origins. The UNHCR executive committee, of which the UK is an original member, has emphasised that decisions on asylum must be made without discrimination as to race, religion, political opinion, nationality or country of origin (Executive Committee Conclusion No. 15(XXX) 1979; also Conclusion No. 22 (XXXII) 1981). Section 19C authorises practices and procedures in relation to immigration and nationality which would be incompatible with the refugee convention too. We hope that the Government will agree to remove or to narrow Section 19C by limiting the exception, if they must, to special treatment on humanitarian grounds.

Attempt to limit the immigration exemption to situations where discrimination was necessary to afford special treatment on humanitarian grounds

House of Lords, Committee Stage
Hansard HL, 11 January 2000, col. 580
Lord Lester of Herne Hill

The noble Lord said: New Section 19C creates a blanket exemption for any directly discriminatory act in relation to any of the wide range of immigration or nationality functions carried out against another person on grounds of nationality, or ethnic or national origin, by a Minister or by officials acting in accordance with the relevant authorisation. That section, which was much debated during the Second Reading of the Bill, delegates considerable power to the Government, by-passing the need for parliamentary approval of racially discriminatory practices and procedures. For the reasons that were debated fairly fully at Second Reading, it has caused great concern, especially among ethnic minorities in this country.

The amendment narrows the ability of the immigration and nationality service to discriminate by limiting it to an act done,

> 'by a relevant person in carrying out immigration and nationality functions in affording persons of a particular nationality, religion or ethnic or national origin'—

those words come from the international treaties to which we are signatories—

> 'special treatment on humanitarian grounds'.

If the Home Office wishes to make special arrangements aimed at providing protection for particular groups seeking shelter in the United Kingdom, such as the Bosnians and Kosovar Albanians who were granted exceptional leave to remain during the recent crisis in the Balkans, it is difficult to understand how that would require any exceptions. We understand from previous contributions by the Minister that that is the main problem with which the Home Office seeks to deal. The reason for affording favourable treatment to some of those groups is surely not based on their ethical or national origins but on their well-founded fear of persecution, the urgency of their humanitarian needs and the need to comply with the United Kingdom's obligations under the refugee convention. The policy is not based on, and is not caused by, their ethnicity. It is not because of Muslim, Kosovar, ethnic or religious origins but for the reasons I have just given. . . .

We all agree with the Home Office that in exercising immigration control one has to draw distinctions which are based, for example, on the nationality of particular people seeking to enter this country. That is not the issue here. We are concerned with the taking of a power which is not in the 1976 Act, even though the 1976 Act already has the powers provided in Section 41. We are concerned with the power to allow the Home Office to discriminate not only in any immigration decisions but also in nationality decisions on the basis of a person's ethnicity. Nothing could do more harm to the reputation of the immigration and nationality service in this country than to give the impression to the ethnic minorities in this country that we are discriminating at the gate, or conferring British nationality and citizenship because of people's ethnicity. I am sure that that is not what we do. Were we to do so, we should be condemned by all the international bodies for breaching international human rights law. Section 41(2) of the Race Relations Act 1976 states:

> 'Nothing in Parts II to IV shall render unlawful any act whereby a person discriminates against another on the basis of that other's nationality or place of . . . residence or the length of time for which he has been present or resident in or outside the United Kingdom . . . if that act is done (a) in pursuance of any arrangements made (whether before or after the passing of this Act) by or with the approval of, or for the time being approved by, a Minister of the Crown; or (b) in order to comply with any condition imposed . . . by a Minister of the Crown'.

Those words were carefully inserted because the immigration and nationality department wished to have them there to give it the freedom that it needed in exercising its public functions. That is why they are in Section 41. I do not understand that there has been any change of circumstances since 1976 to require any wider authorisation to be given than that in Section 41. It is carefully controlled in Section 41 so that it cannot be abused. My amendment is designed to give extra cover without going so far as to authorise discrimination based on ethnicity in immigration or nationality decisions. We very much hope that the Government will be as open minded about this amendment as they were on the previous one. I beg to move.

The Government's response

House of Lords, Committee Stage
Hansard HL, 11 January 2000, col. 583
Lord Bassam of Brighton

The operation of immigration policies necessarily and legitimately involves differential treatment between individuals based on their nationality and, more rarely, their ethnic or national origins. In our view, the existing exemption for immigration and nationality functions strikes the right balance between providing victims of unlawful direct discrimination with an effective right of action and protecting necessary discriminatory activity in the exercise of immigration functions which is required or authorised by Ministers or by legislation . . .

This Bill must make it crystal clear what is unlawful and what is permissible in the public interest. We believe that the existing formulation in Clause 1 (new Section 19C) does so. Activity which is authorised or required by law or by Ministers will be lawful, as will be personal decisions taken by Ministers in the public interest. Unauthorised acts of direct race discrimination will be unlawful, and the Government will have no hesitation in dealing very firmly with them. Failure to provide clarity in this legislation would be unwise, both as an act of policy and to ensure that staff are fully protected when they carry out the duties

Parliament and Ministers have laid upon them. The Government do not share the noble Lord's confidence in the adequacy of the existing legal safeguards provided by the Race Relations Act. Section 41 of the 1976 Act protects discriminatory acts which are carried out 'in pursuance to' statutory provisions or ministerial arrangements. But the courts have adopted a very narrow interpretation of 'in pursuance to'. For acts to benefit from Section 41 they must be actually 'required' by law.

However, the operation of the immigration system necessarily requires the exercise of discretion by Ministers and by appropriately authorised officials in accordance with published, transparent instructions. For example, the Immigration Service at ports requires the ability to target and prioritise certain nationalities for particular scrutiny where it has intelligence that particular national travel documents are being abused or where there is intelligence that individuals or groups of one nationality are presenting themselves as the nationals of another country in order to benefit from compassionate policies or asylum procedures. There is chapter and verse on that. There are many such examples of such activity.

The Immigration Service and Integrated Casework Directorate need the ability to carry out special 'nationality specific' exercises involving the fast tracking of cases and even the use of detention in response to sudden or sustained influxes of certain nationals, most recently from eastern Europe, seeking to circumvent the control. Entry clearance officers need the ability to treat individuals differently on various grounds. Examples include if their country is associated with state-sponsored terrorism or has a track record of hostile intelligence activities or if their country is known to have lax or inappropriate passport issuing arrangements. Such activity is a necessary part of operating the immigration system but may not be considered by the courts as strictly required by law.

There are also many examples of where the immigration system discriminates positively in favour of individuals on the basis of their nationality or ethnic or national origins. One example is the special treatment for Kosovan Albanians during the recent conflict in the Balkans. Kosovan Serbs were not treated the same way, for entirely understandable reasons. There are other examples where guidance to asylum caseworkers directs that the one ethnic or national group from a particular country should be treated differently from another. For example, our policy in relation to persons originating from Bosnia-Herzegovina is to grant exceptional leave where the applicant's ethnic group is no longer in the majority. A Bosnian Croat originating from a Serb area would not be expected to return there, nor would a Bosnian Serb originating from a Muslim area.

Current asylum policy makes a distinction between Kosovan Serbs and Kosovan Albanians where the basis of claim is ethnic origin. The former are a minority and may qualify for asylum, while the latter may be refused and returned. The ethnic or national origin of the applicant in cases involving various other nationalities is also a key consideration in the determination of applications for asylum. It would be impossible to operate a rational asylum determination process if caseworkers were unable to make such distinctions. That is why the Bill makes it clear that discriminatory activity which is required or authorised by law, or by Ministers, cannot be considered to be unlawful.

Impossibility of drawing a distinction between ethnic or national origin and race or colour

House of Lords, Committee Stage
Hansard HL, 11 January 2000, col. 585
Lord Lester of Herne Hill

The Minister. . . . has not yet given a single example of discrimination based on a person's ethnicity as distinct from all the other considerations. We are dealing here with only direct discrimination, not indirect discrimination. I should like to know from the Minister whether there is any example where a person's race — that is what ethnicity is about; it is a part of race — is the basis for treating him worse than someone else. Perhaps I may give an example: the infamous one of the British Asians from East Africa who were refused entry to this country by Mr Callaghan's government by statute. That was held by the European Human Rights Commission to be inherently degrading treatment because it was based on their ethnicity. Under the Bill as it stands there is nothing to stop the Home Office refusing to allow British Asians from East Africa in a similar situation coming here, not on the basis of their colour but of their ethnicity. Surely that is not what the Minister has in mind and surely the Home Office would not dream of discriminating against someone on the grounds of their ethnicity? If that is indeed the case, will the Minister please give some examples of where they have done so? I personally should be deeply shocked if that was so.

The Government's position on the effect of the exemption on its international human rights obligations in the immigration and asylum sphere

House of Lords, Committee Stage
Hansard HL, 11 January 2000, col. 586
Lord Bassam of Brighton

I turn to our international obligations. The noble Lord suggested that the exemption for immigration and nationality functions would breach this country's international obligations under the UN Convention Relating to the Status of Refugees, the International Covenant on Civil and Political Rights and the International Convention on the Elimination of All Forms of Racial Discrimination. The entitlement to immigration, asylum and nationality applicants is detailed in the immigration and nationality enactments listed in Clause 1 of the Bill and in subordinate legislation such as the immigration rules. The exemption does nothing in our view to rescind or restrict rights or entitlements provided in existing legislation; it simply allows that legislation to continue as Parliament, in our view, intended. It also provides the immigration authorities with the necessary latitude to conduct their business rationally, including targeting resources where there is a concerted attempt to abuse the control or where there is a compelling need for special treatment for a particular group on humanitarian grounds. The exemption does not require Ministers to do anything contrary to their international obligations. The discretion which it gives to Ministers still has to be exercised bearing in mind their international obligations. We believe that to be an important point.

Debate about ethnic Chinese people arriving with Malaysian or Singaporean documents although they in fact came from the People's Republic

House of Lords, Report Stage
Hansard HL, 27 January 2000, col. 1692
Lord Avebury

My Lords, the noble Baroness referred to the case of the Chinese who were detected at immigration presenting documents purporting that they were of Malaysian or Singaporean nationality. Can the Minister explain that a little further? If those people were asylum seekers coming from the People's Republic of China, clearly they had good reason for presenting those documents because they would not be able to leave China and come to the United Kingdom as refugees using Chinese passports. As the noble Lord, Lord Bassam, knows well, the problem of false documents has been dealt with extensively on the Floor of the House and in the courts. It has been ruled that the presentation of false documents by an asylum seeker is not a criminal offence and that consideration of it must be deferred until the end of the asylum process. I am mystified, therefore, that the Minister should give that example in support of the Home Office policy on discrimination by the Immigration Service. Conversely, I can see every argument for a provision such as that suggested by my noble friend because there are instances where the Immigration Service positively discriminates in favour of certain nationalities. For example, it is well known that the ports at entry treat Somali nationals favourably because they know what the situation is in Somalia. There is no proper government and people who belong to the wrong group are at risk of being killed by armed factions. Therefore, great sympathy is applied in consideration of applications for asylum by Somali nationals. More or less all of them are accepted as qualifying for exceptional leave to remain, and I have no quarrel with that when I look at the situation in their country of origin. But if it is necessary to allow that kind of thing to happen explicitly, a provision should be put on the face of the Bill while we have the opportunity.

House of Lords, Report Stage
Hansard HL, 27 January 2000, col. 1694
Lord Bassam of Brighton

As I made clear in Committee, we believe that the exemption is necessary to allow the immigration system to handle asylum applications and cases requiring exceptional treatment on compassionate grounds. The noble Lord made clear his view that the courts would not find that the Home Office had acted unlawfully in cases where differential treatment had been provided to different ethnic or national groups because of the situation in their countries of origin. However, as I also made clear, we simply cannot afford any degree of ambiguity to arise in relation to the immigration and asylum system. We are required in practice to operate policies that are country specific, and to treat applications alike without always considering the individual circumstances of a person falling within the relevant ethnic or national group and who is from the country concerned. I listened with care and interest to what the noble Baroness, Lady Prashar, had to say in support of the amendment. Although in a historical sense I can understand her concerns about the issue, it has become clear to us during the course of our examination of the situation that it is necessary, on some occasions, for the Immigration Service to differentiate between individuals on the basis of their ethnic or national origins. I shall go through the example I gave in the letter again because it is important to understand it. From time to time, the Immigration Service detects Chinese nationals with falsified documents that misrepresent them as Malaysian or Singaporean nationals of Chinese ethnic origin. As has been said, were this problem to grow significantly, it would be necessary for the Immigration Service to scrutinise with particular care the documents presented by these nationals of Chinese ethnic origin and to interview them. But with 89.1 million passenger arrivals in the United Kingdom during the last financial year, of which 12.2 million were subject to immigration control, even with the best will in the world the Immigration Service does not have the capacity or the resources to interview every Malaysian or Singaporean seeking to enter the country, irrespective of their ethnic origin. An assessment of risk, based on available intelligence, must be made. Moreover, it has to be said that this risk assessment may sometimes have to be based on the ethnic or national origin of passengers. I give way.

House of Lords, Report Stage
Hansard HL, 27 January 2000, col. 1694
Lord Lester of Herne Hill

I am very worried by the answer and the explanation that has been given. Perhaps I may clarify exactly what we are talking about. If one were dealing with would-be immigrants who were white — that is to say, European in appearance — who came, say, from the Russian Federation, there would be no basis to treat them differently because of their ethnic origin or the kind of grounds mentioned in the letter. The Minister is saying that because people look Chinese we must reserve the right to single them out for special treatment on the basis of their appearance — their ethnic characteristics — and the fact that they are not white. We could not do that with anyone who was white because there are no distinguishing ethnic characteristics of that kind. If that is what is being said, does not the Minister realise that that is quite different from singling out people on the basis of their country of origin or their nationality: it goes to the root of what they are and cannot help being because of their ethnicity, their colour or race. Does the Minister recognise that? Am I correctly understanding what is said in the letter and what is being said by him today?

House of Lords, Report Stage
Hansard HL, 27 January 2000, col. 1695
Lord Bassam of Brighton

My Lords, I am trying to explain to the House that, yes, there will be some circumstances where, on the basis of careful intelligence and a risk assessment, we have to make that judgment based on what is perceived as an individual's ethnicity. Perhaps I may develop the point further. During 1999, the Immigration Service detected more than 5,000 attempts to enter the United Kingdom using forged or counterfeit travel documents or visas. The noble Lord, Lord Avebury, quite understandably referred to the circumstances in which someone might use documents of that sort because he is fearful of the situation in the country from which he originated and this is the best way to effect an escape. However, I urge noble Lords to accept that it is the case that scams are being operated essentially by people who are seeking to come to the United Kingdom because it is an attractive place to live and because it is in their economic interests to come here. These scams are being operated to get round the effect of our immigration legislation. That cannot be acceptable. It is in such extreme circumstances where we suspect that sort of criminality that we feel we need this exemption. That is why we are putting forward this argument.

We do not desire pro-actively to discriminate. But if we do not have the capacity to mount such operations, with a carefully thought-through risk assessment, our system of immigration control will be fundamentally weakened. We do not believe that that is desirable or that that has been Parliament's intention in the past. We do not believe that it accords with legislation that we have recently put on the statute book through the Immigration and Asylum Act 1999. . . . The exemption for immigration and nationality functions in Clause 1 will provide Ministers with the framework within which to provide guidance. The latter is very important in this context and I ask noble Lords to reflect on that. As far as possible the guidance will be published for Parliament and the public to see in line with the Government's commitment to openness and very much in line with our commitment to ensure that we operate our legislation within a framework that combats racism — whether direct or indirect — in all its forms. We must have immigration procedures and practices that will be thoroughly reviewed to ensure that the only discriminatory activity that is necessary and can be justified is covered by clear guidance, approved by Ministers, and that any discriminatory activity which cannot be justified is eliminated. That must be our policy objective.

House of Lords, Report Stage
Hansard HL, 27 January 2000, col. 1697
Lord Lester of Herne Hill

My Lords, guidelines are crucial and they must be transparent. I also believe that they should be subject to parliamentary scrutiny and approval. I add the words 'and approval' because I think that this is quite an exceptional situation where Parliament should act as a watchdog over any approval of ethnic discrimination of this kind. However, perhaps I may try to explain why I am so concerned. Everyone in this House understands that the police must not use their stop and search powers on the basis of racist assumptions. But if they cannot stop black people because of their ethnicity, they cannot take a short cut and say, for example, with regard to the Chinese, 'We think that there is a great deal of criminality of a particular kind among the Chinese community, so anyone who looks Chinese will be stopped and searched for the very important function of detecting and prosecuting crime'. The Home Office has accepted, and we have accepted in this legislation, that that conduct must be unlawful. It is unconscionable for a public officer to treat one person worse than another in exercising the powers of the state because of that person's ethnicity. There is no difference between ethnicity and a person's colour. If you look Chinese, it does not matter whether it is because you look yellow or have Chinese features; it is to do with characteristics that you cannot help. For the Immigration Service to stop and search in precisely that way on the basis of ethnic stereotyping is, I suggest, equally unacceptable. No guidelines are going to make it acceptable. The point is that as a matter of principle immigration officers should not be stopping, searching and interviewing people differently because they are black, Chinese or because of any other ethnic reason. I very much hope that between now and Third Reading we will be able to find an appropriate form of words. It would be very sad if the Bill were to leave this House with a very important fundamental principle still being contentious.

Further debates on the immigration exemption can be found at the House of Lords, Report Stage, *Hansard HL, 27 January 2000, col. 1692* onwards; the *House of Commons, Standing Committee D, 13 April 2000* and House of Commons, Third Reading Debate, *Hansard HC, 30 October 2000, col. 563.*

Race Monitor for the Immigration Exemption

House of Lords, Third Reading Debate
Hansard HL, 3 February 2000, col. 360
Lord Lester of Herne Hill

My Lords, before the Minister sits down, I wonder whether he will also agree to consider whether there might be some machinery, some person, providing adequate safeguards against abuse of discretion within the system so that that might be built into the Government's thinking?

House of Commons, Standing Committee Stage
Hansard HC, Standing Committee D, 13 April 2000 (afternoon)
The Parliamentary Under-Secretary of State for the Home Department (Mr Mike O'Brien)

During the debate in another place, Lord Lester and others expressed concern about the breadth of the exemption for immigration and nationality functions. In particular, there was concern that there should be a mechanism allowing effective scrutiny by Parliament over the operation of the exemptions. We undertook to consider that carefully, and the amendment represents the Government's proposed solution to questions of scrutiny and accountability. The amendment will create a new statutory function — the race monitor — to provide independent oversight of the operation of the exemption for immigration and nationality functions. In appointing the race monitor, the Secretary of State will be debarred from choosing a member of his own staff, which secures and underlines the independence and impartiality of the role. The Secretary of State will be required to consult the Commission for Racial Equality in appointing the monitor. My right hon. Friend the Home Secretary will therefore be able to draw on the commission's considerable expertise in the field of race relations in selecting a candidate with the right skills and background to perform this important task. We have decided to go down the route of creating a specialist race monitor, rather than relying on the commission to exercise its powers under the Act, because of the specialised nature of the immigration, asylum and nationality system. This important function requires a dedicated resource. This amendment will do nothing to restrict the powers of the commission in dealing with these issues. It will add to the oversight and control in the system.

The race monitor will monitor the likely effect of ministerial authorisations to immigration staff to discriminate on grounds of nationality or ethnic or national origin, and acts carried out in accordance with such authorisations. That means that the monitor will examine the justification for such authorisations, their likely effect on the operation of the exemption, and how they actually work in practice. The monitor will report each year his or her findings to the Secretary of State, who will lay the report before each House of Parliament. The monitor's report will provide an accessible focus for informed debate of these matters. The monitor will not monitor discriminatory activity that is required by legislation, because Parliament will already have considered the justification for such discrimination in passing that legislation.

There is a successful precedent for this approach. The Asylum and Immigration Appeals Act 1993 created an independent entry clearance monitor to monitor refusals given by our entry clearance officers overseas in cases in which, as a consequence of restrictions imposed by the 1993 Act, there is no statutory right of appeal. In creating the entry clearance monitor function — a role performed highly effectively by Dame Elizabeth Anson — Parliament recognised the importance of introducing independent oversight over what would otherwise have been an unrestricted executive power. Parliament reaffirmed the entry clearance monitor's function in section 23 of the Immigration and Asylum Act 1999. The option of appointing the same person to perform the race and entry clearance monitor roles will be carefully considered by the Home Office and by the Foreign and Commonwealth Office, though specific statutory authorisation is required.

The Government believe that the approach of establishing a race monitor for the immigration system provides the most effective, workable solution to concerns expressed about the breadth of the exemption for immigration and nationality functions.

House of Commons, Third Reading Debate
Hansard HC, 30 October 2000, col. 544
The Parliamentary Under-Secretary of State for the Home Department (Mr Mike O'Brien)

The race monitor will have free access to all of the IND's papers. He or she will also be able to call on the IND to provide an individual file. However, I make it very clear that the monitor should not be a surrogate appellate authority. It is not the monitor's job to examine an individual case and to make decisions on it. The monitor's job is to look at the broad array of cases and at a selection of cases and to determine whether, as a whole, immigration control is being operated within the spirit of this legislation. The race monitor will, therefore, monitor the immigration service and the IND to ensure that the legislation's spirit is being properly adhered to. The current entry clearance monitor, who provides real accountability to Parliament, provides a very successful precedent for the role of race monitor. The entry clearance monitor will report annually to Parliament, and I know that many hon. Members pay great heed to the views that the monitor expresses. We very much hope that the race monitor will have the same type of credibility and impact, so that Ministers, too, pay great heed to what is said by him or her

NATIONAL SECURITY

House of Lords, Second Reading Debate
Hansard HL, 14 December 1999, col. 134
Lord Bassam of Brighton

The Race Relations Act provides that an act of racial discrimination is not unlawful if done for the purposes of safeguarding national security, and that a ministerial certificate is conclusive evidence that an act was done for precisely that purpose. As far as we are aware, the power has been used only once in almost 25 years. The power to issue such conclusive certificates has been found by the European Court of Human Rights — in relation to equivalent provisions in a different piece of legislation — to be incompatible with Article

6(1) of the ECHR. The Bill removes the power in the Race Relations Act and amends the national security defence so that it will no longer be a complete defence to show that an act was done for the purposes of national security. It will also now need to be shown that the act was justified for that purpose. The Bill also provides for courts to adopt certain special procedures when dealing with cases under the Act that raise national security issues. These provisions are based on similar provisions for tribunal rules made in Schedule 8 to the Employment Relations Act 1999.

See also House of Commons, *Hansard HC, Standing Committee D, 18 April 2000 (afternoon)*.

VICARIOUS LIABILITY OF THE POLICE

House of Lords, Second Reading Debate
Hansard HL, 14 December 1999, col. 133
Lord Bassam of Brighton

In the Act as it stands, employers are held vicariously liable for the discriminatory actions of their employees. That means that where an employee racially discriminates against an individual, the individual can bring proceedings against both the discriminator and against the discriminator's employer. The employer has a defence if he took reasonably practicable steps to prevent employees from doing the act or acts of that description. Police officers are office holders, not employees. Under the Act as it stands, special provision is made to enable them to be regarded as employees in respect of their own treatment, but no provision is made in respect of the exercise of their police functions. Although Section 88 of the Police Act 1996 and Section 39 of the Police (Scotland) Act 1967 make general provision for the vicarious liability of a chief officer of police, the construction of the Race Relations Act means that this does not apply to acts that are unlawful under the Race Relations Act. So there is a clear anomaly here that needs to be addressed in order to bring the police in line with other organisations and with its own general practice. Both the Stephen Lawrence report and the Commission for Racial Equality have made recommendations to this effect. Clause 3 of the Bill, therefore, provides for chief officers of police to be made vicariously liable for acts of discrimination carried out by officers under their control.

POSITIVE DUTIES ON PUBLIC BODIES

Criticism of the initial failure to include positive duties in the Bill

House of Lords, Committee Stage
Hansard HL, 11 January 2000, col. 788
Lord Lester of Herne Hill

The United Kingdom has been criticised by the UN Human Rights Committee for not taking steps with sufficient vigour, and by the UN Committee on the Elimination of Racial Discrimination as recently as 1997. It criticised the United Kingdom for the lack of a similar positive legal duty on bodies working in the fields of health, education, social services, planning and housing as that which applied to local authorities. So we stand condemned by two respected international human rights bodies in the race discrimination field. I do not use emotive or exaggerated language. I simply say that it is unacceptable for the United Kingdom to be pilloried in that way because of the refusal by consecutive governments to take effective action. The time is right. There is no reason why that duty cannot be included in this Bill any more than in the Greater London Authority Act, or in the Northern Ireland Act.

See also Lord Lester's comments in the Second Reading Debate, *Hansard HL, 14 December 1999, col. 140*.

Announcement that positive duties would be included

House of Lords, Report Stage
Hansard HL, 27 January 2000, col. 1673
Lord Bassam of Brighton

The Government have always seen the importance of the duty to promote equality as a positive way of eliminating unjustifiable indirect discrimination in these and all other fields. Our setting of targets for ethnic minority recruitment, retention and promotion, and our guidelines for maintaining race equality inter-policy development and implementation are two examples. We are already committed to placing the promotion of equality by public bodies on a statutory footing. We shall reinforce that commitment by bringing forward a government amendment to the Race Relations (Amendment) Bill to enshrine the principle on the face of the Bill as a positive duty, leaving room for consultation on how exactly the duty will operate in practice and how it will be enforced. Those are two important issues. The amendment will be brought forward at Committee stage in the Commons. Meanwhile, we are considering whether there should be any procedural safeguards consistent with the principle of non-discrimination.

Nature of the general duty

House of Commons, Standing Committee Stage
Hansard HC, Standing Committee D, 2 May 2000 (afternoon)
Simon Hughes MP

A positive statutory duty would ensure that authorities not only react to people who test their racial equality policies, but accept that promoting racial equality is a public benefit and is good service and employment practice. We seek to establish a culture change by inculcating the responsibility of being not passive, but active, particularly because public authorities are role models. The police were the central authority examined by the Lawrence inquiry, and if they can be a good role model and clearly accept their duty to promote equality, there will be a knock-on effect on society and on all those with whom they come into contact. The same applies to central and local government and all other public agencies. Under new clause 3, 'racial equality' would be defined as

> 'equality of opportunity irrespective of membership or perceived membership of any racial group'.

That definition would avoid any narrow categorisation and would apply to any public authority in the conduct of its business. The amendments, including the new clauses and new schedules, draw on the experience gained from the Government of Wales Act 1998 and the Scotland Act 1998. As the Minister will know, the duty in relation to equality is much more advanced in Northern Ireland. As we have discussed previously in Committee, that is the one place in the United Kingdom that has a human rights commission that gives additional support to those who argue for equality of opportunity. Under new clause 2, the duty would apply to every public authority not only in the exercise of its powers, but in the formulation and implementation of its policies and strategies. Every public authority would publish the scheme by which it sought to carry out its positive duty, so that people could have access to it for comment and criticism, to bring about improvements. It cannot be just tokenism: the scheme by which public authorities seek to secure compliance must be worked through and owned, as it were. People understand that that would work a little like a mission statement. There should be a scheme that works out the impact of measures. It is no good having a scheme if it is not tried, tested and evaluated. Public services are becoming much better at doing that in a way that is not burdensome, but gives people regular review opportunities and criteria by which to review. That also allows people to learn lessons: if a policy is having an adverse impact, people can see that it is amended. There should be regulations for secondary legislation. That must be the right way to proceed, so that we do not create clutter by leaving too much to primary legislation, while having the ability to take important measures through the parliamentary process. It is proposed that information should be collected and published, which is necessary to facilitate the public authority in doing its job and to ensure that it is not acting unlawfully. The provision for an annual report is the normal proposal, with which we are all familiar. That could be the annual check, which is published. The report would set out the measures that have been taken, assess their impact and propose measures that might be taken in the year ahead. In the implementation of the duty, public authorities would be subject to the same external audit and inspection proposals as are all other public authorities in the exercise of their duties. I am sure that the Government are happy about that proposition in principle. As I said, public services are becoming much more used to audit and inspection and benefit from it if the right procedure is implemented and works well. I hope that my colleagues do not find that controversial.

EXCLUSION OF MUSLIMS FROM THE DEFINITION OF 'RACIAL GROUP' AND RELIGIOUS DISCRIMINATION

House of Lords, Second Reading Debate
Hansard HL, 14 December 1999, col. 165
Lord Ahmed

There is a further anomaly in that, in the absence of religious discrimination laws, the only protection Muslims, Hindus and Christians enjoyed was under the indirect discrimination provisions of the Race Relations Act. For example, employment cases established that a dress code prohibiting women from wearing any headscarf that directly affects Muslim women can constitute indirect racial discrimination against persons of Pakistani origin. In the past there have been instances in which Muslims, Rastafarians or Hindus believed that they were receiving less favourable treatment by, say, prison officers on the grounds of their religion. Under the Bill as drafted they would have no recourse to redress. I understand that the Government consider that simply adding a reference to religion in existing anti-discrimination legislation would generate more problems than it would solve. One problem is that members of sects, as distinct from members of religions, could claim protection under the new legislation, and that the practices and beliefs of such sects are normally objectionable. I am sure that the noble Lord, Lord Lester of Herne Hill, will agree that it was the courts that defined 'racial groups' in the Race Relations Act; similarly, the definition of religion can surely be left to the courts.

House of Lords, Second Reading Debate
Hansard HL, 14 December 1999, col. 184
Lord Bassam of Brighton

The noble Lord, Lord Ahmed, asked why the Bill did not cover religious discrimination. I am aware that that is a matter that particularly exercises the noble Lord, and it is one in which many of us take a keen interest. The Government are alive to the concerns about religious discrimination and the case put forward that it should be subject to law. This issue raises difficult, sensitive and complex questions. We do not believe that there is a ready answer or quick fix solution to it. We have commissioned research to assess the current scale and nature of religious discrimination and the extent to which it overlaps with racial discrimination in England and Wales.

A SINGLE EQUALITY LAW FOR THE FUTURE

House of Lords, Second Reading Debate
Hansard HL, 14 December 1999, col. 140
Lord Lester of Herne Hill

We hope that the Government will agree to remove those defects. We hope that the Government will also give urgent attention — I emphasise 'urgent' — to the much needed wider reforms of the hotchpotch of anti-discrimination legislation to produce a comprehensive, coherent, user friendly equality law, with more efficient equality compliance and enforcement machinery.

THE ACT AS ONE COMPONENT OF THE CAMPAIGN TO ERADICATE RACISM

House of Commons, Third Reading Debate
Hansard HC, 30 October 2000, col. 563
Mr David Lidington MP

It is not just through Acts of Parliament, legislation, rules and regulations that we will build a successful multiracial society. As I said on Second Reading, legislation has a part to play. As one looks at the current state of the law, it is difficult to argue, if one believes that there should be laws against racial discrimination, that we should have a law that includes the private sector and part of the public sector, but excludes an ill-defined, indeterminate part of the public sector in the way that the 1976 Act does. However, it is in the acts, the decisions, the growing together of individuals, families and communities throughout this country that we will see the creation of a tolerant society that accepts people of different ethnic backgrounds and that appreciates the contribution that people of different ethnic communities bring.

ADDITIONAL HANSARD REFERENCES

Other passages which may be of particular interest to practitioners are as follows:

(i) Debate as the initial 'list' approach taken to public authorities which would be bound by the prohibition on discrimination. This approach was eventually replaced with the Human Rights Act definition of public authority, and the notion of public bodies and 'hybrid' bodies

See: House of Lords, Second Reading Debate, *Hansard HL, 14 December 1999, col. 159*, Lord Haskel; House of Lords, Second Reading Debate, *Hansard HL, 14 December 1999, col. 181*, Lord Lester of Herne Hill; House of Lords, Committee Stage, *Hansard HL, 11 January 2000, col. 533*, Lord Lester of Herne Hill; House of Lords, Report Stage, *Hansard HL, 27 January 2000, col. 1683* onwards; House of Commons, Second Reading Debate, *Hansard HC, 9 March 2000, col. 1206* onwards; House of Commons, Standing Committee Stage, *Hansard HC, Standing Committee D, 13 April 2000 (morning)*; House of Commons, Third Reading Debate, *Hansard HC, 30 October 2000, col. 563.*

(ii) Debate as to the restrictions on remedies available in discrimination cases arising out of criminal proceedings (House of Lords, Committee Stage, *Hansard HL, 13 January 2000, col. 755* onwards; House of Lords, Report Stage; *Hansard HL, 27 January 2000, col. 1703* onwards; House of Commons, *Hansard HC, Standing Committee D, 13 April 2000 (afternoon)*; House of Commons, *Hansard HC, Standing Committee D, 18 April 2000 (afternoon)*).

(iii) Debate as to the test to be applied when race discrimination claims should be adjourned for pending criminal proceedings (House of Lords, Committee Stage, *Hansard HL, 13 January 2000, col. 764* onwards; House of Lords, Second Reading Debate, *Hansard HL, 14 December 1999, col. 132;* House of Commons, *Hansard HC, Standing Committee D, 18 April 2000 (afternoon)*).

(iv) Limitations on the inferences that can be drawn against the respondent to a s. 65 questionnaire when there are pending criminal proceedings (House of Lords, Report Stage; Hansard HL, 27 January 2000, col. 1708 onwards; House of Commons, *Hansard HC, Standing Committee D, 18 April 2000 (afternoon)*).

(v) Discrimination claims arising out of immigration proceedings to be heard in the 'one-stop' immigration appeals system (House of Lords, Second Reading Debate, *Hansard*

HL, 14 December 1999, col. 133, Lord Bassam of Brighton; House of Commons, *Hansard HC, Standing Committee D, 18 April 2000 (afternoon)*).

(vi) Extension in the Act of the provisions prohibiting discrimination in public appointments (House of Commons, *Hansard HC, Standing Committee D, 18 April 2000 (afternoon)*).

(vii) Attempt to add the phrase 'in the purported performance of police functions' to the new provisions on vicarious liability of the police (House of Commons, *Hansard HC, Standing Committee D, 18 April 2000 (afternoon)*).

(vii) Attempt to add the concept of 'acts which occurred as a result or in pursuance of any policing objective set by the Secretary of State' as a statutory defence to discrimination by the police (House of Commons, *Hansard HC, Standing Committee D, 18 April 2000 (afternoon)*).

Appendix 3
Relevant Appendices from the Consultation Paper

APPENDIX 5

Public bodies proposed for addition to Schedule 1A, the general duty, grouped by sponsor Department

- National Audit Office
- Audit Scotland

Cabinet Office
- Political Honours Scrutiny Committee

Department for Culture, Media and Sport
- Theatres Trust
- Treasure Valuation Committee
- Museum of Science & Industry in Manchester
- Horniman Museum
- Geffrye Museum
- Commission for Architecture & the Built Environment
- Resource — The Council for Museums, Archives and Libraries
- The Film Council
- British Library
- Historic Buildings and Monuments Commission for England
- British Museum
- Victoria & Albert Museum
- Natural History Museum
- National Museums & Galleries on Merseyside
- Tate Gallery
- Historic Royal Palaces
- Sport England (English Sports Council)
- National Gallery
- National Maritime Museum
- Imperial War Museum
- British Tourist Authority
- Museum of London
- National Lottery Charities Board
- Arts Council of England
- National Heritage Memorial Fund
- National Portrait Gallery
- Royal Armouries

- Millennium Commission
- Wallace Collection
- English Tourist Board
- New Opportunities Fund
- UK Sports Council
- Broadcasting Standards Commission in respect of its public functions
- Royal Commission on Historical Manuscripts
- Sir John Soane's Museum
- Registrar of Public Lending Right
- National Endowment for Science, Technology and the Arts
- National Museum of Science & Industry
- British Broadcasting Corporation in respect of its public functions
- Channel Four Television Corporation in respect of its public functions
- Independent Television Commission in respect of its public functions
- Sianal Pedwar Cymru (Welsh Fourth Channel Authority) in respect of its public functions
- Radio Authority in respect of its public functions

Department of the Environment, Transport and the Regions

- Advisory Committee on Releases to the Environment
- Building Regulations Advisory Committee
- Disabled Persons Transport Advisory Committee
- Inland Waterways Amenity Advisory Council
- National Forest Company
- National Air Traffic Services Limited
- Environment Agency
- The Health & Safety Executive
- Audit Commission for Local Authorities for England and Wales
- Nature Conservancy Council for England
- Trinity House Lighthouse Service
- Urban Regeneration Agency
- Northern Lighthouse Board
- Local Government Commission for England
- Health & Safety Commission
- Commission for the New Towns
- Civil Aviation Authority — in respect of its public functions
- British Standards Institute
- The Institution of Civil Engineers
- The Institution of Electrical Engineers
- British Waterways Board
- British Transport Police
- Strategic Rail Authority

Department for Education and Employment

- School Teachers' Review Body
- Student Loans Company
- British Educational Communication & Technology Agency
- Construction Industry Training Board
- Qualifications and Curriculum Authority
- Equal Opportunities Commission
- Teacher's Training Agency
- Disability Rights Commission
- Engineering Construction Industry Training Board

- Investors in People UK
- Learning and Skills Council

Department for International Development
- Overseas Service Pensions Scheme Advisory Board
- Commonwealth Scholarship Commission in the UK

Department of Health
- British Pharmacopoeia Commission
- Standing Nursing & Midwifery Advisory Committee
- Unrelated Live Transplant Regulatory Authority
- Committee on the Safety of Medicines
- Standing Medical Advisory Committee
- Medicines Commission
- Administration of Radioactive Substances Advisory Committee
- Advisory Board on the Registration of Homeopathic Products
- Joint Committee on Vaccination and Immunisation
- Standing Dental Advisory Committee
- Standing Pharmaceutical Advisory Committee
- Public Health Laboratory Service Board
- National Radiological Protection Board
- National Biological Standards Board
- Commission for Health Improvement
- English National Board for Nursing, Midwifery & Health Visiting
- Human Fertilisation and Embryology Authority
- Dental Practice Board
- Royal Pharmaceutical Society of Great Britain in respect of its statutory functions and the regulation of the pharmacy profession
- General Medical Council
- United Kingdom Central Council for Nursing, Midwifery and Health Visitors in respect of its public functions
- General Dental Council
- Council for Professions Supplementary to Medicine in respect of its public functions
- General Optical Council
- General Osteopathic Council
- General Chiropractic Council
- Specialist Training Authority of the Medical Royal Colleges
- The Association of Child Psychotherapy
- The British Medical Association
- The Joint Committee on Postgraduate Training for General Practice
- The Royal College of Nursing
- The Royal College of Psychiatrists

Department of Social Security
- Social Security Advisory Committee
- Industrial Injuries Advisory Council
- Central Advisory Committee on War Pensions
- Disability Living Allowance Advisory Board
- War Pensions Committees

Department of Trade and Industry
- Low Pay Commission
- Industrial Development Advisory Board
- National Consumer Council

- Medical Research Council
- Biotechnology & Biological Sciences Research Council
- Natural Environment Research Council
- UK Atomic Energy Authority in respect of its public functions
- Council for the Central Laboratory of the Research Councils
- Advisory, Conciliation & Arbitration Services (ACAS)
- Engineering & Physical Sciences Research Council
- Particle Physics & Astronomy Research Council
- Gas Consumers' Council
- Coal Authority
- Economic & Social Research Council
- Competition Commission
- Design Council
- Post Office Users' National Council
- British Hallmarking Council
- Post Office in respect of its public functions
- British Nuclear Fuels plc in respect of its public functions
- The Association of Authorised Public Accountants
- The Association of Certified Chartered Accountants
- The Engineering Council
- The Insolvency Practitioners Association
- The Institute of Chartered Accountants in England and Wales
- The Institute of Chartered Accountants of Scotland
- The Institute of Trade Mark Agents
- The Law Society

Foreign and Commonwealth Office
- Government Hospitality Fund Advisory Committee for the Purchase of Wine
- Wilton Park Academic Council
- Westminster Foundation for Democracy
- British Association for Central & Eastern Europe
- British-Russia Centre
- Great Britain-China Centre
- British Council
- Marshall Aid Commemoration Commission

Food Standards Agency
- Advisory Committee on Novel Foods and Processes
- Advisory Committee on the Microbiological Safety of Foods
- Expert Group on Vitamins and Minerals
- Food Advisory Committee

Home Office
- Chief Officers of Police
- Advisory Council on the Misuse of Drugs
- Animal Procedures Committee
- Sentencing Advisory Panel
- Firearms Consultative Committee
- Police Negotiating Board
- Horserace Totalisator Board (The Tote)
- Criminal Injuries Compensation Authority
- Police Information Technology Organisation
- Commission for Racial Equality
- Office of the Information Commissioner

- Youth Justice Board for England & Wales
- Gaming Board for Great Britain
- Police Complaints Authority
- Community Development Foundation
- Horserace Betting Levy Board
- Alcohol Education & Research Council
- Board of Visitors to Penal Establishments
- Electoral Commission
- Fire Service Research and Training Trust
- Immigration Detention Centre Visiting Committees
- Selection Panel for Independent Members of Police Authorities

Lord Chancellor's Department
- Law Commission
- Council on Tribunals
- Insolvency Rules Committee
- Land Registration Rule Committee
- Advisory Council on Public Records
- Civil Justice Council
- Civil Procedure Rule Committee
- Crown Court Rule Committee
- Family Proceedings Rule Committee
- Legal Services Consultative Panel
- Legal Services Commission
- The Official Solicitor
- Her Majesty's Magistrates' Courts Service Inspectorate
- Bodies responsible for regulating the provision of legal services (e.g. the Law Society, the Bar Council, the Institute of Legal Executives, Council for Licensed Conveyancers, the Chartered Institute of Patent Agents & the master of facilities)

Ministry of Agriculture, Fisheries and Food
- Hill Farming Advisory Committee for England, Wales and Northern Ireland
- Advisory Committee on Pesticides
- Agricultural Dwelling Houses Advisory Committees
- Veterinary Products Committee
- Wine Standards Board of the Vintners' Company
- Meat & Livestock Commission
- Royal Botanic Gardens, Kew
- Sea Fish Industry Authority
- British Potato Council
- Home-Grown Cereals Authority
- Horticultural Development Council
- Milk Development Council
- Apple and Pear Research Council
- Agricultural Wages Board for England & Wales
- Agricultural Wages Committees for England
- Food from Britain
- Regional Flood Defence Committees
- Covent Garden Market Authority

Ministry of Defence
- Oil & Pipelines Agency

National Assembly for Wales
- Ancient Monuments Board for Wales
- Environment Agency Advisory Committee for Wales
- Hill Farming Advisory Sub-Committee for Wales
- Historic Buildings Council for Wales
- Local Government Boundary Commission for Wales
- Wales New Deal Advisory Task Force
- Welsh Committee for Professional Development of Pharmacists
- Welsh Dental Committee
- Welsh Industrial Development Advisory Board
- Welsh Medical Committee
- Welsh Nursing & Midwifery Committee
- Welsh Optical Committee
- Welsh Pharmaceutical Committee
- Welsh Scientific Advisory Committee
- Countryside Council for Wales
- National Museums and Galleries of Wales
- Welsh Development Agency
- National Library of Wales
- Welsh National Board for Nursing, Midwifery & Health Visiting
- Wales Tourist Board
- Arts Council of Wales
- Qualifications, Curriculum & Assessment Authority for Wales
- Higher Education Funding Council for Wales
- Royal Commission for Ancient & Historical Monuments of Wales
- Welsh Language Board
- Agricultural Wages Committee (Wales)
- Library and Information Services Council (Wales)
- Sports Council for Wales
- National Council for Education and Training for Wales

Office of Water Services
- OFWAT Customer Service Committee (CSCs)

Scottish Executive
- Royal Fine Art Commission for Scotland
- Advisory Committee on Sites of Special Scientific Interest
- Ancient Monuments Board for Scotland
- Building Standards Advisory Committee
- Fisheries (Electricity) Committee
- General Teaching Council for Scotland
- Hill Farming Advisory Committee for Scotland
- Historic Buildings Council for Scotland
- Local Government Boundary Commission for Scotland
- Scottish Industrial Development Advisory Board
- Scottish Law Commission
- Scottish Records Advisory Council
- Scottish Crop Research Institute
- Macauley Land Use Research Institute
- Rowett Research Institute
- Hannah Research Institute
- Scottish Screen
- Scottish Further Education Unit

- Community Learning Scotland
- Moredun Research Institute
- Scottish Natural Heritage
- Scottish Environment Protection Agency
- Scottish Qualifications Authority
- National Museums of Scotland
- Scottish Legal Aid Board
- National Library of Scotland
- Royal Botanic Garden, Edinburgh
- Commissioner for Local Administration in Scotland
- Water Industry Commissioner for Scotland
- The Law Society of Scotland
- Scottish Tourist Board
- National Galleries of Scotland
- Sportscotland (Scottish Sports Council)
- Accounts Commission for Scotland
- Scottish Arts Council
- Royal Commission on the Ancient & Historical Monuments of Scotland
- Scottish Higher Education Funding Council
- Crofter's Commission
- Scottish National Board for Nursing, Midwifery & Health Visiting
- Deer Commission for Scotland
- Scottish Medical Practices Committee
- Scottish Conveyancing & Executry Services Board
- Scottish Agricultural Wages Board
- Scottish Hospital Endowments Research Trust
- Caledonian MacBryane Ltd in respect of its public functions
- Highlands & Islands Airports Ltd in respect of its public functions
- Scottish Transport Group
- Common Services Agency for the NHS in Scotland
- State Hospitals Board for Scotland
- Health Education Board for Scotland
- Mental Welfare Commission for Scotland
- Scottish Council for Postgraduate Medical & Dental Education
- Scottish Hospital Trust
- Scottish Further Education Funding Council
- Learning and Teaching Scotland
- Scottish Dental Practice Board

Treasury

- Financial Services Authority
- Bank of England in respect of its public functions

APPENDIX 6: PART 1

Key central public bodies for which specific duties at paragraph 6.4 are proposed

Crown

- A Minister of the Crown or Government Department
- The National Assembly for Wales
- Audit Scotland
- National Audit Office

Department for Culture, Media and Sport

- British Broadcasting Corporation in respect of its public functions
- Channel Four Television Corporation in respect of its public functions
- Independent Television Commission in respect of its public functions
- Sianal Pedwar Cymru (Welsh Fourth Channel Authority) in respect of its public functions
- Radio Authority in respect of its public functions
- Broadcasting Standards Commission in respect of its public functions

Department of the Environment, Transport and the Regions

- A joint authority established under section 21 of the Local Government Act 1992
- The Common Council of the City of London in its capacity as a local authority or port health authority
- The Sub-Treasurer of the Inner Temple or the Under-Treasurer of the Middle Temple, in his capacity as a local authority
- The London Development Agency
- A regional development agency established under the Regional Development Agencies Act 1998
- A local authority within the meaning of the Local Government Act 1972, namely — in England, a county council, a London borough council, a district council or a parish council
- The Greater London Authority
- The Council of the Isles of Scilly
- A body corporate established pursuant to an order under Section 67 of the Local Government Act 1985 (transfer of functions to successors of residuary bodies, etc)
- A Passenger Transport Executive for a passenger transport area within the meaning of Part II of the Transport Act 1968
- Transport for London
- Urban Regeneration Agency
- The Housing Corporation
- A housing action trust established under Part III of the Housing Act 1988
- A joint authority established under Part IV of the Local Government Act 1985 (fire services, civil defence and transport)
- British Transport Police
- Strategic Rail Authority
- Local Government Commission for England
- Environment Agency
- Audit Commission for Local Authorities for England and Wales
- Health & Safety Commission

Department for Education and Employment

- Equal Opportunities Commission
- Disability Rights Commission
- Learning and Skills Council

Department of Health

- A special health authority established under section 11 of the National Health Service Act 1977
- A Health Authority established under Section 8 of the National Health Service Act 1977
- A primary care trust established under Section 16A of the National Health Service Act 1977
- A National Health Service trust established under Section 5 of the National Health Service and Community Care Act 1990
- Commission for Health Improvement

Home Office

- Chief Officers of Police
- A probation committee constituted under Section 3 of the Probation Service Act 1993 (to be replaced by a local probation board under Section 4 of the Criminal Justice and Court Services)
- The London Fire and Emergency Planning Authority
- A fire authority constituted by a combination scheme under Section 5 or 6 of the Fire Services Act 1947
- A police authority established under Section 3 of the Police Act 1996
- The Metropolitan Police Authority established under section 5B of the Police Act 1996
- The Common Council of the City of London in its capacity as a police authority
- The Service Authority for the National Criminal Intelligence Service
- The Service Authority for the National Crime Squad
- Commission for Racial Equality
- Police Complaints Authority

Lord Chancellor's Department

- A magistrates courts committee established under Section 27 of the Justices of the Peace Act 1997
- Legal Services Commission

Ministry of Agriculture, Fisheries and Food

- The Broads Authority established by section 1 of the Norfolk and Suffolk Broads Act 1988

Ministry of Defence

- Any of the naval, military or air forces of the Crown

National Assembly for Wales

- Higher Education Funding Council for Wales
- A local authority within the meaning of the Local Government Act 1972, namely — in Wales, a county council, a county borough council or a community council
- National Council for Education and Training for Wales
- An Assembly subsidiary as defined by section 99(4) of the Government of Wales Act 1998
- Welsh Development Agency

Scottish Executive

- A Health Board constituted under Section 2 of the National Health Service (Scotland) Act 1978
- Common Services Agency for the NHS in Scotland
- Scottish Enterprise
- State Hospitals Board for Scotland
- Highlands and Islands Enterprise
- Health Education Board for Scotland
- A Special Health Board constituted under Section 2 of the National Health Service (Scotland) Act 1978
- A National Health Service Trust established under Section 12A of the National Health Service (Scotland) Act 1978
- A council constituted under Section 2 of the Local Government etc (Scotland) Act 1994
- A community council established under Section 51 of the Local Government (Scotland) Act 1973
- An office-holder in the Scottish Administration within the meaning given by Section 126(7)(a) of the Scotland Act 1998

- Members of the staff of the Scottish Administration within the meaning given by Section 126(7)(b) of the Scotland Act 1998
- A joint board within the meaning of Section 235(1) of the Local Government (Scotland) Act 1973
- A licensing board constituted under Section 1 of the Licensing (Scotland) Act 1976
- A police authority established under section 2 of the Police (Scotland) Act 1967
- Scottish Higher Education Funding Council
- Scottish Homes
- Scottish Legal Aid Board
- Accounts Commission for Scotland
- Scottish Further Education Funding Council

APPENDIX 6: PART 2

Educational bodies for which the specific duties at paragraphs 6.16 and 6.17 are proposed

- Governing bodies of educational establishments maintained by LEAs, FE and HE institutions within the meaning of Sections 91(3) and (5) of the Further and Higher Education Act 1992
- Managers of a grant-aided school within the meaning of Section 135 of the Education (Scotland) Act 1980
- Board of management of a college of further education within the meaning of Section 36(1) of the Further and Higher Education (Scotland) Act 1992
- Board of management of a self-governing school within the meaning of the Self-Governing Schools, etc (Scotland) Act 1989
- Governing body of an institution within the higher education sector within the meaning of Part II of the Further and Higher Education (Scotland) Act 1992
- Managers of a central institution within the meaning of Section 135 of the Education (Scotland) Act 1980

APPENDIX 6: PART 3

Public bodies with executive functions for which no specific duties are being proposed with regards to policy or service delivery

Department for Culture, Media and Sport

- Museum of Science & Industry in Manchester
- Horniman Museum
- Geffrye Museum
- Commission for Architecture & the Built Environment
- Resource — The Council for Museums, Archives and Libraries
- The Film Council
- British Library
- Historic Buildings and Monuments Commission for England
- British Museum
- Victoria & Albert Museum
- Natural History Museum
- National Museums & Galleries on Merseyside
- Tate Gallery
- Historic Royal Palaces
- Sport England (English Sports Council)
- National Gallery

- National Maritime Museum
- Imperial War Museum
- British Tourist Authority
- Museum of London
- Arts Council of England
- National Heritage Memorial Fund
- National Portrait Gallery
- Royal Armouries
- Millennium Commission
- Wallace Collection
- English Tourist Board
- New Opportunities Fund
- UK Sports Council
- Royal Commission on Historical Manuscripts
- Sir John Soane's Museum
- Registrar of Public Lending Right
- National Endowment for Science, Technology and the Arts
- National Museum of Science & Industry
- National Lottery Charities Board

Department of the Environment, Transport and the Regions

- National Forest Company
- National Air Traffic Services Limited
- The Health & Safety Executive
- Nature Conservancy Council for England
- Trinity House Lighthouse Service
- Northern Lighthouse Board
- Commission for the New Towns
- A joint board which is continued by virtue of Section 263(1) of the Local Government Act 1972
- A body corporate established pursuant to an order under Section 22 of the Local Government Act 1992 (residuary bodies)
- A joint committee constituted in accordance with Section 102(1)(b) of the Local Government Act 1972
- A joint planning board constituted for an area in Wales outside a National Park by an order under Section 2(1B) of the Town and Country Planning Act 1990
- A National Park authority established by an order under section 63 of the Environment Act 1995
- A parish meeting constituted under Section 13 of the Local Government Act 1972
- A port health authority constituted by an order under Section 2 of the Public Health (Control of Disease) Act 1984
- A waste disposal authority established by virtue of an order under Section 10(1) of the Local Government Act 1985
- A water or sewerage authority constituted under Section 62 of the Local Government etc. (Scotland) Act 1994
- Any Charter trustees constituted under Section 246 of the Local Government Act 1972
- Civil Aviation Authority in respect of its public functions
- British Standards Institute
- The Institution of Civil Engineers
- The Institution of Electrical Engineers
- British Waterways Board

Department of Education and Employment

- Student Loans Company
- British Educational Communication & Technology Agency
- Construction Industry Training Board
- Qualifications and Curriculum Authority
- Teacher's Training Agency
- Engineering Construction Industry Training Board
- Investors in People UK

Department for International Development

- Commonwealth Scholarship Commission in the UK

Department of Health

- Public Health Laboratory Service Board
- National Radiological Protection Board
- National Biological Standards Board
- English National Board for Nursing, Midwifery & Health Visiting
- Human Fertilisation and Embryology Authority
- Dental Practice Board
- Royal Pharmaceutical Society of Great Britain in respect of its public functions
- General Medical Council
- United Kingdom Central Council for Nursing, Midwifery and Health Visitors in respect of its public functions
- General Dental Council
- Council for Professions Supplementary to Medicine in respect of its public functions
- General Optical Council
- General Osteopathic Council
- General Chiropractic Council
- Specialist Training Authority of the Medical Royal Colleges
- The Association of Child Psychotherapy
- The British Medical Association
- The Joint Committee on Postgraduate Training for General Practice
- The Royal College of Nursing
- The Royal College of Psychiatrists

Department of Trade and Industry

- National Consumer Council
- Medical Research Council
- Biotechnology & Biological Sciences Research Council
- Natural Environment Research Council
- UK Atomic Energy Authority — in respect of its public functions
- Council for the Central Laboratory of the Research Councils
- Advisory, Conciliation & Arbitration Services (ACAS)
- Engineering & Physical Sciences Research Council
- Particle Physics & Astronomy Research Council
- Gas Consumers' Council
- Coal Authority
- Economic & Social Research Council
- Competition Commission
- Design Council
- Post Office Users' National Council
- British Hallmarking Council
- Post Office in respect of its public functions
- British Nuclear Fuels plc in respect of its public functions

- The Association of Authorised Public Accountants
- The Association of Certified Chartered Accountants
- The Engineering Council
- The Insolvency Practitioners Association
- The Institute of Chartered Accountants in England and Wales
- The Institute of Chartered Accountants of Scotland
- The Institute of Trade Mark Agents
- The Law Society

Foreign and Commonwealth Office
- Westminster Foundation for Democracy
- British Association for Central & Eastern Europe
- British-Russia Centre
- Great Britain-China Centre
- British Council
- Marshall Aid Commemoration Commission

Home Office
- Horserace Totalisator Board (The Tote)
- Criminal Injuries Compensation Authority
- Police Information Technology Organisation
- Office of the Information Commissioner
- Youth Justice Board for England & Wales
- Gaming Board for Great Britain
- Community Development Foundation
- Horserace Betting Levy Board
- Alcohol Education & Research Council
- Board of Visitors to Penal Establishments
- Electoral Commission
- Fire Service Research and Training Trust
- Immigration Detention Centre Visiting Committees
- Selection Panel for Independent Members of Police Authorities
- A licensing planning committee constituted under Section 119 of the Licensing Act 1964

Lord Chancellor's Department
- The Official Solicitor
- Her Majesty's Magistrates' Courts Service Inspectorate
- Bodies responsible for regulating the provision of legal services e.g. the Law Society, the Bar Council, the Institute of Legal Executives, Council for Licensed Conveyancers, the Chartered Institute of Patent Agents & the master of facilities

Ministry of Agriculture, Fisheries and Food
- Wine Standards Board of the Vintners' Company
- Meat & Livestock Commission
- Royal Botanic Gardens, Kew
- Sea Fish Industry Authority
- British Potato Council
- Home-Grown Cereals Authority
- Horticultural Development Council
- Milk Development Council
- Apple and Pear Research Council
- Agricultural Wages Board for England & Wales
- Agricultural Wages Committees for England
- Food from Britain

- Regional Flood Defence Committees
- An internal drainage board which is continued in being by virtue of Section 1 of the Land Drainage Act 1991
- Covent Garden Market Authority

Ministry of Defence
- Oil & Pipelines Agency

National Assembly for Wales
- Countryside Council for Wales
- National Museums and Galleries of Wales
- National Library of Wales
- Welsh National Board for Nursing, Midwifery & Health Visiting
- Wales Tourist Board
- Arts Council of Wales
- Qualifications, Curriculum & Assessment Authority for Wales
- Royal Commission for Ancient & Historical Monuments of Wales
- Welsh Language Board
- Agricultural Wages Committee (Wales)
- Library and Information Services Council (Wales)
- Sports Council for Wales

Office of Water Services
- OFWAT Customer Service Committee (CSCs)

Scottish Executive
- Scottish Crop Research Institute
- Macauley Land Use Research Institute
- Rowett Research Institute
- Hannah Research Institute
- Scottish Screen
- Scottish Further Education Unit
- Community Learning Scotland
- Moredun Research Institute
- Scottish Natural Heritage
- Scottish Environment Protection Agency
- Scottish Qualifications Authority
- National Museums of Scotland
- National Library of Scotland
- Royal Botanic Garden, Edinburgh
- Scottish Tourist Board
- National Galleries of Scotland
- Sportscotland (Scottish Sports Council)
- Scottish Arts Council
- Royal Commission on the Ancient & Historical Monuments of Scotland
- Water Industry Commissioner for Scotland
- Scottish Dental Practice Board
- Commissioner for Local Administration in Scotland
- Crofter's Commission
- Scottish National Board for Nursing, Midwifery & Health Visiting
- Deer Commission for Scotland
- Scottish Medical Practices Committee
- Scottish Conveyancing & Executry Services Board
- Scottish Agricultural Wages Board

- Scottish Hospital Endowments Research Trust
- Caledonian MacBryane Ltd in respect of its public functions
- Highlands & Islands Airports Ltd in respect of its public functions
- Scottish Transport Group
- Mental Welfare Commission for Scotland
- Scottish Council for Postgraduate Medical & Dental Education
- Scottish Hospital Trust
- The Law Society of Scotland
- Learning and Teaching Scotland

Treasury
- Financial Services Authority
- Bank of England in respect of its public functions

APPENDIX 6: PART 4

Advisory NDPBs subject to the general duty and for which specific duties are not being proposed

Cabinet Office
- Political Honours Scrutiny Committee

Department for Culture, Media and Sport
- Theatres Trust
- Treasure Valuation Committee

Department of the Environment, Transport and the Regions
- Advisory Committee on Releases to the Environment
- Building Regulations Advisory Committee
- Disabled Persons Transport Advisory Committee
- Inland Waterways Amenity Advisory Council

Department for Education and Employment
- School Teachers Review Body

Department for International Development
- Overseas Service Pensions Scheme Advisory Board

Department of Health
- Standing Dental Advisory Committee
- Unrelated Live Transplant Regulatory Authority
- Standing Pharmaceutical Advisory Committee
- Standing Medical Advisory Committee
- Medicines Commission
- Joint Committee on Vaccination and Immunisation
- Committee on the Safety of Medicines
- Advisory Board on the Registration of Homeopathic Products
- Administration of Radioactive Substances Advisory Committee
- Standing Nursing & Midwifery Advisory Committee
- British Pharmacopoeia Commission

Department of Social Security
- Central Advisory Committee on War Pensions
- Industrial Injuries Advisory Council
- Disability Living Allowance Advisory Board
- Social Security Advisory Committee

- War Pensions Committees

Department of Trade and Industry
- Industrial Development Advisory Board
- Low Pay Commission

Foreign and Commonwealth Office
- Wilton Park Academic Council
- Government Hospitality Fund Advisory Committee for the Purchase of Wine

Food Standards Agency
- Advisory Committee on the Microbiological Safety of Foods
- Advisory Committee on Novel Foods and Processes
- Expert Group on Vitamins and Minerals
- Food Advisory Committee

Home Office
- Advisory Council on the Misuse of Drugs
- Animal Procedures Committee
- Firearms Consultative Committee
- Police Negotiating Board
- Sentencing Advisory Panel

Lord Chancellor's Department
- Advisory Council on Public Records
- Land Registration Rule Committee
- Family Proceedings Rule Committee
- Crown Court Rule Committee
- Council on Tribunals
- Civil Justice Council
- Insolvency Rules Committee
- Law Commission
- Legal Services Consultative Panel
- Civil Procedure Rule Committee

Ministry of Agriculture, Fisheries and Food
- Veterinary Products Committee
- Hill Farming Advisory Committee for England, Wales and Northern Ireland
- Agricultural Dwelling Houses Advisory Committees
- Advisory Committee on Pesticides

National Assembly for Wales
- Welsh Nursing & Midwifery Committee
- Wales New Deal Advisory Task Force
- Environment Agency Advisory Committee for Wales
- Welsh Scientific Advisory Committee
- Welsh Optical Committee
- Welsh Medical Committee
- Welsh Industrial Development Advisory Board
- Welsh Dental Committee
- Welsh Committee for Professional Development of Pharmacists
- Local Government Boundary Commission for Wales
- Historic Buildings Council for Wales
- Hill Farming Advisory Sub-Committee for Wales
- Ancient Monuments Board for Wales
- Welsh Pharmaceutical Committee

Scottish Executive

- Ancient Monuments Board for Scotland
- Scottish Industrial Development Advisory Board
- Scottish Records Advisory Council
- Scottish Law Commission
- Royal Fine Art Commission for Scotland
- Local Government Boundary Commission for Scotland
- Historic Buildings Council for Scotland
- Hill Farming Advisory Committee for Scotland
- General Teaching Council for Scotland
- Building Standards Advisory Committee
- Advisory Committee on Sites of Special Scientific Interest
- Fisheries (Electricity) Committee

Appendix 4
The New Style Questionnaire under the Race Relations Act 1976, s. 65

RACE RELATIONS ACT 1976

ASKING QUESTIONS UNDER THE PROVISIONS OF SECTION 65 OF THE RACE RELATIONS ACT 1976, AS AMENDED BY THE RACE RELATIONS (AMENDMENT) ACT 2000

CONTENTS

A complainant should obtain TWO copies of this booklet, one to send to the respondent and the other to keep.

Before completing the questionnaire or the reply form (as appropriate), the complainant and the respondent should read Part I of the guidance and (again as appropriate) Part II or III.

Issued by The Home Office and
The Department for Education and Employment

GUIDANCE ON THE PROCEDURE UNDER SECTION 65 OF THE RACE RELATIONS ACT 1976

PART 1 — INTRODUCTION

1. The purpose of this guidance is to explain the questions procedure under section 65 of the Race Relations Act 1976 ('the Act').[1] This guidance has been updated to take into account the provisions of the Race Relations (Amendment) Act 2000 ('the Amendment Act') which came into force on 2 April 2000. The procedure is intended to help a person

[1] The prescribed forms, time limits for serving questions and manner of service of questions and replies under section 65 are specified in The Race Relations (Questions and Replies) Order 1977 (SI 1977 No. 842).

(referred to in this guidance as the **complainant**) who thinks he has been discriminated against by another (the **respondent**) to obtain information from that person about the treatment in question in order to

(a) decide whether or not to bring legal proceedings, and

(b) if proceedings are brought, to present his complaint in the most effective way.

A questionnaire has been devised which the complainant can send to the respondent and there is also a matching reply form for use by the respondent (both are included here). The questionnaire and the reply form have been designed to assist the complainant and respondent in identifying information which is relevant to the complaint. It is not, however, obligatory for the questionnaire or the reply form to be used; the exchange of questions and replies may be conducted, for example, by letter. *This questionnaire should not be used in respect of race relations complaints relating to immigration decisions that are to be considered as part of one-stop immigration and asylum appeals (see section 57A of the Act, inserted by section 6(2) of the Amendment Act).*

2. This guidance is intended to assist both the complainant and the respondent. Guidance for the complainant on the preparation of the questionnaire is set out in Part II; and guidance for the respondent on the use of the reply form is set out in Part III. Guidance is also provided in the margins of the questionnaire. The guidance is not part of the questionnaire. The main provisions of the Act are referred to in the appendix to **this** guidance. Further information about the Act will be found in the various leaflets published by the Commission for Racial Equality which may be obtained from:

Central Books
Telephone: 020 8986 5488
Fax: 020 8533 5821
E-mail: cre@centralbooks.com

Further information is also available from the CRE's website at www.cre.gov.uk and from The Home Office website at www.homeoffice.gov.uk. The CRE's leaflet on the employment provisions of the Act may also be obtained, free of charge, from any employment office or Jobcentre of the Employment Service. The CRE's leaflets may also be obtained from local racial equality councils.

How the questions procedure can benefit both parties

3. The procedure can benefit both the complainant and the respondent in the following ways:

(1) If the respondent's answers satisfy the complainant that the treatment was not unlawful discrimination, there will be no need for legal proceedings.

(2) Even if the respondent's answers do not satisfy the complainant, they should help to identify what is agreed and what is in dispute between the parties. For example, the answers should reveal whether the parties disagree on the facts of the case, or, if they agree on the facts, whether they disagree on how the Act applies. In some cases, this may lead to a settlement of the grievance, again making legal proceedings unnecessary.

(3) If it turns out that the complainant institutes proceedings against the respondent, the proceedings should be that much simpler because the matters in dispute will have been identified in advance.

What happens if the respondent does not reply or replies evasively?

4. The respondent cannot be compelled to reply to the complainant's questions. However, by virtue of section 65 of the Act, this questionnaire and any reply are (subject to the provisions of the section) admissible in proceedings under the Act and a court or tribunal may draw any such inference as is just and equitable from a failure without reasonable excuse to reply within a reasonable period, or from an evasive or equivocal reply, including an inference that the person questioned has discriminated unlawfully. The respondent's attention is drawn to these possible consequences in the note at the end of the questionnaire.

5. New section 65(4A) of the Act, inserted by section 5(2) of the Amendment Act, provides that, in proceedings under new section 19B of the Act, a court will not be able to draw the inferences in paragraph 4 above if:

(a) at the tine of doing the relevant act the respondent was carrying out public investigation or public prosecutor functions; and

(b) he or she reasonably believes that a reply or a different reply would be likely to prejudice any criminal investigation, any decision to institute criminal proceedings, or any criminal proceedings, or would reveal the reason behind a decision not to prosecute, or not to continue, criminal proceedings.

The Act does not prevent a complainant from seeking a reply at a later date when the circumstances set out above may no longer apply.

Period within which questionnaire must be served on the respondent

6. There are different time limits within which a questionnaire must be served in order to be admissible in any ensuing legal proceedings. Which time limit applies depends on whether the complaint would be under the employment, training and related provisions of the Act (in which case the proceedings would be before an employment tribunal), or whether it would be under the functions of a public nature, education, goods, facilities and services or premises provisions (in which case proceedings would be before a designated county court or, in Scotland, a sheriff court).

Employment tribunal cases

7. In order to be admissible under the questions procedure in any ensuing employment tribunal proceedings, the complainant's questionnaire must be served on the respondent either:

(a) before a complaint about the treatment concerned is made to an employment tribunal, but not more than 3 months after the treatment in question; or

(b) if a complaint has already been made to a tribunal, within 21 days beginning when the complaint was received by the tribunal.

However, where the complainant has made a complaint to a tribunal and the period of 21 days has expired, a questionnaire may still be served provided the permission of the tribunal is obtained. This may be done by sending to the Secretary of the Tribunals a written application, which must state the names of the complainant and the respondent and set out the grounds of the application. However every effort should be made to serve the questionnaire within the period of 21 days as the permission of the tribunal to serve the questionnaire after the expiry of that period will not necessarily be obtained.

Court cases

8. In order to be admissible under the questions procedure in any ensuing county or sheriff court proceedings, the complainant's questionnaire must be served on the respondent before proceedings in respect of the treatment concerned are brought, but not more than 6 months after the treatment.[2] However, where proceedings have been brought, a questionnaire may still be served provided the permission of the court has been obtained. In the case of county court proceedings, this may be done by obtaining form N244 from the county court office, and completing it and sending it to the court, with the appropriate fee, and the respondent. In the case of sheriff court proceedings, this may be done by making an application to a sheriff.

PART II — GUIDANCE FOR THE COMPLAINANT

NOTES ON PREPARING THE QUESTIONNAIRE

9. Before filling in the questionnaire, you are advised to prepare what you want to say on a separate piece of paper. If you have insufficient room on the questionnaire for what you want to say, you should continue on an additional piece of paper, which should be sent with the questionnaire to the respondent.

---

[2] Where a person has applied in writing to the CRE for assistance in respect of his case, the time limit of 6 months is extended by 2 months. It is open to the CRE to extend the period by a further month.

Paragraph 2

10. You should give, in the space provided in paragraph 2, as much relevant factual information as you can about the treatment you think may have been unlawful discrimination, and about the circumstances leading up to that treatment. You should also give the date, and if possible and if relevant, the place and approximate time of the treatment. You should bear in mind that in paragraph 4 of the questionnaire you will be asking the respondent whether he agrees with what you say in paragraph 2.

Paragraph 3

11. In paragraph 3 you are telling the respondent that you think the treatment you have described in paragraph 2 may have been unlawful discrimination by him against you. It will help to identify whether there are any legal issues between you and the respondent if you explain in the space provided **why** you think the treatment may have been unlawful discrimination. However, you **do not have** to complete paragraph 3; if you do not wish or are unable to do so, you should delete the word 'because'. If you wish to complete the paragraph, but feel you need more information about the Race Relations Act before doing so, you should look to the appendix to this guidance.

12. If you decide to complete paragraph 3, you may find it useful to indicate—

(a) what **kind** of discrimination you think the treatment may have been i.e. whether it was direct discrimination, indirect discrimination, or victimisation (for further information about the different kinds of discrimination see paragraph 1 of the appendix)

(b) which provision of the Act you think may make unlawful the kind of discrimination you think you may have suffered. (For an indication of the provisions of the Act which make the various kinds of discrimination unlawful, see paragraph 2 of the appendix.)

Paragraph 6

13. You should insert here any other question which you think may help you to obtain relevant information. (For example, if you think you have been discriminated against by having been refused a job, you may want to know what were the qualifications of the person who did get the job and why that person got the job.)

14. Paragraph 5 contains questions which are especially important if you think you may have suffered direct discrimination because they ask the respondent whether racial considerations had anything to do with your treatment. Paragraph 5 does not, however, ask specific questions relating to indirect discrimination or victimisation. If you think you may have suffered indirect discrimination you may find it helpful to include the following question in the space provided in paragraph 6:

Paragraph 6:

'Was the reason for my treatment the fact that I could not comply with a condition or requirement which is applied equally to people regardless of their racial group?
If so—

(a) what was the condition or requirement?
(b) why was it applied?'

15. If you think you may have been victimised you may find it helpful to include the following question in the space provided in paragraph 6:

'Was the reason for my treatment the fact that I had done or intended to do, or that you suspected I had done or intended to do, any of the following:

(a) brought proceedings under the Act; or
(b) gave evidence or information in connection with proceedings under the Act; or
(c) did something else under or by reference to the Act; or
(d) made an allegation that someone acted unlawfully under the Act?'

Signature

16. The questionnaire must be signed and dated. If it is to be signed on behalf of (rather than by) the complainant, the person signing should—

(a) describe himself (e.g. 'solicitor acting for (*name of complainant*)'), and
(b) give his business (or home, if appropriate) address.

WHAT PAPERS TO SERVE ON THE PERSON TO BE QUESTIONED

17. You should send the person to be questioned the whole of this document (i.e. the guidance, the questionnaire and the reply forms), with the questionnaire completed by you. **You are strongly advised to retain, and keep in a safe place, a copy of the completed questionnaire** (and you might also find it useful to retain a copy of the guidance and the uncompleted reply form).

HOW TO SERVE THE PAPERS

18. You can either deliver the papers in person or send them by post. If you decide to send them by post you are advised to use the recorded delivery service so that, if necessary, you can produce evidence that they were delivered.

WHERE TO SEND THE PAPERS

19. You can send the papers to the person to be questioned at his usual or last known residence, business address, or the office or establishment where he works or is normally attached. If you know he is acting through a solicitor you should send them to him at his solicitor's address. If you wish to question a limited company or other corporate body or a trade union or employers' association, you should send the papers to the secretary or clerk at the registered or principal office of the company, etc. You should be able to find out where its registered or principal office is by enquiring at a public library. If you are unable to do so, however, you will have to send the papers to the place where you think it is most likely they will reach the secretary or clerk (e.g. at, or c/o, the company's local office). It is your responsibility, however, to see that the secretary or clerk receives the papers.

USE OF THE QUESTIONS AND REPLIES IN EMPLOYMENT TRIBUNAL PROCEEDINGS

20. If you decide to make (or already have made) a complaint to an employment tribunal about the treatment concerned and if you intend to use your questions and the reply (if any) as evidence in the proceedings, you are advised to send copies of your questions and any reply to the Secretary of the Tribunals before the date of the hearing. This should be done as soon as the documents are available; if they are available at the time you submit your complaint to a tribunal, you should send the copies with your complaint to the Secretary of the Tribunals.

PART III — GUIDANCE FOR THE RESPONDENT

NOTES ON COMPLETING THE REPLY FORM

21. Before completing the reply form, you are advised to prepare what you want to say on a separate piece of paper. If you have insufficient room on the reply form for what you want to say, you should continue on an additional piece of paper, which should be attached to the reply form sent to the complainant.

22. Here you are answering the question in paragraph 4 of the questionnaire. If you **agree** that the complainant's statement in paragraph 2 of the questionnaire is an accurate **description** of what happened, you should delete the second sentence.

23. If you **disagree** in any way that the statement is an accurate description of what happened, you should explain in the space provided in what respects you disagree, or your version of what happened, or both.

Paragraph 3

24. Here you are answering the question in paragraph 5 of the questionnaire. If, in answer to paragraph 4 of the questionnaire, you have agreed with he complainant's description of his treatment, you will be answering paragraph 5 on the basis of the facts in his description. If, however, you have disagreed with that description, you should answer paragraph 5 on the basis of your version of the facts. To answer paragraph 5, you are advised to look at the appendix to this guidance. You need to know:—

(a) how the Act defines discrimination — see paragraph 1 of the appendix,

(b) in what situations the Act makes discrimination unlawful — see paragraph 2 of the appendix; and

(c) what exceptions the Act provides — see paragraph 3 of the appendix.

25. If you think that an exception (e.g. the exception for employment where being of a particular racial group is a genuine occupational qualification) applies to the treatment described in paragraph 2 of the complainant's questionnaire, you should mention this in paragraph 3a of the reply form and explain why you think the exception applies.

Signature

26. The reply form should be signed and dated. If it is to be signed on behalf of (rather than by) the respondent, the person signing should—

(a) describe himself (e.g. 'solicitor acting for (*name of respondent*)' or 'personnel manager of (*name of firm)*'), and

(b) give his business (or home, if appropriate) address.

SERVING THE REPLY FORM ON THE COMPLAINANT

27. If you wish to reply to the questionnaire you are strongly advised to do so without delay. **You should retain, and keep in a safe place, the questionnaire sent to you and a copy of your reply**.

28. You can serve the reply either by delivering it in person to the complainant or by sending it by post. If you decide to send it by post you are advised to use the recorded delivery service, so that, if necessary, you can produce evidence that it was delivered.

29. You should send the reply form to the address indicated in paragraph 7 of the complainant's questionnaire.

THE RACE RELATIONS ACT 1976 SECTION 65(1)(a)

QUESTIONNAIRE OF PERSON AGGRIEVED (THE COMPLAINANT)

Name of person to be questioned (the respondent)	To ....
Address	of ....
Name of complainant	1 I ....
Address	of .... consider that you may have discriminated against me contrary to the Race Relations Act 1976.

Give date, approximate time, place and factual description of the treatment received and of the circumstances leading up to the treatment (see paragraph 10 of the guidance)	2 On
Complete if you wish to give reasons, otherwise delete the word 'because' (see paragraphs 11 and 12 of the guidance)	3 I consider that this treatment may have been unlawful because
This is the first of your questions to the respondent. You are advised not to alter it	4 Do you agree that the statement in paragraph 2 is an accurate description of what happened? If not in what respect do you disagree or what is your version of what happened?
This is the second of your questions to the respondent. You are advised not to alter it.	5 Do you accept that your treatment of me was unlawful discrimination by you against me? If not a why not? b for what reason did I receive the treatment accorded to me? and c how far did considerations of colour, race, nationality (including citizenship) or ethnic or national origins affect your treatment of me?
Enter here any other questions you wish to ask (see paragraphs 13–15 of the guidance)	6
*Delete as appropriate if you delete the first alternative, insert the address to which you want the reply to be sent	7 My address for any reply you may wish to give to the questions raised above is *that set out in paragraph 1 above/the following address
See paragraph 16 of the guidance	Signature of complainant .... Date ....

NB By virtue of section 65 of the Act, this questionnaire and any reply are (subject to the provisions of the section) admissible in proceedings under the Act and a court or tribunal may draw any such inference as is just and equitable from a failure without reasonable excuse to reply within a reasonable period, or from an evasive or equivocal reply, including an inference that the person questioned has discriminated unlawfully

THE RACE RELATIONS ACT 1976 SECTION 65(1)(b)

REPLY BY RESPONDENT

Name of complainant	To ....
Address	of ....
Name of respondent	1 I ....
Address	of ....
Complete as appropriate	hereby acknowledge receipt of the questionnaire signed by you and dated .... which was served on me on (date) ....
*Delete as appropriate	2 I ***agree/disagree** that the statement in paragraph 2 of the questionnaire is an accurate description of what happened.
If you agree that the Statement in paragraph 2 of the questionnaire is accurate, delete this sentence. If you disagree complete this sentence (see paragraphs 22 and 23 of the guidance)	I disagree with the statement in paragraph 2 of the questionnaire in that
*Delete as appropriate	3 I **accept/dispute** that my treatment of you was unlawful discrimination by me against you.
If you accept the complainant's assertion of unlawful discrimination in paragraph 3 of the questionnaire delete the sentences at a, b and c. Unless completed a sentence should be deleted (see paragraphs 24 and 25 of the guidance)	a My reasons for so disputing are b The reason why you received the treatment accorded to you is c Considerations of colour, race, nationality (including citizenship) or ethnic national origins affected my treatment of you to the following extent:—
Replies to questions in paragraph 6 of the questionnaire should be entered here	4

Delete the whole of this sentence if you have answered all the questions in the questionnaire. If you have not answered all the questions, delete 'unable' or 'unwilling' as appropriate and give your reasons for not answering	5 I have deleted (in whole or in part) the paragraph(s) numbered .... above, since I am **unable/unwilling** to reply to the relevant questions of the questionnaire for the following reasons:—
If, at the time of doing the relevant act, you were carrying out public investigation or public prosecutor functions; and you reasonably believe that to respond, or to give a different response, would be likely to prejudice any criminal investigation, any decision to institute criminal proceedings, or any criminal proceedings, or would reveal the reason behind a decision not to prosecute, or not to continue, criminal proceedings, you should refer to section 5(2) of the Race Relations (Amendment) Act 2000. This provides that, in such circumstances, you may be able to decline to respond to a section 65 questionnaire without the risk of adverse inferences being drawn.	
See paragraph 26 of the guidance	Signature of respondent .... Date ....

APPENDIX

NOTES ON THE SCOPE OF THE RACE RELATIONS ACT 1976, AS AMENDED BY THE RACE RELATIONS (AMENDMENT) ACT 2000

Definitions of discrimination

1. The different kinds of discrimination covered by the Act are summarised below.

Direct discrimination arises where a person is treated less favourably than another is (or would be) treated because of his (or someone else's) colour, race, nationality (including citizenship) or ethnic or national origins.

Indirect discrimination arises where a person is treated unfavourably because he cannot comply with a condition or requirement which

(a) is (or would be) applied regardless of colour, race, nationality (including citizenship) or ethnic or national origins, and

(b) is such that the proportion of persons of a particular racial group (i.e. one defined by reference to colour, race, nationality (including citizenship) or ethnic or national origins) who can comply with it is considerably smaller than time proportion of persons not of that group who can comply with it, and

(c) is to the detriment of the person in question because he cannot comply with it, and

(d) is such that the person applying it cannot show that it is justifiable regardless of the colour, race, nationality (including citizenship) or ethnic or national origins of the person to whom it is applied

Victimisation arises where a person is treated less favourably than other persons are (or would be) treated because that person has done (or intends to do or is suspected of having done or intending to do) any of the following:—

(a) brought proceedings under the Act; or

(b) given evidence or information in connection with proceedings brought under the Act; or

(c) done anything else by reference to the Act (e.g. given information to the Commission for Racial Equality); or

(d) made an allegation that someone acted unlawfully under the Act.

Victimisation does not, however, occur where the reason for the less favourable treatment is an allegation which was false and not made in good faith.

Unlawful discrimination

2. The provisions of the Act which make discrimination unlawful are indicated in the table on the next page. Complaints about discrimination which is unlawful under the provisions in Group A (the employment provisions) must be made to an employment tribunal. Complaints about discrimination which is unlawful under the provisions in Group B must be made to a county court or in Scotland, a sheriff court.

Exceptions

3. The Act provides for a number of exceptions in relation to employment, housing, the provision of goods and services, and public functions.

PROVISIONS OF THE RACE RELATIONS ACT 1976 (AS AMENDED) WHICH MAKE DISCRIMINATION UNLAWFUL

	Section of Act
GROUP A	
Discrimination by employers in recruitment and treatment of employees	4
Discrimination against contract workers	7
Discrimination against partners	10
Discrimination by trade unions, employers' associations etc	11
Discrimination by bodies which confer qualifications or authorisations needed for particular kinds of jobs	12
Discrimination in the provision of training	13 and 15
Discrimination by employment agencies	14
GROUP B	
Discrimination by bodies in charge of educational establishments	17
Discrimination (other than that covered by section 17) by local education authorities	18
Discrimination by planning authorities	19A
Discrimination (other than that covered by other provisions of the Act) by public authorities	19B
Discrimination in the provision of goods, facilities or services to the public or a section the public	20
Discrimination in the disposal of premises	21
Discrimination by landlords against prospective assignees or sublessees	24
Discrimination by clubs or associations with 25 or more members (other than clubs or associations covered by section 11 or 20)	25
Discrimination by, or in relation to, barristers	26A
Discrimination by, or in relation to, advocates	26B

Appendix 5
Precedents for statements of case

1. Particulars of claim for claim under the Race Relations Act 1976, s.19B and wrongful arrest/false imprisonment

IN THE [ ] COUNTY COURT

BETWEEN:

MR A — Claimant

and

(1) THE CHIEF CONSTABLE OF THE ANYWHERESHIRE POLICE
(2) PC BLOGGS
(3) WPC SMITH
(4) MR DRUNKEN YOB — Defendants

PARTICULARS OF CLAIM

The parties

1. The Claimant, whose date of birth is 8 December 1978, is British born, of Afro-Caribbean origin. He is a student at Newtown University.

2. The First Defendant is sued as chief officer of police for the Anywhereshire police area. The officers referred to herein, including the Second and Third Defendants, are officers who were at all material times acting under his direction and control and in purported performance of their police functions.

3. Insofar as the claim is for unlawful discrimination contrary to the Race Relations Act 1976, as amended by the Race Relations (Amendment) Act 2000, the acts and omissions of the officers referred to herein occurred during the course of their holding of police office, and the Second Defendant is vicariously liable for the same by virtue of section 76A of the Act.

The facts

4. At about 10 pm on Saturday 14 July 2001 the Claimant left the library at Newtown University in order to meet his friend, Mr B at a fast food café on Main Street, Newtown.

They had both been studying that evening, revising for their final year examinations which began the following Monday. Mr B is also British born, of Pakistani origin.

5. At about 11.25 pm, as the Claimant and Mr B were leaving the fast food café, a group of four white males came towards them, having recently left the Rat and Piano public house. One of the white males was the Fourth Defendant. They were all apparently drunk.

6. The Fourth Defendant saw that the Claimant was carrying his books and began taunting him about studying on a Saturday night. He used abusive language calling him a 'teacher's pet' and a 'swotty black bastard'. The Claimant and Mr B told the man to mind his own business. Mr B made a comment to the effect that at least they had been using their time more effectively than getting drunk. The Claimant and Mr B continued walking towards the bus station. All four white males followed them.

7. Within seconds, the Fourth Defendant grabbed the Claimant from behind and began punching him in the face. Mr B was also punched by one of the other white males. The other two white males then joined in the attack. During the attack the Fourth Defendant and at least one of the other white males used racist language such as 'darkie bastard' and 'nigger'. Both the Claimant and Mr B suffered injuries, namely cuts and bruising to the face.

8. The Second and Third Defendants were passing by in their patrol car and arrived at the scene. They immediately separated the men and asked the Fourth Defendant what had happened. He pointed to the Claimant's books which were now scattered on the floor and told the Second Defendant that the Claimant had tried to steal them from him. The Claimant repeatedly sought to deny this but the Second and Third Defendants did not listen and made no attempt to look inside the books, where the Claimant's name was printed. The Second Defendant told the Claimant he was 'nicked' and escorted him to the Newtown police station.

9. The Claimant was not interviewed until 2pm the following day. In interview, he made it clear that he was the victim of the assault and that he wished to press charges against the Fourth Defendant. After the interview the Claimant was released on bail.

10. The Claimant attended the police station on several occasions thereafter. He was not told until 1 September 2001 that he was not going to be charged.

11. At no time have the Second or Third Defendants or any other officers from the Anywhereshire police area taken a statement from the Claimant as to the attack, despite his requests that they do so. To the best of the Claimant's knowledge, at no time have the Second or Third Defendants or any other officers from the Anywhereshire police area arrested, interviewed or charged the Fourth Defendant.

The Claimant's claims

12. On 14 July 2001, the Fourth Defendant intentionally assaulted the Claimant in the manner particularised at paragraph 7 above. The said assault constituted trespass to the Claimant's person by the Fourth Defendant.

13. On 14 July 2001, and repeatedly thereafter, the Claimant has sought the assistance of the Anywhereshire police as the victim of a racially aggravated assault by the Fourth Defendant. Accordingly, he was a member of the public seeking the services of the West Yorkshire Police within the meaning of section 20 of the Race Relations Act 1976.

14. Further, the Anywhereshire police are a public authority within the meaning of section 19B of the Race Relations Act 1976, as amended by the Race Relations (Amendment) Act 2000.

15. It is the Claimant's case that the Second or Third Defendants assumed he had been the perpetrator of the assault and arrested him on grounds of his race and/or colour. This constitutes a 'detriment' within the meaning of section 1(1)(a) of the Race Relations Act 1976.

16. Further, it is the Claimant's case that the Second or Third Defendants and/or other officers from the Anywhereshire police area did not investigate the allegations he was making against the Fourth Defendant, on grounds of his race and/or colour. This constitutes a further detriment.

17. The Claimant contends that he has been subject to direct discrimination within the meaning of section 1(1)(a) of the Race Relations Act 1976, namely less favourable treatment on grounds of his race than a person of another race receives or would receive.

18. The Claimant therefore claims that the First, Second and Third Defendants unlawfully discriminated against him in that they:

i. refused or deliberately omitted to provide the Claimant with their services as police officers; contrary to section 20(1)(a) of the Race Relations Act 1976;

ii. refused or deliberately omitted to provide the Claimant with services of the like quality, in the like manner and on like terms as are normal compared to other members of the public, contrary to section 20(1)(b) of the Race Relations Act 1976;

iii. unlawfully discriminated against him in the exercise of their functions as public authorities, contrary to section 19B(1) of the Race Relations Act 1976.

19. When the Second Defendant arrested the Claimant, he did not have reasonable suspicion of the commission by him of an arrestable offence, or any other lawful authority to arrest him. Further or alternatively, the arrest was unlawful in that the Claimant was not informed of the ground for the arrest at the time of, or as soon as is practicable after, the arrest. The Claimant was detained from his arrest at around 12pm until after 3pm the following day. Accordingly, the Claimant claims wrongful arrest and false imprisonment.

20. As a result of these matters, the Claimant has suffered personal injury, distress, injury to his feelings, loss of liberty, loss and damage.

PARTICULARS OF PERSONAL INJURY

[insert details]

FURTHER PARTICULARS OF LOSS

The Claimant was imprisoned from around 12pm on 14 July 2001 until around 3pm on 15 July 2001. He felt acute distress and humiliation at being arrested in front of people who had gathered at the scene, some of whom were other students. He suffered the distress and anxiety of facing a wrongful prosecution from 14 July 2001 until 1 September 2001. The ongoing distress and anxiety, upset, anger and embarrassment he felt interfered with revision for his examinations and he achieved lower results than he would otherwise have done as a result of the stress he was under.

As the aforementioned torts have damaged the Claimant's feelings of dignity and pride, he is entitled to and does seek aggravated damages.

As the aforementioned torts consisted of arbitrary, oppressive and unconstitutional behaviour by officers of the Crown, the Claimant is entitled to and does seek exemplary damages.

In support of his claims for aggravated and exemplary damages, the Claimant relies on the matters aforesaid, the fact he believes his race has been the main motivation for the police's treatment of him, the lack of an apology by the police and the manner in which the proceedings are conducted by the Second, Third and Fourth Defendants as appropriate.

PARTICULARS OF SPECIAL DAMAGE

Please see attached schedule.

21. Further, the Claimant claims interest on such sums as the Court finds to be due at such a rate and for such a period as the Court shall allow pursuant to section 69 of the County Court Act 1984.

AND THE CLAIMANT CLAIMS:

i. Damages, including:
  a. aggravated damages;
  b. exemplary damages; and
  c. damages under the Race Relations Act 1976, including damages for injury to feelings

to the value of [£].

ii. A declaration that the First, Second and Third Defendants unlawfully discriminated against him contrary to sections 20(1)(a) and/or 20(1)(b) and/or 19B(1) of the Race Relations Act 1976;

iii. Interest pursuant to section 69 of the County Court Act 1984 as aforesaid;

iv. Costs.

DATED THIS DAY OF

STATEMENT OF TRUTH

I believe/the Claimant believes that the facts stated above are true.

Full Name: ______________________________

Signed: ______________________________

2. Particulars of claim for claim of indirect discrimination, alleging that the way in which the catchment area for a popular school was drawn was indirectly discriminatory, in that it excluded an area with a high Pakistani population

IN THE [ ] COUNTY COURT

BETWEEN:

MRS C — Claimant

and

RANDOMSHIRE COUNTY COUNCIL — Defendants

PARTICULARS OF CLAIM

1. The Claimant is of Pakistani origin. Her two children, F and R, are twins, born on 10 August 1991.

2. The Claimant and her family live on the Nomansland estate, between the B2731 and A43 in Randomshire. The vast majority of inhabitants on the Nomansland estate are of Pakistani origin.

3. For the academic year 2000–2001 F and R were pupils in their final year at Noname school in Nomansland. They are keen to attend Random Grammar School, located in the centre of Randomtown, for the academic year commencing in September 2001.

4. On 1 July 2001, the Claimant was informed that F and R were not eligible to seek admission to the school on the basis that the family live on the Nomansland estate. The catchment area imposed by the Defendant for the school only runs from the centre of town north to the B2731 and not beyond. The population of the catchment area is 80% white. Very few Pakistani families live there.

5. The Claimant contends that to be eligible for F and R to attend Random Grammar School, the family are required to live south of the B2731. This constitutes a 'requirement or condition' within the meaning of section 1(1)(b) of the Race Relations Act 1976.

6. Given the population of the catchment area, the proportion of Pakistani people who can comply with the condition or requirement is considerably smaller than the proportion of people who are not from the Pakistani racial group who can comply with it.

7. The Defendant is a public authority within the meaning of section 19B of the Race Relations Act 1976, as amended by the Race Relations (Amendment) Act 2000.

8. The drawing up of the catchment area is a 'function' of the Defendant in its capacity as a public authority.

9. Accordingly, the Claimant contends that she has been subject to unlawful indirect direct discrimination contrary to sections 1(1)(b) and s. 19B of the Race Relations Act 1976, as amended by the Race Relations (Amendment) Act 2000.

10. As a result of these matters, the Claimant has suffered loss and damage.

PARTICULARS OF LOSS

Please see attached schedule (e.g. Cost of trips to council meetings to discuss the issue?).

11. Further, the Claimant claims interest on such sums as the Court finds to be due at such a rate and for such a period as the Court shall allow pursuant to section 69 of the County Court Act 1984.

AND THE CLAIMANT CLAIMS:

i. Damages under the Race Relations Act 1976, including damages for injury to feelings [to the value of £ — if appropriate];
ii. A declaration that the Defendant unlawfully discriminated against her contrary to sections 1(1)(b) and s.19B of the Race Relations Act 1976, as amended by the Race Relations (Amendment) Act 2000;
iii. Interest pursuant to section 69 of the County Court Act 1984 as aforesaid;
iv. Costs.

DATED THIS DAY OF

STATEMENT OF TRUTH

I believe/the Claimant believes that the facts stated above are true.

Full Name: ______________________

Signed: ______________________

Index